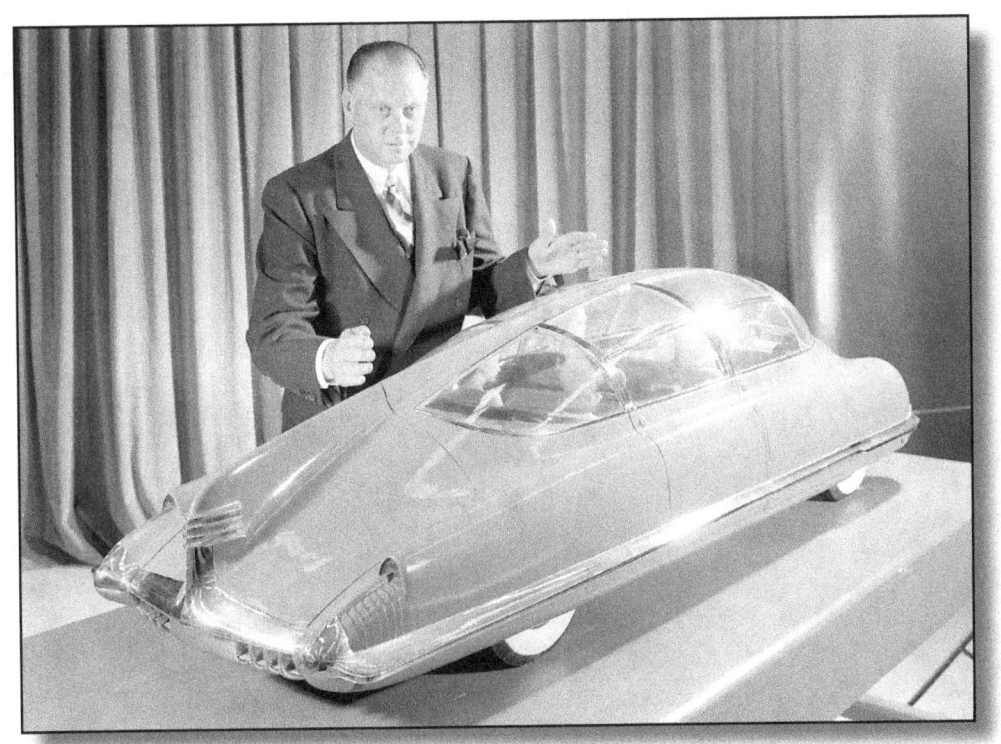

THE CARS OF
HARLEY EARL©

Features GM's Revolutionary Concept & Production Cars

DAVID W. TEMPLE

CarTech®

CarTech®, Inc.
6118 Main Street
North Branch, MN 55056
Phone: 651-277-1200 or 800-551-4754
Fax: 651-277-1203
www.cartechbooks.com

© 2016 by David W. Temple

All rights reserved. No part of this publication may be reproduced or utilized in any form or by any means, electronic or mechanical, including photocopying, recording, or by any information storage and retrieval system, without prior permission from the Publisher. All text, photographs, and artwork are the property of the Author unless otherwise noted or credited.

The information in this work is true and complete to the best of our knowledge. However, all information is presented without any guarantee on the part of the Author or Publisher, who also disclaim any liability incurred in connection with the use of the information and any implied warranties of merchantability or fitness for a particular purpose. Readers are responsible for taking suitable and appropriate safety measures when performing any of the operations or activities described in this work.

All trademarks, trade names, model names and numbers, and other product designations referred to herein are the property of their respective owners and are used solely for identification purposes. This work is a publication of CarTech, Inc., and has not been licensed, approved, sponsored, or endorsed by any other person or entity. The Publisher is not associated with any product, service, or vendor mentioned in this book, and does not endorse the products or services of any vendor mentioned in this book.

Edit by Paul Johnson
Layout by Monica Seiberlich

ISBN 978-1-61325-234-5
Item No. CT556P

Library of Congress Cataloging-in-Publication Data Available

Written, edited, and designed in the U.S.A.
Printed in the U.S.A.

Frontispiece: *Harley Earl is shown discussing the 1948 rear-engine Corsair proposal seen here in 3/8 scale. (Photo Courtesy of GM Media Archive)*

Title Page: *Clare "Mac" MacKichan (conversing with a stylist) was deeply involved in the designs of the first-generation Corvettes, the Corvette-based dream cars for the 1954 GM Motorama, and the 1955–1957 Chevrolets. Note the upholstery samples on the desk in the foreground.*

Contents Page: *This 1957 Corvette was ordered with the 270-hp 2 x 4-barrel carburetor option and 4-speed transmission. Over half of the 6,339 Corvettes built that year had either the 245- or 270-hp dual 4-barrel 283s. The two-tone color scheme of Venetian Red with the Shoreline Beige side cover was an option.*

Back Cover Photos:

Top: *According to GM's booklet,* Flight of the Firebirds, *with the 1958 GM Firebird III, Harley Earl "envisioned an entirely different type of car, 'which a person may drive to the launching site of a rocket to the moon,'" when he considered the styling for the next turbine car. A GT-304 turbine engine, considerably more advanced than those of the previous Firebirds, powered it.*

Bottom: *This 1955 Bel Air was one of the most significant models in GM history. When the new Tri-Fives were launched in 1955, they carried a myriad of innovations, including the new Gen-I small-block. This convertible was one of 41,292 built for the model year, and it carried many options. Among the dealer accessories and factory options are grille guard, outside rearview mirror, radio, wire wheel covers, fuel-filler door guard, and Continental Wheel Carrier. Powering the Gypsy Red and Shoreline Beige car is a 265 V-8 with Powerglide. This car scored 998 points out of a possible 1,000 at the 2011 International Chevy Classics show held in Springfield, Missouri. (Photo Courtesy Eckler's Chevy Classics magazine and Colin Date, editor)*

TABLE OF CONTENTS

Preface and Acknowledgments 6
Foreword by Ken Pickering 8
Chapter One: The Early Days 9
Chapter Two: The LaSalle 20
Chapter Three: The Art and Colour Section 33
Chapter Four: The Modern Concept Car 44
Chapter Five: An American Sports Car 60
Chapter Six: Tri-Five Chevrolets 77
Chapter Seven: Tail Fins, Chrome, Gadgets and More! 89
Chapter Eight: The GM Motorama 131
Chapter Nine: Parade of Progress 152
Chapter Ten: Harley Earl's Damsels of Design 156
Chapter Eleven: Harley Earl's Personal F-88s 164
Chapter Twelve: Styling the 1959s 172
Conclusion 190
Index 191

PREFACE AND ACKNOWLEDGMENTS

Mentioning the name Harley Earl to enthusiasts of GM's cars today results in at least something beyond a blank stare. That was not true 20 or even 10 years ago. Still, exactly who the man was and what he accomplished remains unclear to many. Earl retired at the start of the 1959 model year and passed away about a decade later. This was at a time when the number of car collectors in the United States was still relatively few (at least compared to today) and GM cars of the post–World War II era through 1959 were far removed from the iconic status they have had for many years now. Yet, those cars were styled under the man who invented the concepts of styling mass-produced automobiles.

At General Motors, Harley Earl ruled much like a dictator. He could be both a tyrant and a gentleman. He was tall and imposing, yet he stuttered just enough to be self-conscious. He was flamboyant, gifted, an imperfect perfectionist, a visionary, and truly unique. Earl worked long hours and was dedicated to achieving perfection in the execution of his style. Only rarely did he miss the mark.

GM Vice President of GM Styling, Harley Earl, kept the company at the forefront of styling automobiles for three decades. Here he poses with Cadillac's flagship model for 1954, the El Dorado. (Photo Courtesy GM Media Archive)

Earl's decades-long career began many years earlier when in his teens he began working for his father, who had founded a carriage-building business. With the advent of the automobile, though, it became a custom-car business with clients from the new Hollywood movie-making industry. As an adult Harley was given control of the company, which was later bought by Don Lee, a man who ran GM distributorships in California. From there, Earl met the Fisher Brothers, which in turn led to him being hired as a *freelancer* to style one of GM's most important models, the LaSalle. That car's success earned Earl an invitation from company president Alfred P. Sloan Jr. to come to work for General Motors to set up a styling department, which was labeled the "Art and Colour Section" to explicitly establish the purpose of the organization. Over time the name changed to "GM Styling" (or sometimes referenced as "GM Styling Section") then finally to "GM Design" during Earl's career at the company.

The time had passed when just seeing a car in motion was considered miraculous; the automobile became more common and more sophisticated mechanically; for the most part, all of them (with the exceptions of the ultra-expensive models) were just about the same in that regard, thus more or less leveling the playing field for the well-established automakers. Something was needed to make the playing field uneven again, something to give General Motors an advantage. That something was styling.

A styling department was a new concept and one Earl would have to essentially invent. He met with resistance at first but proved himself and his ideas to result in more sales. The basic idea behind his efforts was very simple: A beautiful car had more eye appeal than one that was just a utilitarian "plain brown wrapper." Why buy the plain brown wrapper when a beautiful car could be had at just as an affordable price. Beauty in the automobile became supremely important. The competition had to catch up quickly by establishing their styling departments. Some from Earl's Art and Colour Section eventually went on to work for the competition, such as Virgil Exner (Studebaker, followed by Chrysler Corp.) and Frank Hershey (Ford Motor Company). In effect, Harley Earl was responsible for the styling (either directly or indirectly) of nearly every car starting in the 1930s and well beyond. Harley Earl firmly believed that art had a place in industry (from packaging to anything mechanical) and he proved this firmly held belief. Under his leadership GM's share of the automobile market climbed to 52 percent. From the start (even as market share grew) Earl had to fight engineers, accountants, and sometimes even company president Harlow Curtice to push his ideas through to production.

Earl, after three decades of success in styling automobiles, finally lost his way. His old sources of inspiration were not quite working any longer. Automotive historian Michael Lamm once said, "Harley Earl was beginning to outlive his era. People do it and designers do it." Earl lasted three decades; none of his successors came close to matching his record with the exception of his handpicked successor, Bill Mitchell, who began working under Earl in the mid-1930s. Upon the departure of Earl, Mitchell took charge of GM Styling/GM Design for nearly 20 years.

With this book, you will have a glimpse of the work done under the watchful eye of the "stylemaster," Harley Earl. The word "glimpse" is used here because an exhaustive look would take many hundreds of pages. You can find some additional insights from Lamm's recently re-released book, *A Century of Automotive Style*, which he co-wrote with the late David Holls, one of Earl's many talented stylists. This book was one of many important sources referenced in the production of *The Cars of Harley Earl*.

Finally, of particular note is that this book was produced through the cooperation of many people: Sidney Allen (owner, 1955 Chevrolet 210 and 1958 Impala convertible), Mike Ames (owner, 1934 Cadillac V-8 and 1954 Buick Skylark), Daniel Bazin, Karen and Eric Bernard (owners, 1958 Buick Century), Angelo Van Bogart (editor for *Old Cars Weekly* and owner, 1955 Cadillac), Joe Bortz (Bortz Auto Collection), Terry Boyce, Brad Brooks, Josh Burdick, Tom Burns, Gene Bussian, Tom Chinn (owner, 1958 Corvette), Mike Cibulas (Oldsmobile Club of America), Allan Clark (Cadillac & LaSalle Club), Dr. Thomas Clark (owner, 1957 Corvette), Joseph Chow (owner, 1959 Buick Le Sabre), Carlos Cortez (University of Texas at San Antonio, UTSA Libraries Special Collections), Tim Coy (Cadillac & LaSalle Club), Colin Date (editor, *Chevy Classics*), Christo Datini (GM Heritage Center), Wayne Ellwood, David Fletcher (owner, 1957 Bel Air convertible), Alan Forbush (owner, 1958 Chevrolet Del Ray), Karin Fowler, Michael Hancock (owner, 1954 Chevrolet 150), Magnus Karlsson (Bilsport Classic Sweden), Don Keefe (Keefe Media), Bill Kinsella (owner, 1942 Oldsmobile), Gary Klecka (owner, 1955 Buick 76R Riviera), Wolfgang Kupka (owner, 1959 Cadillac Eldorado Brougham), John Kyros (GM Media Archive), Brian Laurance (Buick Club of America), Ed Lucas (FEL Enterprises), Nancy Martin (Charles Chayne family archives), David McGee, Jack Milford, Bob Najjar, Nick Pagani (owner, 1950 Olds Ninety-Eight convertible), Ken Pickering (GM, retired), Steve Plunkett (owner, multiple 1930s, 1940s, and 1950s Cadillacs), Debra Powless, Larry and Tammy Reid (owner, 1950 Olds Ninety-Eight convertible), Bill and Shelagh Rathgeber (owners, 1955 Pontiac Laurentian), John Richmond, Chris Ritter (AACA Library), Clint Ruby (owner, 1955 Cadillac Eldorado Special), Steve Shore (owner, 1952 Buick Special), Brett Snyder, Bill Stewart (owner, 1958 Oldsmobile Fiesta), Steve Stewart (editor for the *Self-Starter*, Cadillac & LaSalle Club), Stephen Struck, Scot Taylor (owner, 1959 Olds Ninety-Eight Sport Sedan), and Hampton Wayt.

Although the names of Phil Aubrey, Christo Datini, Jim Jordan, John Kyros, Brian Laurance, and Ken Pickering are already included in this list, they deserve an extra *thank you* for their assistance with obtaining information and photos for this book. Of course many thanks to everyone!

David North, a designer for General Motors from 1959 to 1991, rendered this work titled, "Harley J. Earl, Dean of Automobile Designers. (Photo Courtesy GM Media Archive)

FOREWORD

By Ken Pickering, General Motors 1949–1989

To my mind, we have witnessed three great innovators in this past 100 years, men of great vision who have changed the very basic ways we live. I believe these men exhibited pure genius during their business careers.

Walt Disney started out with a cartoon about a little rodent named Mickey Mouse and went on to build a giant empire of breakthrough motion pictures and trend-setting theme parks.

At Apple Inc., Steve Jobs was in every sense a true visionary. He created products that we had never before seen and changed our culture in many ways.

And then there was Harley Earl, the man who created the specialized business of automobile styling and design. His method of styling or designing an automobile became the model for the entire industry. Harley Earl also championed the annual model change and made us all anticipate the new model introductions. Earl developed the methods that are still followed today by all automotive companies, both domestic and internationally sourced.

Almost every other person who led the design operations at competing automobile companies during this same period learned their craft under his tutelage. Harley Earl had a remarkable career from the founding of GM Art and Colour in 1927 to his retirement as vice president in charge of GM Design in 1958.

David Temple is an expert in the field of automobiles and has written much about the General Motors models of this period. He is also uniquely qualified to write this story about Harley Earl, his invention of the GM Motorama, and the special models he created for this

Ken Pickering, an engineer, worked under Harley Earl during his last few years as VP of Design. Pickering is seen here with his award-winning 1956 Corvette, a car he personally customized. The grille was salvaged from a trashcan at Design! (Photo Courtesy Ken Pickering)

spectacular annual event.

In my 40 years with General Motors, I had the privilege to spend most of my career at GM Styling. I remember well working on some of the Motorama models mentioned by David in this book, and I also have vivid memories of several years of a close personal work association with Harley Earl. He was the ruthless ruler of his kingdom and a fearless leader in General Motors.

We will all enjoy and benefit from David Temple's insights about Harley Earl, the man, and his groundbreaking work in automobile styling and design.

ABOUT THE AUTHOR

David W. Temple is an automotive historian and seasoned writer as well as an avid researcher and expert on the life and times of Harley Earl. He is the preeminent writer and researcher to reveal the story behind the story, and the most insightful review of Harley Earl cars. He is also the author of the widely celebrated *Motorama: GM's Legendary Show and Concept Cars*. He has amassed an incredible archive of information and photos on Harley Earl's noted designs and innovative cars. He has worked as a freelance automotive journalist and photographer for nearly 30 years. During his career, Temple has specialized in 1950s and 1960s American cars. He has penned many magazine articles that have appeared in *Cars & Parts, Collectible Automobile, Auto Restorer,* and others. He has also authored *Full Size Fords: 1955–1970*.

THE EARLY DAYS

CHAPTER 1

"Let me say quickly that when I refer to myself I am merely using a shortcut to talk about my team. There are 650 of us, and collectively we are known as the Styling Section of General Motors."
– *"I Dream Automobiles" by Harley Earl,* The Saturday Evening Post, *August 7, 1954*

On June 23, 1927, a monumental event officially occurred, which began the transformation of the automobile from a mere assemblage of mechanical systems engineered for the purpose of transportation to that of a work of art and a status symbol for the car buyer. Because of this moment in time, the automobile evolved from a mere contrivance for transportation to a mechanized system wrapped in a carefully thought-out design for the purpose of enticing people to buy the car because it *looked good*. The concept of styling as a means to sell cars came to General Motors by way of a man named Harley Jefferson Earl, or Mr. Earl (typically pronounced as one word, "Mistearl"), to those he hired to work in the new Art and Colour Section of General Motors. Styling became one of the most important attributes of the automobile and General Motors led the way in this regard. In fact, sales of GM cars rose from a 12 percent market share in the 1920s to 52 percent by 1956. Styling was a major reason for that tremendous growth.

As with all turning points in history, a series of events converged leading to this moment in mid-1927. Harley Earl was born on November 22, 1893, in Los Angeles and grew up in Hollywood before the advent of the movie industry there. He was the second of five children born to Jacob and Abbie Earl and the only one to follow in his father's footsteps. Jacob, who had experience as a woodworker and lumberjack, established the Earl Carriage Works in 1889 in Los Angeles, where he repaired and built horse-drawn wagons and carriages. With the automobile gaining in popularity, Jacob began constructing car bodies and in 1908 renamed his company the Earl Automobile Works.

Son Harley is said to have worked in his father's shop after school, and that is likely true. Certainly, at an early age he developed an interest in designing cars. In 1980, Harley's brother, Art Earl, gave an interview to author Michael Lamm for the book Lamm co-wrote with Dave Holls, *A Century of Automotive Style*. In it, Art stated that Harley's interest in clay modeling was demonstrated on a camping trip to Bailey's Ranch (at Palomar Mountain) in

This portrait of Harley Earl dates from 1927, the year in which he joined General Motors. About one year earlier, General Motors hired him to produce designs for its new LaSalle, a kind of junior Cadillac. His work on that project led directly to his position as head of GM's new styling department. (Photo Courtesy GM Media Archive)

1910. Heavy rain had fallen in the area leaving the clay soil malleable. Art said, "He'd pick up a big chunk of clay and would work it down to the sort of car he wanted. I guess we had 20 or 30 of these little cars of different shapes: roadsters and touring cars. . . . But it started to rain again. We got two more inches of rain in about half an hour and it melted all of our clay cars."

Harley Earl on Styling

Many may be surprised to learn that the man who has been labeled over the years "The da Vinci of Detroit" and headed Styling for General Motors for more than three decades could not draw well and even said so: "I am sure that a good many high-school students can top me in freehand sketching." However, he could communicate to those artists of GM's Styling Section what he wanted done and in so doing influenced the design of tens of millions of cars over the span of his career.

In the August 7, 1954, issue of *The Saturday Evening Post*, Harley Earl explained how cars were designed in the days prior to the Art and Colour Section and how he completely changed the old methods: "Fisher Body would draw up the body and the hood, and then it would model the body . . . then the divisions would take that drawing and they would put on their front end and their fenders and wheels, and they . . . would put them together. Well, when I worked on the LaSalle, we didn't do it that way. We made it all one; built it right together as one unit rather than separate it."

Earl not only understood the importance of an integrated design, but also how important being able to show how a design will appear when built by the use of full-scale clay models. He reportedly said, "A picture is worth a thousand words, but a model is worth a thousand pictures." He used the concept during his earliest days as a designer and continued the practice at General Motors.

The 1954 article, "I Dream Automobiles" by Harley J. Earl as told to Arthur W. Baum, provided readers with an excellent account of how automobiles were designed at that time. In the first part of the story, Earl notes the excitement the public experienced at a new model introduction, but that was not something he shared with them because by the time those cars appeared at dealerships they were already "at least 27 months" old to him. (This was the time General Motors needed to prepare a car to go from drawing board to assembly line, as well as the tooling required to build it.)

"I have to live two to three years apart from a great American interest. I can't talk to the neighbors about their new cars with anything like their fresh enthusiasm. I like it that way. I have my own new cars, too. They are beauties to me; even though they may be mere scratches on a paper pad or full-scale pro-

One of Harley Earl's ways of inspiring imaginative thinking from his staff was competition. Seen here is one of the many designs offered for one of those competitions held in the Design Auditorium on the 11th floor of the Argonaut Building in June 1952. (Photo Courtesy GM Media Archive)

jections on one of our car-size blackboards. It hasn't been too long ago that we settled what your 1957 car will look like. Although I suspect that our Styling Section is sometimes referred to in other GM divisions as the Beauty Parlor, we look upon our design job as a serious one. It is obviously important to the company that three years from now the public shall accept and like what we are doing today. Most of our thousands of hours of work every year are small refinements and revisions to improve the comfort, utility, and appearance of our automobiles. But we also need explosive bursts of spanking-new themes, and somehow we get them," Earl explained.

Within the article, Harley Earl detailed for the reader some of the constraints of automobile design by pointing out the limits imposed by engineers as well as federal regulations. As to the former he used the rather uncomplicated example of pursuing a three-wheeled automobile design, something he knew engineers would find "inherently dangerous" so the "engineers wouldn't encourage us." As to regulations Earl explained how they affect styling using the example of trying to provide a car with a single headlight to which the states would "prohibit it since many of them control the number, brightness, position, and height of headlights."

Other design criteria highlighted by Mr. Earl included practical limits on the length of a car: "Parking problems have already dictated maximum reasonable lengths . . ."and he also noted, "Just plain artistry also is limiting. . . ."

Harley Earl made the most of the limits of artistry with lower, longer, wider proportioning of automobiles, if not in actual design then by creating the appearance of such: "My primary purpose for twenty-eight years has been to lengthen and lower the American automobile, at times in reality and always at least in appearance. Why? Because my sense of proportion tells me that oblongs are more attractive than squares just as a ranch house is more attractive than a square, three-story, flat-roofed house or a greyhound is more graceful than an English bulldog."

The Corvette sports car gave Earl a chance to design something completely different from large automobiles. As with the latter, inspiration for design features came from various European models. His annual trips to the European auto shows (something he had done even prior to joining General Motors) served to provide ideas to adapt to American cars. Sometimes, though, inspiration came by chance as in the case of the Firebird I turbine car, as he wrote in "I Dream Automobiles": "The Firebird tickles me because of its origin. In our 1953 Motorama, the spotlight model of the dream cars was the Le Sabre, and just after it had been first shown to company officials, I was on an airplane trip. I picked up a magazine and noticed a picture of a new jet plane, the Douglas Skyray. It was a striking ship, and I liked it so well that I tore out the

Color, whether it involved paint or fabric, was as important a consideration in styling an automobile as any. This photo from 1956 shows the paint and fabric color sample charts for GM Coach. (Photo Courtesy GM Media Archive)

picture and put it into my inside coat pocket.

"Subsequently, a traveling companion, also a GM officer, stopped at my seat to congratulate me on the Le Sabre. 'But,' he added, 'now what will you do for next year?' At that moment, I had absolutely nothing in mind. But I patted the pocket where the picture of the Skyray was tucked away. 'I have it right here,' I said. I was joking. I was merely answering his banter in kind. Then, bingo, I decided I had kidded myself into something. The result . . . is that the Firebird is an earthbound replica of the Skyray airplane." With this story, Harley Earl proved what he had stated earlier in that article, "First-class minds will seize on anything out of the ordinary."

Harley's interest went further than design, though. He demonstrated his love of racing cars in a surreptitious way; at least it was secret for about a day. In 1911, Jacob Earl bought a Mercer roadster. Mercer was well known for performance; its Model 35R Raceabout could be driven consistently at 70 mph and reach a speed in excess of 90 mph. Harley was apparently aware of such facts. He borrowed his father's Mercer for a weekend stock car race and won it. The story of how Jacob learned of his son's victory has several versions. One is that he was reading the newspaper, turned to the sports section, and read the story of Harley winning the 100-mile race in a "special new Mercer." A second version, as detailed in *A Century of Automotive Style*, is that Jacob found the speedometer pegged at 80 mph. Being aware that his son had driven his car the previous day, he asked him what had happened, to which Harley suggested the speedometer needle must have stuck as the result of hitting a bump in the road. In yet another version, a customer walked into the Earl Automobile Works the following Monday and congratulated Jacob on his son's victory in the stock car race! Jacob did not understand at first, so the matter was clarified. As the story goes, he then had some "choice words" for young Harley.

Regardless of exactly what happened, Harley had a taste of racing cars and loved it. He wrote about the origins of his enjoyment of racing in an article for the August 7, 1954, copy of *The Saturday Evening Post*, titled "I Dream Automobiles": "My father produced a very tough steel, which was in demand by race drivers for steering knuckles. That led to my hanging around the racetrack at Santa Monica, where the crop of young drivers of that time included Ralph De Palma and Barney Oldfield." He even sketched the cars racing at the Santa Monica track, although sometimes doing so with "lines that I thought were an improvement."

In 1912, Harley Earl graduated from Hollywood High School. His father was hoping he would become a lawyer and with his urging, Harley enrolled at the University of Southern California. However, after excelling in athletics (setting a pole-vaulting record) during his first year there, Harley Earl dropped out to go to work in his father's shop where he served as the chief designer. Three years later Harley was back in school, but this time at Stanford University. According to Lamm and Holls, Harley's father was hoping his son would study law, but as before, Harley excelled in sports, both track and rugby. This time fate seems to have set Harley Earl on the career path he was to follow. While playing rugby one afternoon, Harley took a hard hit from the cleats of another player, causing a leg injury later resulting in an infection. The infection became so serious, the doctor recommended amputation, but Harley refused. Fortunately his choice was the right one, but he was out of action at school while he recovered at home. This is where the record of his education becomes a bit murky. As stated in *A Century of Automotive Style*, Stanford ultimately gave Harley credit for two years of undergraduate pre-law. However, according to Harley Earl's account in the aforementioned article he penned for *The Saturday Evening Post*, he studied engineering while attending Stanford.

Now back at home, Harley resumed working at his father's shop. He also found a new hobby, golf, and saw more of his high school sweetheart, Sue Carpenter, whom he later married. The clientele of the Earl Automobile Works also flourished during this period thanks to the successful new movie industry of Hollywood. Film producers such as Cecil B. DeMille (who lived only a short distance from the Earls), along with movie stars, including Roscoe "Fatty" Arbuckle, Douglas Fairbanks, Mary Pickford, and Tom Mix, became customers. Others outside the movie business included multimillionaire oil tycoon Edward L. Doheny Jr., who drilled the first successful oil well in the Los Angeles city oil field.

A car built for Fatty Arbuckle was a first for Harley Earl. In, "I Dream Automobiles," Earl wrote, "The factory produced special broughams, landaus, and other models for what you might call the carriage trade. But the first automobile body that I undertook was built behind my father's back while he was away in the mountains for a long rest, and I was left in charge of the business. I think I am justified in saying that my career started in a big way. My first order for a special auto body was from Fatty Arbuckle."

In January 1919, Harley Earl's work caught the attention of a *Los Angeles Times* reporter who was visiting the Los Angeles Auto Show, where some of the custom-bodied cars designed by Earl were on exhibit: "The most startling local models at the show are those built by the Earl Auto

Harley Earl married his high-school sweetheart, Sue Carpenter, in 1917. This undated photo was likely taken at their home in Grosse Point, Michigan. (Photo Courtesy GM Media Archive)

One of many special-bodied Cadillacs created by Harley Earl and his craftsmen at the Don Lee Coach & Body Works, a 1921 Speedster. (Photo Courtesy GM Media Archive)

Works, whose sensational Chandler [Town Car] and Marmon [Phaeton] are attracting huge crowds. These cars are designed by Harley J. Earl, a local man... who has sprung into prominence as a maker of motor fashions almost overnight." Whether the reporter realized it or not, by the use of the word "fashions" he had touched upon the concept Harley Earl would use at General Motors; just as clothing went in and out of fashion, so would automobiles by design.

On July 13, 1919, Earl Automobile Works, which had become one of the largest producers of custom car bodies, was sold to one of the company's major customers, Don Lee, a Cadillac distributor and owner of nearly four dozen dealerships throughout California. Earl served as chief designer for the Don Lee Coach & Body Works where 90 to 100 craftsmen designed and built as many as 300 custom-car bodies per year. As time passed, more and more of those cars were Cadillacs, reaching an output of 100 (one-third of the company's business) by 1925.

During the early 1920s, Frederick Fisher, one of the founders of Fisher Body, which by then was a division of General Motors, began taking annual vacations to the Los Angeles area. On some of those trips, a friend, Jimmy Baldwin, who was a Chevrolet dealer, joined him. Baldwin's son, Andy, knew Harley Earl from their days at Stanford University. While on a vacation to Los Angeles in 1922 with Fisher, Andy called his friend Harley to suggest they have lunch together and play golf afterward. He also said he was bringing along another gentleman, Fred Fisher. This became a routine leading to Harley Earl becoming well acquainted with the upper echelon at Cadillac.

During the years in which Harley Earl began working at his father's company and on through to the time he became a prominent custom-car builder, Earl's future employer came into existence and grew rapidly. William Durant officially established General Motors Company when he filed papers of incorporation for his new company. Durant, who was known as "the king of carriage makers" as a result of his successful venture, the Dort-Durant Company, soon added Buick and Oldsmobile to his new company. In 1909, Oakland and Cadillac were added to the growing roster.

Durant also acquired for the ever-increasing General Motors such companies as A. C. Spark Plug, DELCO, Harrison Radiator, McLaughlin Motor Company, and a 60 percent interest in Fisher Body. McLaughlin, by the way had been a joint venture with Buick even prior to the formation of General Motors. The McLaughlin cars were built and sold in Canada and exported to other countries. In 1931, the German company, Opel, joined the GM family. General Motors had grown into an international venture.

Not all of these acquisitions transpired under Durant's presidency, however. Unfortunately, his numerous purchases over a short time eventually put his company in financial jeopardy. Worried creditors instituted stricter financial demands and made matters more difficult for General Motors and Durant, and he was soon forced out of General Motors. Alfred P. Sloan Jr. once stated that "Mr. Durant was a great man with a great weakness; he could create but not administer." Sloan, incidentally, was serving as president of Hyatt Roller Bearing when General Motors bought that company (and he later became president after Durant's successor, Pierre S. du Pont, resigned).

Durant did not exit the automotive business, though. In 1911, he, along with Louis Chevrolet, set up the Chevrolet Motor Car Company, and by 1918 Durant had used it to acquire General Motors through a reverse merger. But by 1920, he was again forced out of General Motors, this time permanently.

In 1925, Lawrence Fisher was the president of Cadillac and near Christmastime that year, he made a phone call to Harley Earl, which led to a major change in the way automobiles were mass-produced. Harley Earl and Larry Fisher had become good friends and also played golf together. Not surprisingly, they also discussed the subject of styling automobiles. This topic had been on the minds of Lawrence Fisher and Alfred Sloan, so the conversation between Lawrence and Harley was not merely casual. They recognized that styling could be a great sales tool for the mass-produced automobile, and Harley Earl had proven himself as a highly gifted designer. His

The 1927 LaSalle (Model 303 Roadster shown) is considered to be the first production car to have been designed entirely by a stylist. Harley Earl, the car's designer, is shown in the driver's seat with Cadillac Chief Larry Fisher standing on the far side. (Photo Courtesy GM Media Archive)

The Fisher Brothers and Fisher Body

Brothers Frederick and Charles Fisher (the oldest two of seven brothers), along with their uncle Albert Fisher, founded the Fisher Body Company.

In 1902, Fred became a draftsman at C. R. Wilson Company, and two years later his brother Charles joined him. The company was the largest maker of horse-drawn carriage bodies in the world and also built automobile bodies for some of the earliest automakers, including Cadillac, Oldsmobile, Ford, and others. In 1908, they went to work for their uncle, Albert, in his carriage shop, the Standard Wagon Works, which had supplied a small number of car bodies to Ford. Not long afterward, the two brothers, along with their uncle, partnered to form the Fisher Body Company, which was capitalized at $50,000; of that figure, $30,000 came from Uncle Albert.

Brothers Frederick and Charles Fisher, the eldest two of seven brothers, along with their uncle Albert founded the Fisher Body Company. In 1919, the Fishers sold a 60 percent interest in their highly successful business to General Motors. By 1926, General Motors took full ownership. "Body by Fisher" remained a stand-alone division of General Motors for decades. Here Fisher brothers (front left to right) Lawrence, Charles, William, Howard, and Edward are shown at the 1927 groundbreaking ceremonies for the Fisher Building. (Photo Courtesy GM Media Archive)

The new business venture soon thrived; early customers included Cadillac, Oldsmobile, EMF, Ford, Herreshoff Motor Company, and others. One of the partners of EMF suggested Fisher build a closed car body; Charles began experiments in that regard. The closed body was expensive to produce, but the Fishers recognized that driving automobiles would not become a year-round means of transportation without finding a way to produce closed bodies at a reasonable cost. Albert, however, objected to the idea to the point he wanted out of the firm. Fisher's connection to Herreshoff was fortuitous at this point. Louis Mendelssohn, a major shareholder in Herreshoff, bought out Albert Fisher's interest for $30,000 and oversaw the financial concerns of the business. He later negotiated the sale of Fisher to General Motors.

As a result of increasing demand for closed bodies, a separate closed-body engineering section was created, which led to the Fisher Closed Body Company (formed in December 1910). Within two years Fisher Body Company expanded into Canada, locating in Walkersville, Ontario, just across from downtown Detroit; brother Lawrence joined Frederick and Charles as superintendent of paint and trim.

Soon thereafter, Alfred and Edward were added to the family business, followed by William.

As the business grew, Fred and Charles developed new manufacturing techniques to keep pace with increasing demand for automobile bodies. In 1914, the company produced approximately 105,000 bodies. In 1916, Fisher merged all of its operations and the Fisher Body Corporation was incorporated in New York with a stock authorization of $6 million.

After World War I ended, Fisher discussed manufacturing entire automobiles, but while that prospect was being deliberated, Ford, General Motors, and Studebaker began considering the acquisition of Fisher. General Motors, which was continually increasing its orders from the company, ultimately bought Fisher Body in two phases, each occurring in 1919 (leading to General Motor's control of production, finances, and 60 percent of the stock with day-to-day management concerns left to the Fisher brothers) and in 1926 (when General Motors traded more than 664,000 shares of its own stock for the remaining 40 percent of Fisher). Fisher's body production climbed past 135,000 units in 1919 and one year later soared to approximately 575,000 then passed the one million mark for 1921. About three decades later, it had produced in excess of 35 million auto bodies.

About one year before General Motors assumed full ownership, the Fisher Division of General Motors acquired Fleetwood Body Corporation. While Fleetwood's plant was small and outdated, its reputation in the coach-building industry was excellent, thus the name brought prestige to General Motors. Fleetwood then became Cadillac's in-house coachbuilder, and General Motors promoted the Fleetwood label about as much as the Fisher name. The Cadillac V-12 and V-16 models of the early 1930s were engineered and bodied by Fleetwood under the direction of Lawrence Fisher.

For 1935, the Fisher Body Division of General Motors became the first automaker to replace the fabric roof insert with a one-piece, full metal top dubbed "Turret Top." Prior to this, roofs were only partially constructed of steel with the central portion filled with a rubberized fabric because up until the debut of the Turret Top, the technology to stretch the metal as required without cracks forming had not been discovered.

The following year, Fisher introduced full-steel bodies formed by welding the steel inner and outer panels into a shock-resistant structure; wood bodies with steel outer panels had become obsolete. As the Styling Section of General Motors led by Harley Earl pushed the styling envelope to produce new shapes in metal, Fisher Body adapted, thus helping to give General Motors the top spot among the automakers of the 1950s.

General Motors introduced its Turret Top steel bodies for 1935 and Silver Streak hood trim, which remained a traditional feature through 1956. The Turret Top was an all-steel roof, an innovation previously impractical to manufacture, thus requiring inserts of rubberized fabric. This image from a 1936 Pontiac brochure shows illustrations of the Master Six and Deluxe Six series coupes.

approach of integrating every aspect of the design of a car (the grille, the hood, the trunk, and every other piece of the body) was an important part of Harley Earl's success. Their telephone conversation was about an invite to come to Detroit to design a new model dubbed LaSalle, a car conceived to fill a large price gap between Buick and Cadillac. The price gap was troubling because those wanting to make the move up from Buick to Cadillac could purchase a Packard instead for a price in between the top two GM brands. On January 6, 1926, Mr. Earl boarded a train to Detroit and over the span of three months provided the designs for the new LaSalle. (The LaSalle is detailed in the next chapter.) One

This photo was taken on the 11th floor of the Argonaut Building from which Styling worked until the opening of the Design Center in 1956. The view is facing the east wall; the west wall contained a turntable and a theater curtain as seen in many photos of the dream cars shown at the GM Motorama. The executive offices, including Harley Earl's, were to the right side, and there was a small studio behind this wall where overseas and other special projects were done. (Photo Courtesy GM Media Archive)

Alfred P. Sloan Jr.

Alfred P. Sloan Jr. was born May 23, 1875, in New Haven, Connecticut. He was one of five children born to Alfred Sr. and Katherine Sloan. In 1895, he received a degree in electrical engineering from MIT (completing the curriculum in just three years) and was the youngest member of his graduating class. Soon thereafter, Alfred Sr. (who had achieved financial success as a coffee and tea importer and wholesale grocer), along with another man, was persuaded by young Alfred to invest $5,000 in Hyatt Roller Bearing Company, a business that was not doing well. He was placed in charge of the floundering company, but he was sure he could solve Hyatt's problems. Six months later Hyatt had amassed $12,000 in profits. In 1898 he married Irene Jackson of Roxbury, Massachusetts.

Then in 1901, at the age of 26, Sloan was named president of Hyatt and the company grew to be one of the most successful bearing manufacturers. Sloan smartly convinced Hyatt to produce antifriction bearings for automobiles, and Oldsmobile soon became the company's first automotive customer. (Previously, automobiles had used heavily greased wagon axles.) The list of customers quickly grew via the addition of a number of additional automobile manufacturers. In fact, under Sloan's leadership, Hyatt grew rapidly.

In 1916, GM president William Durant bought Hyatt, along with four other manufacturers of automobile parts and accessories (including Remy Electric and Dayton Engineering Laboratories), with Mr. Sloan as president of the group now named United Motors Corporation. In late 1918, General Motors took over United Motors as its own parts division, and Sloan became a vice president of the growing automotive manufacturing giant. At the time Durant bought Hyatt, the bearing company had a gross income of $10 million and profits of $4 million.

Alfred Sloan Jr. was elected president of General Motors in 1923, after the departure of Pierre S. du Pont from that position. Among the many things Sloan did, as president, was to seriously consider the importance of styling in the design of an automobile. On July 8, 1926, he penned a letter to Henry Bassett, the general manager of Buick, in which he wrote, "The question arises: Are we as advanced from the standpoint of beauty of design, harmony of lines, attractiveness of color schemes and general contour of the whole piece of apparatus as we are in the

Alfred Sloan Jr. was elected president of General Motors in 1923. Years earlier he headed Hyatt Roller Bearing, which supplied antifriction bearings to various automakers. General Motors later acquired the company. At that time, Sloan came to General Motors and recognized the marketing value of styling automobiles. He was instrumental in hiring Harley Earl. (Photo Courtesy GM Media Archive)

soundness of workmanship and the other elements of a more mechanical nature? That is the point I am raising and I believe it is a very fundamental one. At the present time one of our very important lines is being revamped from the appearance standpoint."

The letter was quoted in Alfred Sloan's 1964 book, *My Years with General Motors*, and in the paragraph that followed he stated, "The action I mentioned in the last line of the letter was to make styling history. Lawrence P. Fisher, who was then the general manager of Cadillac, shared with me a belief in the importance of appearance. He had been visiting some of the dealers and distributors around the country, among them Don Lee of Los Angeles, California. Don Lee owned, in conjunction with his sales operations, a custom body shop in which he built special bodies on both foreign and American cars and paid a visit to the shop where custom bodies were built. There he met their young chief designer and the director of the custom body shop, Harley J. Earl . . . [Earl] was doing things in a way Mr. Fisher had never seen before. For one thing he was using modeling clay to develop the forms of various automobile components. Also he was designing the complete automobile, shaping the body, hood, fenders, headlights, and running boards and blending them together into a good-looking whole. This, too, was a novel technique." Sloan went on to define the ultimate importance of this meeting: "Mr. Fisher's interest in this young man's talent was to result in actively influencing the appearance of more than 50 million automobiles from the late 1920s to 1960."

Sloan also established the hierarchy of cars at General Motors. It was a great marketing strategy for selling cars. The theory was that the entry-level buyer would be able to move up over time as the buyer's income rose, thus moving from a Chevrolet to an Oakland then Oldsmobile and so on. Furthermore, when a gap developed in GM's lineup of cars, Sloan filled it so as to avoid losing market share.

From 1937 to 1956, Mr. Sloan was the chairman of the board of General Motors. Upon his resignation from the chairmanship, Sloan was named honorary chairman of the board, a title that he held until his death on the afternoon of February 17, 1966, at Memorial Sloan-Kettering Center Hospital, which he helped establish.

For much of his life, Alfred P. Sloan Jr. dedicated a large part of his time to philanthropic activities, as a private donor to many causes and organizations and through the foundation he established in 1934.

year later, the LaSalle made its debut. It was a sales success and proved what Alfred Sloan had believed for some time: Styling was an important way to market cars.

Sloan approached GM's executive committee on June 27, 1927, with a plan to establish a new department for the purpose of considering the use of art and color in the design of automobiles, a department first labeled "The Art and Colour Section," with Harley Earl as its director.

Harley Earl was given the responsibility "to direct general production body design and to conduct research and development programs in special car designs," wrote Sloan in his book, *My Years with General Motors*. The original staff consisted of 50 people, 10 of whom were designers and the rest shop workers and clerical and administrative assistants.

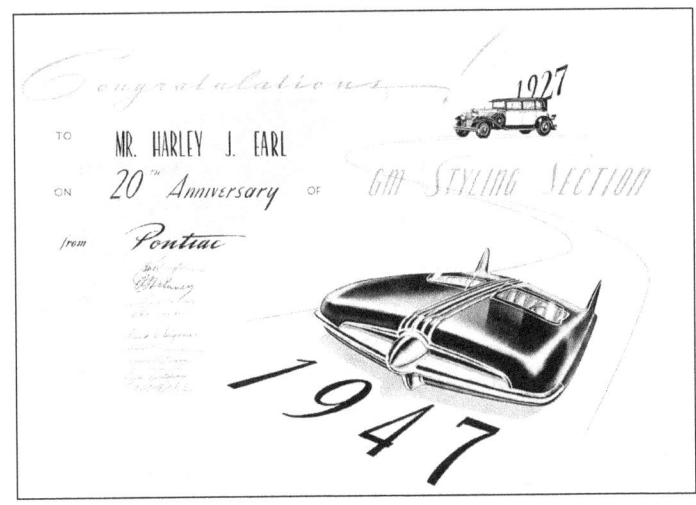

The year 1947 marked the 20th anniversary of Harley Earl joining General Motors to head the new Art and Colour Section, later renamed GM Styling. This artful congratulatory message came from the Pontiac Studio. (Photo Courtesy GM Media Archive)

Actor/comedian Roscoe "Fatty" Arbuckle had his new 1919 Pierce-Arrow Model 66-A4 built with special coachwork by Harley Earl at the Don Lee Coach and Body Works. It was the third custom car that Earl designed for Arbuckle.

Chapter One *The Early Days*

Harley Earl pioneered the modern concept car with the 1938 Buick Y-Job, which served as his personal transportation for many years. The Y-Job featured numerous advanced mechanical and styling ideas for the time. (Photo Courtesy GM Media Archive)

Earl's Art and Colour Section merged perfectly with Sloan's thinking regarding the concept of annual model year changes, which were meant to entice the public to buy new cars through just enough differences to make the next new model seem better while avoiding making too radical a change too soon. Earl's talents led him to being appointed a vice president in 1940.

One of the many innovations that originated within the Art and Colour Section was the conception of what is generally considered the first modern concept car, the 1938 Buick Y-Job (a car detailed in Chapter Four). Concept cars are designed and built by automotive manufacturers to this day.

Harley Earl oversaw the creation of dozens of concept cars (then called dream cars) during his command of styling, including the 1951 GM Le Sabre, 1954 Chevrolet Nomad, a series of cars powered by turbine engines, and many more that were seen across the country as exhibits of the extravagant traveling auto show dubbed the GM Motorama. He also had many production cars modified for VIPs.

As his 65th birthday approached (General Motors had a mandatory age-65 retirement policy at the time), Harley Earl retired from General

Harley Earl is seen in this photo demonstrating the Le Sabre's hideaway convertible top, which was stowed underneath a pivoting panel. The design did away with the need for a conventional top boot. The same concept had appeared on the previous Y-Job, as well as the 1953 Corvette. (Photo Courtesy GM Media Archive)

One of the more advanced research projects that Harley Earl initiated was GM's turbine car research program. Shown here are all versions of the experimental Firebirds: I, II, and III, from left to right. Each demonstrated not only turbine power, but several other advanced ideas such as self-driving. The 1958 Firebird III project was among the last concept cars Earl would oversee.

Among the many cars displayed at the 2015 Amelia Island Concours d'Elegance was this 1931 model custom-built for actor Buck Jones. It is likely the first Cadillac to receive tail fins. The unique car is undergoing restoration.

Harley Earl had this 1952 Cadillac custom convertible built for Harold Boyer, the head of Cadillac Motor Car Division's Cleveland tank plant after their discussion of what Boyer's idea of the ultimate car would be, which was "part Cadillac, part sports car." Harley Earl oversaw the design of many cars built for VIPs, as well as for his own use.

Motors at the end of 1958, leaving his handpicked successor, Bill Mitchell, in charge of GM Design. Even though Harley Earl left General Motors at the end of November 1958, he did not actually retire. Earl continued to work at the consulting firm he established in 1945, Harley Earl & Associates. In 1964, it was merged with Walter B. Ford Design Associates to become Ford and Earl. Earl's contract with General Motors required him not to perform any design work for their competition. He, therefore, created attractive packaging for Nabisco and Ban Roll-On Deodorant, designed aircraft interiors, and showrooms, and so on. He also served as a consultant to General Motors.

Earl moved to Palm Springs, Florida, upon his retirement from General Motors. As a fan of automotive racing, he stayed close to racing events at Sebring and the new NASCAR spectacle, the Daytona 500, which was first run in February 1959. Earl drove his one-off 1959 Oldsmobile F-88 Mk. III for onlookers during pre-race activities.

Earl's seemingly boundless imagination was extinguished due to complications of a stroke he suffered in February 1969; he passed away on April 10 of that year at the age of 75.

The chapters that follow this one spotlight the cars designed by Harley Earl, the man who invented the career, automobile stylist. However, a comprehensive analysis of every car is not practical in just one volume such as this. Therefore, for the most part, this book will detail the more significant cars created under his watch, such as the Cadillac Aerodynamic Coupe, Eldorado, Corvette, Bel Air, Century, Skylark, Eighty-Eight, and of course, the LaSalle. These are among the most treasured automobiles to collectors of automotive art.

Harley Earl headed General Motors' styling department from mid-1927 to late-1958. His interest in styling was not limited to automobiles; his office was state of the art in that regard. He is shown seated at his desk with a scale model of the 1951 GM Le Sabre. (Photo Courtesy GM Media Archive)

CHAPTER 2

THE LASALLE

"This, gentlemen, is the LaSalle we will not be building."
— Harley Earl, August 1933, executive preview of the 1934 models

In an article published in the winter 1967 issue of *Automobile Quarterly*, Harley Earl, who was interviewed for the story, recalled the beginnings of the LaSalle: "About 1926, Cadillac thought of coming through with the LaSalle and several people had worked on it to create what they wanted. They had a price on the car and they wanted it not to be quite as conservative as the Cadillac. They were shooting at more of a two-car family; that was their philosophy. Fred Fisher recommended that they permit me to do one, just to get a different angle. That's when Larry Fisher came into the picture and he asked me to come back to Detroit.

"When you are a designer, you kind of think, 'Well, if I were building one for myself from the chassis up, what would I do?' The Hispano was a car I was deeply in love with, from stem to stern. I didn't want to take too big a chance and do something that didn't look like anything.

"So I went back and sketched some stuff for them and they asked me to stay and finish it. The models and sketches took about three months, from sketch to mock-up. Mr. Sloan brought in the heads of the departments and asked if they saw anything that would be a problem, like tearing dies. They made some little dies and stretched metals. They didn't have any trouble. . . .

"About a month later Mr. Sloan asked me to come back to New York to discuss a permanent job."

The Need for the LaSalle

LaSalle (or sometimes spelled La Salle) was born because of a critical predicament for General Motors. For years Cadillac ruled the high-priced field, but by about the mid-1920s, Packard had moved ahead of Cadillac. However, that was not all that was wrong at General Motors. In 1921, Alfred Sloan headed an advisory staff, a special

A four-passenger Sport Phaeton was among the many styles offered in the 1929 LaSalle line of cars. Note the contrasting red accents and chassis. Chassis were black in standard form, but for an extra charge could be painted another color. (Photo Courtesy Cadillac & LaSalle Club)

committee created to evaluate the company's product policies. What was found was troubling; only Buick and Cadillac were profitable! All lines had to be improved and new products offered as needed to compete in every price class. One of the first things done was to terminate divisions Scripps-Booth and Sheridan (acquired under Durant's presidency), which contributed little to General Motors, thus they were dropped.

Sloan, as president of General Motors starting in 1923, continued improving GM's product lines and cost issues, but still had to solve the problem of being competitive in all price classes. In 1924, the touring car (the dominant body style at the time) prices were as follows: Chevrolet, $510; Oldsmobile, $750; Oakland, $945; Buick "4," $965; Buick Six, $1,995; and Cadillac, $2,995. Price gaps had developed between the various car lines, as well as a product gap between the Buick Six and Cadillac. Many of those able to move up market from a Buick Six chose to purchase a Packard, which sold for a lower price than a Cadillac. One solution to the price gap problem was to produce a new model beginning with the 1926 models labeled Pontiac, based upon the Chevrolet and to be sold by Oakland as a companion model. Other gaps were filled later (starting with the 1929 model year) with the Viking as a companion model built by Oldsmobile and the Marquette name (discontinued in 1912) was revived and built by Buick.

The LaSalle concept emerged in 1925 as the solution for filling the product gap existing between the upper level Buick and Cadillac. Once the LaSalle came into existence, it was priced just above the Buick Six so as to add sales for General Motors and not take away any from Cadillac. The model was more stylish and youthful than the reserved Cadillac; indeed, it was so different that there was very little parts interchange with a Cadillac. The LaSalle, as explained in Chapter One, became the first car to be designed at the direction of a stylist, Harley Earl. Production of the LaSalle continued through 1940, with major styling changes occurring three times after the inaugural 1927 model year, 1934, 1937, and 1939. The Viking and Marquette did not last as long; each was terminated after the 1931 model year. Pontiac ultimately replaced Oakland, also at the end of the 1931 model year.

Hispano-Suiza Influence

Harley Earl designed what became the 1927 LaSalle with inspiration from the Hispano-Suiza (now manufactured in France instead of Spain). This included the grille, winged radiator emblem, hood louvers, and headlights; he also used experiences gained as a custom-car builder. (Incidentally, Earl was not the only one commissioned by General Motors to provide designs. The firm of Hibbard and Darrin was also asked.) Fittingly, the car's namesake was the noted French explorer Robert de La Salle (1643–1687). Cadillac, the division responsible for building the LaSalle, was also named for a French explorer, Antoine de la Mothe Cadillac (1658–1730). The fact that Earl's inspiration was named for a French explorer was purely coincidental. However, his choice for inspiration was not by happenstance.

Ron Van Gelderen and Matt Larson explain in the book, *LaSalle: Cadillac's Companion Car*: At the time, "Anything French was immediately linked to new design, high fashion, color, and excitement. It was reasoned that the French foreign design characteristics of the new automobile should capitalize on this fashionability to attract those in the market niche as potential purchasers of the new LaSalle. LaSalle had all of the attributes advertising agencies would be able to promote with an uncommon flair to meet the vogue of the times." Furthermore, the Hispano-Suiza was perceived as one of the most exciting cars built at that time, if not *the* most.

LaSalle Series 303

The official introduction of the new LaSalle Series 303 occurred on March 5, 1927, the 269th anniversary of the birth of Antoine de la Mothe Cadillac. An advertising blitz commenced on March 3 with newspaper ads; the popular *Saturday Evening Post* featured a double-page ad in its issue that week, too. Among the selling points of the new car was its Cadillac engine (a Cadillac design) and the "finest workmanship of Fisher Body craftsmen" as applied to all Cadillac models. The March issue of *Motor* magazine also published a four-page article on the LaSalle. The author wrote that when he "first laid eyes on these new models lined up in a row stretching down one side of the exhibition room at the Cadillac factory, his first impression was that here was just about the most beautiful line of cars he had ever seen. But a moment later he discovered that on the other side of the room was a line of Cadillacs, and he realized that the Cadillacs were just as attractive.

"The two lines of cars are quite distinct in their appearance characteristics, and yet there is a definite resemblance. The word 'European' has become a popular term to apply to new models, and while Cadillac officials did not use this term in talking of the LaSalle line, nevertheless the instant the writer saw these new cars he was impressed with their foreign air. They have all the smartness of the leading foreign cars coupled with a neatness that is characteristic of American cars. . . . "

Famed aviator Charles Lindberg, the first to fly solo across the Atlantic, drove a new 1927 LaSalle. If that fact did not add prestige to the LaSalle name, nothing did! (Photo Courtesy GM Media Archive)

Pricing

The price gap that emerged between Buick and Cadillac was filled with Fisher-bodied LaSalles ranging from $2,495 for the four-passenger Phaeton to $2,795 for the five-passenger Imperial Sedan. Prices for Fleetwood-body versions spanned from $3,600 (two-passenger Coupe) to $5,000 (five-passenger Town Cabriolet with front compartment wing windows).

Features

Features of the 1927 LaSalle Series 303 included a V-8, two-tone paint with the hood and cowl typically being finished in a darker color than the body (a novelty at the time), and a choice of wheel types.

Even though a lighter, smaller version of the Cadillac 90-degree V-8 powered it, the LaSalle's engine was a fresh design, which differed internally, had a reduced displacement (via slightly shorter stroke), and produced somewhat less horsepower. LaSalle engines used side-by-side connecting rod attachments on the crankshaft journals, thus eliminating the fork and blade connecting rods of the older Cadillac engine, which had used this arrangement since its inception in 1915.

Displacement of the LaSalle V-8 measured 303 ci and was rated at 75 bhp. (The series designation based upon engine displacement was a European trait.) For comparison, the Cadillac Series 314 engine displaced 314.5 ci and produced 80 bhp. The LaSalle engine was not as complex and was more economical to build than that of the Cadillac. Thus, an enlarged version of the LaSalle V-8 went into the 1928 Cadillacs.

A pulley attached to the end of the camshaft held a belt to turn a six-bladed fan. Thermostatically controlled external shutters helped to maintain proper engine temperature. The heads of the LaSalle engine were finned as another means of thermal control.

Fuel flow to the carburetor was established via a vacuum tank with vacuum sourced from the intake manifold. This setup did away with the possibility of fuel flow being interrupted by mechanical or electrical failure. However, the potential weak point in the system was a long up-hill climb in which intake manifold vacuum dropped too low. To eliminate that mode of fuel starvation, a supplementary vacuum pump driven by an eccentric on the camshaft was included. A one-way valve kept the pump's labor restricted to the vacuum tank. Fuel mixture was controlled by a thermostatic system on the "vertical carburetor," thus minimizing the use of the choke.

Braking was performed by two independent systems (a rather advanced idea at the time), although by mechanical actuation. Hydraulic line failure was still viewed as too much of a risk by engineers. Internal expanding shoes were used for the front brake drums while external contracting bands were applied to the rear drums.

At introduction, five body styles were offered on a 125-inch wheelbase, which was 7 inches shorter than that of the smallest Cadillac. Eventually, additional body styles were made available. Fisher built three bodies, which sat on a 134-inch wheelbase. Furthermore, four semi-custom special-order Fleetwood styles were offered.

The 125-inch wheelbase Fisher Body offerings comprised a two-passenger Coupe (with leather or fabric back), two-passenger Roadster with rumble seat, two-passenger Convertible Coupe with rumble seat, four-passenger Victoria Coupe (leather back), four-passenger Phaeton, four-passenger Dual-Cowl Phaeton (introduced in July 1927), a five-passenger Sedan (leather back), and a five-passenger Town Sedan (metal back, introduced in July 1927).

In September 1927, the following style changes were made: The two-passenger Coupe, style 7410, was replaced by style 8140; the four-passenger Victoria Coupe, style 7390, was replaced by style 8130; and the five-passenger Sedan, style 7380, was replaced with style 8120. These style replacements comprised only a minor change to the curve at the rear of the roof, which was slightly lessened to give the appearance of a lower body.

Body types mounted on the long wheelbase (all of which were announced in August 1927) consisted of a seven-passenger Sedan (style 8060, metal back), seven-passenger Imperial Sedan (style 8070, metal back, division window between front and rear compartments), and a five-passenger Imperial Sedan (style 8090, leather back, blind quarters, division window).

Fleetwood's series was composed of a two-passenger Coupe (style 3110), five-passenger Sedan (style 3120), and a five-passenger Town Cabriolet (style 3130).

A large number of color combinations were available for the LaSalle thanks to the arrival three years earlier of DuPont Chemical Company's fast-drying, polychromatic Duco finishes. While the two-tone scheme of a darker hood and cowl with a lighter color for the body was typical, solid black as well as solid La Force Gray were also offered. Black was the standard color for the fenders and chassis, but the chassis could be painted another color for an additional $15. Paint color selections are known to have changed throughout the year, but no complete listing of all possible standard offerings is available.

LaSalles were assembled in Detroit in what had once been the plant used by Chrysler to build DeSotos. Prior to this, the Saxon Motor Car Company used the plant.

Excellent Performance

Although the 1927 LaSalle's V-8 was of lower horsepower, it was still an impressive performer. As reported in

Cadillac's in-house publication, *Clearing House*, on June 20 of that year, a nearly stock roadster (headlights, windshield, and running boards removed along with mechanical adjustments for high-speed driving) was driven at an average speed of 95.2 mph (103 mph was the highest speed attained) over a distance of 951.87 miles on GM's Milford Proving Grounds 3.78-mile-long test track over a nearly 10-hour period with only nine brief pit stops totaling less than 7½ minutes. (A fractured oil line terminated the test.) By achieving this, the LaSalle was judged as qualified to serve as the official pace car for the 1927 Indianapolis 500 run on May 30.

1928–1931: Only Mild Changes

The 1928 sales brochure for that model year's LaSalle stated, "A year ago LaSalle was a new name, even though it was sponsored by the oldest and finest in the fine car field. Today it still symbolizes (as it did when it first appeared) a new tomorrow in motorcar design, apparel and performance so far in advance of current practice that LaSalle is destined to be the symbol of good taste in motoring for long years to come." Apparently the public agreed with the flowery language. Sales of the LaSalle for 1927–1928 were very good, with 26,804 units being built.

The total production is given in this way because Cadillac used continuous serial numbers with no distinction between the 1927 and 1928 models. Up to that time, overall production numbers were tabulated through the calendar year, not model year. Research by the Cadillac & LaSalle Club has determined the change point for the 1928 model year took place on January 3. Future LaSalles had very distinct model year divisions. Furthermore, overall production figures quoted included chassis upon which went a custom-built body constructed by a coachbuilder. Some were ordered for commercial use.

An additional 160 units were built at the Oshawa, Ontario, plant. For the first nine months of production, one of every four Cadillac-built cars was a LaSalle.

The success of the 1927 LaSalle meant the 1928 models needed only very minor updates. In fact, the LaSalle was little changed through the 1932 model year. For 1928, 16 additional narrow hood louvers brought the total to 28 and horsepower was advertised as 80. The Series 303 engine was not changed. Prices went down slightly (by typically $20) for Fisher-bodied models, while prices for the Fleetwood-built cars ranged from $4,275 to $4,800.

Several body styles were added to the Fisher series: a five-passenger Sedan (metal back, style 8110) with the first one shipped December 31, 1927, and five others announced in January composed of a five-passenger Family Sedan (style 8110-A), a five-passenger Business Coupe (style 8110-A), two-passenger Business Coupe (style 8140-A), five-passenger Coupe (metal back, style 8050), seven-passenger Family Sedan (metal back, style 8060-A), and a five-passenger Cabriolet Sedan (style 8080). The latter three types were on the 134-inch wheelbase chassis.

Incidentally, Fisher built a single, unlisted Touring version on a 134-inch chassis; exactly when is unknown. The five-passenger Sedan (style 3120, 125-inch wheelbase) in the Fleetwood series was dropped and the five-passenger Transformable Town Cabriolet with front door crank-operated windows (style 3751) was added to the Fleetwood series. Total Fleetwood units built for 1927–1928, incidentally, amounted to only 58.

Standard equipment for 1927–1928 included five painted wood wheels with a rear-mounted spare (except Sport Phaeton, which came standard with six wire wheels, two of which were fender-mounted spares). Optional equipment included unpainted wood, wire or disc wheels, fenderwells for two spares (standard for Sport Phaeton), folding trunk rack (standard issue for Sport Phaeton), running board searchlight (standard for Sport Phaeton), and a special trunk. Sometime after the introduction of the LaSalle, a set of high-compression (5.1:1 ratio) heads was offered for Roadster and Phaeton versions for a charge of $125. When these heads were chosen, wire wheels were recommended due to the higher speed and acceleration; cost of the wheels was $95.

Color choices for the LaSalle continued to be dramatic and were supposedly based on those appearing in nature. Some of the more striking pairings of colors included lavender with green wheels, yellow-gold with orange fenders, and taupe with blue window reveals. Upholstery was of leather, cloth, or mohair.

Cadillac and LaSalle shared a sales catalog for the first time this model year. Prior marketing strategy had kept the two apart. By this point, LaSalle was taking away some sales from Cadillac, which probably explains the change in the marketing approach.

During the final years of the roaring 1920s, the long wheelbase versions of the LaSalle had proven to be more in demand than expected. Therefore, the 1929 model lineup was changed to accommodate this reality; all body styles (with the exceptions of the Roadster, the two Phaetons, and two Fleetwood versions) were built on the 134-inch wheelbase chassis.

The Fleetwood series now comprised four fully custom bodies (all five-passenger types): a Transformable Town Cabriolet (style 3051) on the 125-inch wheelbase, a Town Cabriolet with collapsible rear quarters also on the 125-inch wheelbase (style 3130) and the two body styles on the 134-inch wheelbase: a Transformable Town Cabriolet (style 3751), and an All-Weather Phaeton (style 3780).

Fisher Body offerings numbered 14 and comprised the following: four-passenger Phaeton (style 1185), four-passenger Sport (style 1185-B), two-passenger Roadster (style 1186), seven-passenger Sedan (style 8530), seven-passenger Imperial Sedan (style 8540), five-passenger Sedan (style 8550), five-passenger Family Sedan (style 8555), five-passenger Coupe (style 8570), two-passenger Convertible Coupe (style 8580), two-passenger Coupe (style 8590), five-passenger Convertible Landau Cabriolet (style 8600), five-passenger Imperial Convertible Landau Cabriolet (style 8605), five-passenger Town Sedan (style 8610), and the five-passenger Imperial Town Sedan (style 8615).

As the series designation "328" suggests, the LaSalle's engine was enlarged to 328 ci via an increase in the bore size to 3.25 inches, netting an additional 6 hp. General Motors installed the "Synchro-Mesh" transmission in the LaSalle, which Cadillac started using in the prior model year. The Synchro-Mesh transmission allowed the engine to reduce RPM until the gears in the transmission components were at the right speed to safely engage when either shifting up or down to avoid grinding.

Other advertised changes for the 1929 model year included an improved steering gear, Security-Plate (shatterproof) glass, more fully adjustable front seat, Pneumatic Control (hydraulic shocks) for maximum quietness, and chrome-plating for components previously plated with nickel. Furthermore, new color schemes were made available throughout the model year.

Production reached a record total of 22,961 units (available records account for 22,950 units, an unexplained 11-unit gap). The total figure included such rarities (in the Fisher Body series) as the five-passenger Imperial Town Sedan, of which a mere 17 were built, the five-passenger Imperial Convertible Landau Cabriolet, of which only 37 were built, and a single LaSalle hearse. The LaSalles with Fleetwood bodies were even more rare, accounting for a grand total of 25 units of the overall production.

While the 1927–1931 LaSalles underwent little change over those years, the 1930–1931 versions were the most changed of this group. The 1930 model year brought an end to the shorter wheelbase cars; all body styles in what was now the Series 340 were mounted atop a 134-inch-wheelbase chassis, just 6 inches shorter than the wheelbase of the upper-level Cadillacs.

LaSalles this year moved away from the Hispano-Suiza look and came to appear more like a Cadillac. The bodies were said to be "lower, longer, and racier in appearance than ever before." Fisher Body styles dropped to seven, while the custom-bodied Fleetwood series increased to eight.

Those from Fisher were composed of the five-passenger Town Sedan (style 30-252), two-passenger Coupe (style 30-258), five-passenger Sedan (style 30-259), seven-passenger Sedan (style 30-262), seven-passenger Imperial Sedan (style 30-263), two-passenger Convertible Coupe (style 30-268), and five-passenger Coupe (style 30-272).

The Fleetwood special custom bodies were the five-passenger Transformable Cabriolet (style 3351), five-passenger Brougham (style 3364), two-passenger Roadster, which were known as Fleetcliffe (style 4002), seven-passenger Touring, called Fleetlands (style 4057), five-passenger Phaeton, known as Fleetshire (style 4060), five-passenger All-Weather Phaeton, called the Fleetway (style 4080), and a couple of five-passenger Sedanettes both also known as Fleetwinds, with one a Cabriolet (style 4081 and the other style 4082).

Only one each of the Transformable Cabriolet and Brougham was built; only 42 Sedanette Cabriolets and 45 Sedanettes were sold. The remaining body styles accounted for a few hundred sales each; in all, Fleetwood output amounted to 1,278 cars, which was the high-point of Fleetwood production until 1934 when all LaSalles were built by Fleetwood.

As indicated in the revised series name, a 340-ci V-8 now powered the LaSalle. The displacement grew via another increase in bore size to 3 5/16 inches; the stroke remained the same. Output was now rated at 90 hp. High-compression heads were again offered for domestic models, but this time the ratio was increased to 5.3:1 (versus the 5.1:1 previously offered). However, the V-8 of the LaSalle was eclipsed by the release of the new Cadillac V-16 series with a displacement of 452 ci.

Standard equipment included wood wheels with 6.50 x 19-inch US Royal black sidewall tires and a rear spare tire carrier. An optional 18-inch wood, wire, or disc wheel with 7.00 x 18-inch U.S. Royal tires was offered. Some Fleetwoods (Roadster, Phaeton, and Touring) were to receive "Sport Type" colors. However, these sport-type colors (combinations 101 through 105) were available for the other members of the Fleetwood styles.

The Great Depression stunned the country just a few weeks after the 1930 models were released, and as a result made GM's pricing structure more complicated. Even so, LaSalle kept General Motors competitive with automakers with cars in a similar price range such as the Chrysler Imperial 80, Franklin 11-B, Kissel 8-75, Packard Six, and Peerless 6-72, and so on. However, production fell significantly to 14,986 units.

Only subtle styling changes were seen in the 1931 LaSalle lineup now known as the Series 345 (later re-dubbed as Series 345-A once the Series 345-B appeared the following year). This year, the same engine powered the LaSalle and the Cadillac. Displacement measured 353 ci and provided a small boost in horsepower over the 1930 LaSalle engine. Clearly the series designation had departed from the standard of representing engine size.

Fisher Body types remained unchanged, but the style numbers were altered and began with 31-6xx. Prices for each dropped substantially, ranging from about 9 percent to about 14 percent depending upon the model. Fleetwood Body offered six of the eight body styles from the prior model year while only the Transformable Cabriolet and Brougham were dropped.

However, the style numbers changed. The five-passenger Town Car (of which only one was built) was style 4151; the two-passenger Roadster (150 built and the most common) was style 4602. The remaining models' style numbers changed only in the second digit with that going from a "0" to a "6." Fleetwood cars accounted for 330 of the 10,995 LaSalles built for the 1931 model year. Even with the substantial price decrease, the total was over 25 percent less than 1930 production. Cadillac sales actually exceeded those of LaSalle just as they had the previous model year. LaSalle had lost its separate identity; the separate identity was a critical marketing point that had helped to make the model viable.

Popular options this time included a chrome-plated radiator screen and the Heron hood ornament. Other options available were chrome-plated wire wheel spokes, chrome-plated folding trunk rack, hot air heater (with single or double registers), radio, rumble seat windshield, fabric tire cover, and chrome-plated tire cover.

1932: Facelift

The 1932 model year brought a mix of price decreases and price increases depending upon the body style. It also brought back two wheelbases (130 and 136 inches) and some extensive restyling. Even so, production figures were bleak (3,386), all of them Fisher Body cars because the Fleetwood-built LaSalles were not offered this time.

Shutters and screens were eliminated from the grille shell, which surrounded a waffle-patterned radiator. Headlights had a tie-bar between them with a "LaS" emblem mounted at the center. Front fenders had a longer sweep into the running boards. The running boards had the appearance of being an integral part of the front fenders as a result of this. Bodylines were more rounded than earlier LaSalles. The doorsills were lower. Wheel size was reduced from 18 inches to 17. The lower doorsills and reduced wheel diameter, in combination with a lower height for the body, made for a much sleeker and refined-looking car. A double-molded beltline offered the opportunity for a multitude of color combinations.

The symmetrically shaped dash with easy-to-read round dials, chrome trim surrounds, and wooden upper panel was yet another styling change for 1932. LaSalles were equipped with this dash through 1934 and Cadillac kept it in use through 1937.

Reportedly, Harley Earl judged the 1932 LaSalles as one of his personal favorites.

With the freshly restyled LaSalles came some body style changes and style identification numbers. Eight body styles were available: two-passenger Coupe (style 32-678), two-passenger Convertible Coupe (style 32-668), five-passenger Town Coupe (style 32-672), five-passenger Sedan (style 32-659), five-passenger Town Sedan (style 32-652), seven-passenger Sedan (style 32-662), seven-passenger Imperial Sedan (style 32-663), and a unique five-passenger Phaeton (style 256) composed of a Fisher-built Cadillac body mounted on a LaSalle chassis. The two-passenger Convertible Coupe replaced the two-door Roadster to fill the demand for a more weather-tight automobile.

Engine displacement stayed at 353 ci, although horsepower increased to 115 at 3,000 rpm. Improved carburetion and a mechanically operated fuel pump were further refinements for the V-8.

An adjustable ride control dubbed Full-Range Ride Regulator was standard this year. It was operated via a handle under the dash and set the hydraulic shocks for either a soft, firm, or normal ride. A gauge on the dash provided the driver with the ability to see the setting chosen. Also included was a freewheeling and vacuum-operated automatic clutch.

1933: Major Restyle

The 1933 LaSalle Series 345-C received new styling features, but the body was generally about the same. Of the styling alterations, the most prominent was the skirted front fenders, which concealed the bottom of the fenderwells for the side-mounted spares. The grille shell was greatly altered; it was painted rather than plated and was peaked at the center instead of flat. It completely surrounded the radiator but was not closely related to its shape anymore. This change, done strictly for styling purposes, forced the radiator filler to be relocated under the hood. Headlights were mounted on vertical stanchions (but with trumpet horns still attached) and the tie-bar between them was eliminated.

LaSalle's V-8 went unchanged this year, but the Synchro-Mesh transmission was improved. The freewheeling feature was not continued but was still available upon request; it was fitted to many of the 1933 models.

Body style offerings were largely identical to those of the previous model year, but the body codes began with 33- with the exception of the Cadillac-bodied cars, which again included the Phaeton, style 8-256 (one built), as well as a five-passenger Coupe, style 8-272 (two built), and an All-Weather Phaeton, style 8-273 (two built). In addition, four five-passenger Town Coupes, style 8-222, with body by Fleetwood were built. Interestingly, style 8-222 was an offering in the 1932 Cadillac lineup. Also offered was style 8-155, a Fisher Body Cadillac two-passenger Roadster on the 130-inch wheelbase LaSalle chassis, but none appear to have been built.

LaSalle was represented at the 1933 World's Fair in Chicago by six closed-bodied cars in non-standard paint schemes. One of them, a two-passenger Coupe, still exists. In all, production totaled a disappointing 3,482 units.

1934: Reprieve via Styling

The 1934 LaSalles were "Sleek, smooth, powerful, and aristocratic, the new LaSalle has character and individuality . . . beauty and strength." And according to GM's brochure on the newly designed car, "None but the superb craftsmanship of Fleetwood custom builders could transform expressionless wood and metal into this masterpiece." Yet, the LaSalle was supposed to be discontinued after 1933. Other companion models (Buick's Marquette and Oldsmobile's Viking) were dropped; Pontiac was kept, but Oakland was terminated.

The decision to suspend production of the LaSalle had already been made by the time Harley Earl told his group of stylists to develop some fresh ideas for the 1934 LaSalle, in hopes the model could be reinstated. Earl then left for his annual tour of the European auto shows. While Harley Earl was away, Jules Agramonte, who had come over from Fleetwood, created an airbrush rendering composed of features influenced by the narrow-fronted, fixed–front wheel English beach racers of the day such as a tall, slender grille, a narrow and tapered hood, headlights attached to the radiator shell, and skirted front wheels. He showed it to one of his superiors, Harry Shaw, and suggested it could become the new LaSalle. Shaw disagreed and told him to file it away.

However, Shaw went on a vacation immediately afterward and Agramonte knew Mr. Earl was returning from Europe. He also knew Earl often came to the studios at night to look over the stylists' work. Agramonte decided to leave his rendering of the proposed LaSalle lying on his desk in plain sight. As expected, Earl made his late-night visit and found the LaSalle rendering. According to Earl, it was one of the most exciting days of

Stylists of GM's Art and Colour Section are shown at work on designs for the 1934 LaSalle in this photograph. At center right is an instrument panel design. Note scale clay model at top center. By this point, Harley Earl had pushed through his philosophy that every element of an automobile should be styled. (Photo Courtesy Cadillac & LaSalle Club)

his life when he spotted the breathtaking design, which would be the next LaSalle if he had his way.

According to the book *LaSalle: Cadillac's Companion Car*, "It was perfect; slender and light, with the most beautiful fender forms anyone had ever seen. It was like a modern racing plane. This car had no vestige with the old traditional 'carriage trade' vehicles. Just like the original 1927 LaSalle, it was the right new car design for the times, but this time it was an original design and . . . totally American."

Harley Earl ordered Agramonte to develop the design further and then to build clay models. After the LaSalle was refined and in clay form, a highly accurate sample body made from scrimmed wood and metal was constructed. All details were present, including the biplane bumpers, chevrons on the leading portion of the front fenders, and hood portholes. The next phase of the process would either revive the LaSalle or put an end to it permanently: the executive review of the new 1934 cars of each division.

In August 1933, William Knudsen (president of General Motors), Lawrence Fisher (Cadillac Division president), Ernest Seaholm (chief engineer), John Chick (Cadillac general sales manager), and Nicholas Dreystadt (works manager) gathered in the auditorium of the Argonaut Building. To them, Harley Earl presented each new model from the divisions of General Motors, but saved the LaSalle for last. Just before raising the curtain in dramatic fashion to reveal the LaSalle, Earl announced to the group, "This, gentlemen, is the LaSalle we will *not* be building." (Another account claims Earl said, "Gentlemen, if you decide to discontinue the LaSalle, this is the car you are not going to build.") Everyone was greatly impressed with the LaSalle they "were not going to build." So, the decision to discontinue it was reversed.

Management's "one-eighty" regarding production of the LaSalle created a bit of a problem, though. No one was expecting this change and, therefore, the production line was not ready for the radically redesigned car. Using the nearly idle Fleetwood plant solved the matter. Sales of the Fleetwood-built V-12 and V-16 models had decreased greatly, leaving the skilled craftsmen with little to do. It was only their skills that kept them from having already been laid off. Thus, for the duration of the 1934 model year, all LaSalles, which were designated as Series 350, wore the prestigious Fleetwood badge.

The original design for the 1934 LaSalle (prior to the planned cancellation) was much like the 1933 version, but with headlights mounted on pylons atop the fenders, a wide grille angled back, and fenders flowing back into the running boards, as in 1933. Another feature, the biplane bumpers, was carried forward for production. In the end, very little from 1933 was carried over; the torpedo hood ornament, the double broadleaf dash, and the art deco–style dome light bezel were the only features kept. It was so different that none of the LaSalle body panels interchanged with any other GM car. The 1934 LaSalle was so different from its contemporaries that other automakers (even European ones) looked to it for styling inspiration.

Agramonte's design resulted in a streamlined shape with pontoon front fenders, which flowed more downward ahead of the wheels, thus hiding the front chassis. Racing aircraft, which had fixed landing gear streamlined with pontoon-shaped fairings, influenced the shape. This time, the front fenders were truncated in back rather than sweeping into the running boards. Headlights were mounted on the radiator shell. Especially notable is the tall, narrow grille and radiator shroud, as well as the long, tapered hood.

The result of this styling was a narrow engine compartment, which did not allow the Cadillac V-8 to fit. The solution to this was a different engine. Replacing the V-8 was a straight-8 displacing 240 ci and producing 95 hp at 3,700 rpm. To keep costs down, an entirely new engine was ruled out, so in the end a block based upon the Oldsmobile's straight-8 block was used. By the time it was machined and fully assembled by Cadillac workmen, it had little in common with an Olds engine. The straight-8 and the 119-inch wheelbase of the LaSalle were traits in common with the Oldsmobile. Because of these similarities, the myth began that the LaSalle had an Oldsmobile 8 chassis, and even today the completely inaccurate claim is made that the 1934 LaSalle had more in common with the 1934 Oldsmobile than the Cadillac.

Steel, 16-inch disc wheels were fitted with painted wheel covers color-coordinated to the body color, or full chrome wheel covers. Rear fender shape mimicked that of the front.

In keeping with the streamlined theme, the spare tire was now concealed either in the luggage compartment of the four-door models or in a compartment beneath the rumble seat of two-door models. Nine standard color choices were offered for U.S.-built cars and included such colors as Admiral Blue with Freedom Blue wheels, Richmond Maroon with Vincennes Red wheels, and Lamar Tan with Sealing Wax Red wheels. (Canadian cars had far more color choices, 25 of them.) As in the past, the customer could specify any durable color at no extra charge. An opalescent finish was available at extra cost.

Further enhancing the streamlined appearance of the LaSalle was the mid-year availability of a set of rear wheel shields (fender skirts) as an option costing $25. They were ornamented with a hubcap at the center. However, the fender shields had been fitted to a number of special-order cars and the World's Fair convertible before being officially offered.

The design was beautiful, but it challenged the technology of the day. Presses were not able to produce all of the complex shapes, so a lot of the bodywork had to be done by hand. Fortunately, the Fleetwood employees were highly skilled at such labor. This was the final year for the body to be built over wood framing.

Body styles of the LaSalle Series 350 were limited to four: the five-passenger sedan (style 34-159), two-passenger convertible coupe (style 34-168), two-passenger coupe (style 34-178), and the five-passenger Club Sedan with blind quarters (style 34-182). The French builder Van den Plas built at least one European custom-bodied LaSalle (a Cabriolet).

New mechanical updates other than the engine included hydraulic brakes (two years ahead of Cadillac), knee-action independent coil spring suspension, torsional rear stabilizer bar to help prevent side sway, and the mid-year introduction of Hotchkiss drive (replacing the torque-tube) along with improvements to the transmission.

The streamlined shape of the new LaSalle probably had much to do with its selection as the pace car for the 1934 Indianapolis 500. Prices decreased significantly from those of 1933. The lowest was $1,595 (two-passenger Coupe) and all other models were priced at $1,695.

Many two-tone paint schemes were offered for LaSalles throughout the years of production. However, single-tone paint was recommended by the factory to emphasize the streamlined styling of the all-new 1934 models. This LaSalle Convertible Coupe has an uncommon two-tone combination. Only 600 of the type were built for the model year. (Photo Courtesy Worldwide Auctioneers)

Despite its newness, its impact of automotive styling, and the extra publicity from pacing the Indy 500 race, total 1934 LaSalle production amounted to only 7,232, even though the 1934 body was supplied into March 1935.

1935–1936

"In appearance, the LaSalle is smarter than the style-setting LaSalle of last year, the car that established the streamlined trend for the entire industry," said the 1935 LaSalle brochure. It looked very much like the 1934 models, but nearly every panel was different. Technology had advanced enough to allow the presses, along with more ductile steel, to form the complex shapes of the body and to make a roof completely of steel; it was dubbed the "Turret-Top." It completely eliminated the wooden roof slats and the leather or fabric insert. Fisher Body once again built the LaSalle bodies.

The most immediately noticeable differences between the previous Series 350 and the new Series 50 models were a V-type windshield and new one-piece bumpers. The biplane bumpers proved to be fragile and, therefore, less practical. Most everything else received subtle alterations. Two-door body styles received a fender-mounted spare, but the four-door styles stayed with the spare mounted inside the trunk. The wheelbase grew 1 inch, to 120.

Body style offerings numbered five this time and comprised the five-passenger Standard Sedan (style 35-5009), five-passenger Touring Coupe (style 35-5011), five-passenger Touring Sedan (style 35-5019), two-passenger Convertible Coupe (style 35-5067), and two-passenger Convertible Coupe (style 35-5077). Also offered was a commercial chassis with a 121-inch wheelbase (style 35-50). Other than the commercial chassis (53 ordered), the least produced was the Standard Sedan with only 100 being built.

Mechanical upgrades included a more powerful straight-8, up 10 hp to 105 at 3,600 rpm, a new Stromberg duplex downdraft carburetor, and a variable output generator.

Production increased to 8,653 units for 1935. A substantial price decrease from 1934 likely accounts for the greater number of sales. Still, Packard did better thanks to a more economical model dubbed the One-Twenty introduced that year. Priced as much as $250 less than a comparable LaSalle, the One-Twenty found in excess of 25,000 buyers.

For 1936, the LaSalle Series 50 was little changed. One of the most obvious changes to the exterior was made per many customer requests: the doors of the two-door and the front doors of the four-door models were now hinged in front and opened from the rear. Hood ventilators were completely redesigned with six instead of five sets within a raised rectangular shape. Upon the rectangular form appeared the name "LASALLE" in chromed letters. A more convex grille with nine horizontal bars rather than six and only two vertical hash marks appearing on the catwalks were additional styling updates.

Inside was a new instrument panel layout, which was nearly identical to that of the Cadillac. Its symmetrical design simplified the process of changing it to right-hand drive for export cars. Most of the instrumentation was grouped at the center of the dash.

Body styles included a five-passenger Touring Coupe (style 36-5011), five-passenger Touring Sedan (style 36-5019), two-passenger Convertible Coupe, and a two-passenger Coupe. Aside from the commercial chassis priced at $950, the lowest priced LaSalle was the two-passenger Coupe at $1,175 while the two-passenger Convertible Coupe took the top spot at $1,255.

The 1936 LaSalle was priced about $1,000 less than the least expensive Cadillac. It was no longer intended to fill a price gap but was simply meant to keep the luxury car division from losing money. While the economy began to recover, the LaSalle did, too, but not in proportion to the improvement of the economy. Sales amounted to 13,004 units, an improvement of more than 50 percent above those of 1935. Unfortunately, it was not good enough. Packard outsold the LaSalle by about a four-to-one ratio.

1937–1938

In an attempt to become competitive, the 1937 LaSalle was again made all Cadillac by giving it a 322-ci version of the Cadillac Series 60's V-8 and heavily promoting it as a car completely built by Cadillac. The LaSalle now shared its B-body with Cadillac's Series 60 (a more compact model added for 1936), as well as the Buick Century.

The 1937 LaSalle received a 124-inch wheelbase this time and much of the additional length was ahead of the firewall. Even though it was all-new, styling elements from the 1934–1936 model years were still present. Up front was a tall, narrow, one-piece die-cast grille, though this time with a bold V-8 emblem attached rather than a "LaS" used since the model's inception. The LaS emblem was relocated to the center of the front bumper. This time there were no hash marks on the catwalks. The long hood had horizontal louvers with six stainless steel trim pieces spanning virtually the entire length. Pontoon-like fenders, again with a trio of chromed chevrons in front and bullet-like headlight housings, were familiar LaSalle traits carried forward from 1934.

While LaSalle's new longer body gave it a narrower appearance, there was more room under the hood, thus making possible the fitting of Cadillac's V-8. This V-8 was a "Monobloc," a first for Cadillac. It was slightly lighter than the previous Cadillac V-8 and produced 125 hp at 3,400 rpm. With the increased output, the rear axle ratio was reduced. Also new was the installation of an oil bath air cleaner, a hypoid rear axle, and a simplified exhaust with one large muffler instead of two.

Other than promoting the LaSalle as being "completely Cadillac built," advertising also focused on its economical pricing. Prices ranged from $995 to $1,485; they would never be so low again for the LaSalle. Series 37-50 LaSalles were offered in several styles this time and included the five-passenger Touring Sedan two-door (style 37-5011), five-passenger Touring Sedan four-door (style 37-5019), two-passenger Sport Coupe (style 37-5027), five-passenger Convertible Sedan (style 37-5049), two-passenger Convertible Coupe (style 37-5067), and a Flower Car (style 37-5067F), of which only six were built. A 160-inch wheelbase commercial chassis (style 37-50) was also offered, bringing 949 orders.

Ten standard colors were offered and included black with black wheels (or optionally, Flare Red or Clearwater Green for the wheels), Admiral Blue with matching wheels, Peruvian Gray with Flare Red wheels, or Santaupe Metallic with Kashan Blue wheels. Standard upholstery choices for closed-bodied cars were Bedford cord or plain Broadcloth in tan or gray and for convertible bodies, leather in black, tan, gray, or green.

Once again, the LaSalle was chosen to pace the Indianapolis 500. A few weeks prior to the running of the race, race car driver Ralph De Palma set a new speed record on the Indy track while driving a Convertible Coupe for 500 miles in 6 hours 5 minutes 0.59 seconds.

LaSalle sales surged, totaling 32,005, the highest they would ever be. Even so, the LaSalle remained well behind the sales race with the lower series Packards. However, LaSalle sales edged out those of the Lincoln Zephyr by nearly 2,150 units. The relative success of this year's LaSalle came at the expense of lost Cadillac Series 60 sales.

LaSalle for 1938 had only mild styling changes. A slightly larger

Integrating the headlights into the fender was an idea that kept cropping up with stylists. This 1937 LaSalle showed how the feature would appear. In the end, the same argument about the lights being more prone to breakage by flying debris put an end to the proposal, at least for a little while longer. (Photo Courtesy GM Media Archive)

This proposed 1938 LaSalle Sixty Special ultimately became the basis for the Cadillac Sixty Special. The design originated because Harley Earl was seeking another trendsetting car like the 1927 LaSalle. (Photo Courtesy GM Media Archive)

V-type grille and a slightly different front bumper were among the frontal changes. More noticeable were the headlights with longer housings mounted on fluted, vertical stanchions. The length of the hood was accentuated with a newly designed set of slender ventilators running along its side panels. It was also changed in the way it opened ("alligator" style) leaving the side panels in place. Lifting the hood ornament released the hood. The chevrons were deleted from the front fenders, which were subtly reshaped with a faster taper toward the rear side and a more vertical drop in back, giving a more squared-off appearance.

Changes to the interior were more significant. The gearshift lever was relocated from the floor to the steering column and the dash was redesigned with the use of plastic for the first time. Plastic was a new material and it offered a way to cost-effectively make more complicated decorative designs with a jewel-like appearance.

Styles offered for 1938 were the five-passenger Touring Coupe (style 38-5011), five-passenger Touring Sedan (style 38-5019), two-passenger Coupe (style 38-5027), five-passenger Convertible Sedan (style 3-5049), two-passenger Convertible Coupe (style 38-5067), and again a 160-inch wheelbase commercial chassis (style 38-50) of which 900 were ordered.

One LaSalle model that received consideration for production was the Sixty Special. However, Cadillac incorporated this design and it proved to be very popular. It came about because Harley Earl wanted another LaSalle that would become yet another trendsetter. A recently hired stylist, Bill Mitchell, was assigned by Earl to head the design effort. Some elements of the styling for the Sixty Special came from European influence, this time the Panhard Panoramic, which Earl and William Knudsen saw at the 1934 Paris Salon held late that year.

Sales figures for the 1938 LaSalle came to 15,501 units. Prices had increased significantly since the previous model year and had done so at the time the country's economy had slumped again. The lowest priced model, the two-passenger Coupe, sold at a base price of $1,295. It was the second most popular model with 2,711 being built, while the most popular was the five-passenger Touring Sedan, which accounted for 9,768 sales.

1939

A considerably restyled LaSalle appeared for the 1939 model year. The freshly redesigned body again sat on a 120-inch wheelbase, yet despite it being 4 inches shorter; the overall length of the car actually appeared to have increased. Although new, the styling themes of the past remained such as a tall, narrow grille, V-type windshield, and similar fender shaping. However, large

The LaSalles received a major redesign for 1939. New styling features included a tall, vertical diecast grille, along with a grille in front of the so-called catwalk on either side of the center radiator grille. Shown is a Convertible Coupe, one of 1,020 produced. (Photo Courtesy Cadillac & LaSalle Club)

side grilles now appeared, the glass area was greatly increased, and running boards were deleted, but still available as an option.

Speaking of optional equipment, a particularly interesting one was the Sunshine Turret-Top available for two- and four-door sedan models. It was an easily operated sliding steel panel, which provided increased ventilation as well as a view of the sky. This option added $37.50 to the base price of either model. Only 23 LaSalles were so equipped, according to *LaSalle: Cadillac's Companion Car*.

Fourteen standard colors were offered this year, including schemes such as Cavern Green with Triton Green wheels, or Trinidad Gray Iridescent with Corsican Red wheels. The center grille and hood ventilators were white and chrome while the side grilles were black and chrome.

Body styles offered were the five-passenger Touring Sedan two-door (style 39-5011), five-passenger Touring Sedan two-door with the Sunshine Turret-Top (style 39-5011A), five-passenger Touring Sedan four-door (style 39-5019), five-passenger Touring Sedan four-door with the Sunshine Turret-Top (style 39-5019A), two-passenger Coupe (style 39-5027), five-passenger Convertible Sedan (style 39-5029), two-passenger Convertible Coupe (style 39-5067), and a commercial chassis with a 156-inch wheelbase (style 39-50), of which 874 were sold. Sales of the 1939 LaSalles totaled 23,002 units and that was enough to finally exceed those of the Packard One-Twenty.

1940: The End

In its final year of production, the LaSalle was offered in not one, but *two* series: the Series 50 and Series 52. Series 50 cars still had the 1939 body, but with a newly styled front end. Headlights (with sealed-beam units for the first time) were now integrated into the front fenders. A belt molding ran the length of the hood all the way to near the back of the car. Running boards were a delete option. When deleted, they were replaced by a set of three horizontal stainless-steel moldings. Surprisingly, fender-mounted spares (Series 50 only) were made available again, but few cars were ordered with the option.

Five body styles (all on a 123-inch wheelbase) were offered: the five-passenger Touring Sedan two-door (style 40-5011), five-passenger Sedan four-door (style 40-5019), two-passenger Coupe (style 40-5027), five-passenger Convertible Sedan (style 40-5029), two-passenger Convertible Coupe (style 40-5067), and a 159-inch commercial chassis (style 40-50) of which 1,030 were produced. The five-passenger Touring Sedans, built with the Sunshine Turret-Top, had an "A" added to the style numbers, as was the case for 1939. A total of 149 were built, but only nine of them were the two-door version. Another low-production car was the five-passenger Convertible Sedan of which only 125 were built. A curious style was mentioned only in the *Cadillac-LaSalle Series Chassis Parts List*, 40-5019F, which was a five-passenger Imperial Sedan. Only four such cars were built.

Pricing ranged from $1,180 (two-passenger Coupe) to $1,730 (five-passenger Convertible Sedan).

The Series 52 Special used the C-body, the same as that for the Cadillac Series 62. It is often referred to as the "torpedo body." None of the body panels of the Series 52 interchanged with those of the Series 50. The 1940 sales brochure for this model said, "As you can see, the Sedan is entirely new in styling: low, wide, and with windows of exceptional size. Notice the absence of protruding hinges and the smart simplicity of exterior details." (The reference to "protruding hinges" was noting the fully concealed door hinges of the Series 52 versus the exposed ones of the Series 50.) Series 52 models lacked a belt molding, had less chrome, and could also be ordered without running boards as a no-charge delete option.

At the start of the model year, the Series 52 Special was available in only two body styles: a two-passenger Coupe (style 40-5227C) and five-passenger Touring Sedan (style 540-219). In March 1940, two additional styles were offered: two-passenger Convertible Coupe (style 40-5267) and five-passenger Convertible Sedan (style 40-5229). Only 75 of the latter were produced. The five-passenger four-door Touring Sedan was the most produced of all (including Series 50 offerings), with 10,181 being built.

The Sunshine Turret-Top was available for LaSalle as well as Oldsmobile, Buick, and Cadillac two- and four-door sedan models. It was an easily operated sliding steel panel providing increased ventilation as well as a view of the sky. Only 23 LaSalles were so equipped. (Photo Courtesy GM Media Archive)

If the 1941 LaSalle had entered production, it would have been offered in three series, each corresponding with those of the Cadillac: Series 61, 62, and 63. All proposals were four-door sedans. Left to right are the Series 51 fastback, Series 50, and the Series 52 torpedo body. (Photos Courtesy GM Media Archive)

Two-tone interiors were offered for the Series 52 convertible models and were identical to those of the corresponding models in the Cadillac Series 62 line. The interior of the closed models of the Series 52 was similar to that of the Series 50. All interiors of the Series 52 models were made by Fleetwood and were noted as such via a tag attached to the lower side of the passenger seat. Also special to the Series 52 was a power convertible top for two-door version only. Because rearward visibility was poor with the top up, a driver's side outside rearview mirror was standard equipment.

Standard color choices numbered 14 for the Series 50, most of which were iridescent shades such as Oxblood Maroon Iridescent, Chicory Green Iridescent, and Beaumont Blue Iridescent. As for the Series 52, a total of 16 standard color options, including four two-tone patterns, were offered. However, an extraordinarily long list of 314 special order colors was made available for closed-bodied Series 52 models, while "only" 40 special order colors were offered for the convertible models. Many of them were two-tone schemes. Standard color choices numbered 16, of which four were two-tone patterns.

Prices for the Series 52 ranged from $1,320 (two-passenger Coupe) to $1,825 (five-passenger Convertible Sedan).

The 322 V-8 for both series of LaSalles was now rated at 130 hp at 3,400 rpm

In all, 24,130 Series 50 and 52 LaSalles (including chassis) were built, putting it ahead of the Lincoln Zephyr again, although still behind Packard's One-Twenty. On August 26, 1940, the last LaSalle, a Series 52 Special Sedan, left the assembly line, thus finally ending GM's companion car arrangement. The legacy of the LaSalle was its trend-setting styling, which helped establish General Motors as the style leader for years to come.

The Canceled 1941 Models

If the 1941 LaSalle had entered production, it would have been offered in three series, each corresponding with those of the Cadillac: Series 61, 62, and 63. According to *LaSalle: Cadillac's Companion Car*, all proposals were four-door sedans and no other styles appear to have been planned for production, judging by the lack of any documentation or photos of prototype versions showing additional body styles.

As explained in *LaSalle: Cadillac's Companion Car*, the planned LaSalle Series 51 fastback became the Cadillac Series 61, the Series 52 torpedo body became the Cadillac Series 62, and the Series 50 became the Cadillac Series 63. Harley Earl told Dave Holls, who ultimately became VP of GM Design, that the Cadillac Series 63 body originally intended for the LaSalle would have been exclusive to that model.

The decision to terminate the LaSalle was evidently made at the last moment. Hubcaps for the 1941 models had actually begun to be stamped. Some LaSalle enthusiasts own surviving examples of them.

Conclusion

While the LaSalle initially filled the market void, which had existed between Cadillac and Buick, keeping it priced accordingly meant fluctuating prices, as those for the models bracketing it changed as price structures and economic conditions changed. Regardless of the price changes, the LaSalle seldom made a profit for General Motors, a fact that contributed to the cancellation of the 1941 models.

Author Maurice Hendry in his book, *Cadillac, Standard of the World: The Complete History*, explained the demise of the LaSalle this way: "It was priced fairly close to the Cadillac, yet low enough to have competition from Buick, which was GM's strongest medium-priced make. For prestige purposes, with Packard, Lincoln, and Chrysler becoming more and more involved in the medium-priced field, it was good psychology for Cadillac to abandon it altogether and go all-out to conquer the high-price field, which they soon did."

THE ART AND COLOUR SECTION

CHAPTER 3

"The world stands aside for the man who knows where he is going."
— Harley Earl to his stylists

Harley Earl entered his 10th-floor office, looked out the window, and pondered where to start and how to organize his Art and Colour Section. Aside from his experiences with The Earl Automobile Works and Don Lee Coach & Body Works, there were few guidelines available because this was a new concept in the automobile industry. He had not brought anyone from California with him because he realized if he had done so, the rest of his staff would feel like outsiders and those from the California group would always be favored. Earl needed a staff, but where was he to look? Fortunately, Earl had some help to get this new endeavor started.

Ernest Seaholm was Cadillac's chief engineer at the time. According to the book, *General Motors Styling, 1927–1958: The Genesis of the World's Largest Design Studio* by Tracy Powell, Earl discussed the matter with Seaholm, who suggested starting with Ralph Pew. Pew had contributed sketches and engineering data to the original LaSalle design. Seaholm offered to transfer him to Earl's Art and Colour department either permanently or at least temporarily until Earl's organization was staffed as needed. After learning of Pew's impending transfer to Art

The first models designed under Harley Earl as head of GM Art and Colour Section were for Chevrolet, Buick, and Cadillac. Shown is a 1929 Cadillac 341-B Dual Cowl Phaeton. Fisher built its body. Note storage access panels between the running boards and doors, a typical feature of the era. (Photo Courtesy Cadillac & LaSalle Club)

Chapter Three *The Art and Colour Section*

Shown here is a 1930 Cadillac Town Sedan Series 353. The two-tone blue CCCA Grand National winner is far and away one of the most stylish and luxurious cars of the period.

This Fleetwood-bodied 1934 Cadillac Series 355D V-8 coupe is one of only six known to have been built. Its V-style slanted grille, bullet-shaped headlamps, pontoon fenders, and angled windshield gave the car a very streamlined and sporty appearance. The wheelbase spans 146 inches. The original price was $3,895.

This literally unique 1934 Cadillac Series 452D Victoria Convertible Coupe was purchased new by Hugh Fenwick (1905-1991) of Aiken, South Carolina, for $8,150. Fenwick was a businessman and at one time president of Vultee Aircraft. At the time it was built, it was the longest car ever produced; the wheelbase spans 154 inches. This special car is currently a part of the Steve Plunkett collection in Canada. (Photo Courtesy Steve Plunkett and Paul Sontrop)

The 1941 Cadillacs are among the most-coveted models of the pre–World War II era. Styling was all new this model year. One novel feature of the car was the fuel-filler hidden under the left-side taillight. Fender skirts and spotlights were extra-cost accessories. The Series 62 convertible, like the one shown here, accounted for 3,100 sales. (Photo Courtesy Steve Plunkett and Paul Sontrop)

Styling updates for the 1942 Cadillacs included the front fender shape extended across the doors and circular parking lights. Illustrated here is a Series 62 convertible coupe. (Photo Courtesy Cadillac & LaSalle Club)

and Colour, John Lutz, a builder in the body-building department thought Earl's department would offer some interesting new work and asked to be moved there, too. The Fisher brothers often came by to see how Earl was doing; they, too, offered one of their workers, Howard O'Leary, who knew many GM employees, which was a great advantage because Earl knew almost no one there. Then steadily, Earl's staff began to grow, soon reaching a half-dozen with the addition of Frank Humer, an expert on body layout. Next came two draftsmen, a wood worker, a metalworker, and so on, until Harley Earl had a staff of nearly 50 people by January 1928. All of these people were drawn to the Art and Colour Section because it offered a sort of new frontier in making automobiles, a job full of adventure. They were right.

Getting Accepted

Acquiring a staff for the Art and Colour Section was just one matter with which to deal. Getting the new group accepted by the other departments was another and a more serious one.

In January 1928, Earl had a staff. However, "production men ran the auto business" and Art and Colour was an "interloper" to be "disregarded," wrote Tracy Powell in his book on GM Styling. "Why not put a grille in front of the radiator," someone suggested to a division official. The answer was, "It would cost money. What would it do?" The attitude of many within the company was that styling was just a waste of money and time. They could not see how something like a grille could give an automobile eye appeal to a customer. However, Harley Earl found there was one engineer at General Motors who had vision, O. E. Hunt, who was Chevrolet's chief engineer. Hunt approached Earl about acquiring some assistance in designing a facelift for the following year's car. Hunt, who had established an impressive reputation within General Motors, helped earn Harley Earl's Art and Colour department a little more respect.

During the rest of 1928, Art and Colour began to perform work on the rest of the GM line of cars. With the launch of the LaSalle being a great success, other companion models

The Oakland was in its final year in 1931. Its companion model, Pontiac, took over the slot where Oakland had been positioned (between Chevrolet and Oldsmobile) after outselling the Oakland by wide margins. (Photo Courtesy GM Media Archive)

Chrome-plated ventilator doors add a sporty touch to this 1931 Cadillac Series 355-A Convertible Coupe. The V-16 cars had these doors on a raised panel, while V-8 and V-12 models were as seen here. Passenger capacity is five with the rumble seat. (Photo Courtesy Cadillac & LaSalle Club)

(Pontiac with Oakland, Marquette with Buick, and Viking with Oldsmobile) were being styled by Earl's department. The Pontiac was so good that when the companion model concept was dropped for all but Cadillac-LaSalle, Oakland was dropped rather than Pontiac.

Later in 1928, an important meeting was held in New York between Alfred Sloan, Lammot du Pont II (then chairman of General Motors), Howard O'Leary, and Harley Earl, resulting in the expansion of the role of Art and Colour. As explained in Powell's book, "At the beginning there had been no idea expressed that Art and Colour would do more than furnish ideas to Fisher. Growth was in the air. All agreed that styling properly encompassed more than the shapes of fenders and radiator frames. Trim selection and paint choices were put into the Section."

Growth was, indeed, ahead for the Art and Colour Section.

The Harley Earl Way

Harley Earl could not draw well, and he said so. However, Earl could get his designers to draw for him and he could see what was right and what was wrong with every line of a drawing and clay model. Even a minuscule fraction of an inch aberration did not escape Earl's eye. He had a keen sense of proportion and also had his own special language to convey his ideas; this language was one the stylists had to learn how to correctly interpret if they wanted to remain employed at GM's styling studios.

According to the book by C. Edson Armi, *The Art of American Car Design*, published in 1988, "Although Harley Earl was known throughout the industry as a perceptive critic, his design contribution was limited to verbal themes. Those who knew him best remember his communicating ideas about visual form but almost never originating a visual form himself . . . the process he developed for extracting original shapes from others and the system he invented to structure that process stem from a lack of original visual ability on the one hand and a critical, synthetic, and administrative genius on the other.

"One of Earl's closest aides attributes his way of dealing with employees to his frustration at not being able to express his ideas visually. He invented words to represent the visual forms in his head and, because of the communication barrier, once understood, they became a permanent part of everyone's vocabulary . . . when he would call something a Blitz line . . . that became a Blitz line. Earl issued typical instructions in a language unto itself: 'I want that line to have a deflunky, to come across, have a little hook in it, and then do a little Rashoon or a Zong.'"

Armi stated that Bill Mitchell said of his boss' process that his "inability to communicate visually explains his synthetic, or 'director's,' concept of design: 'When he wanted something, it would be very difficult to work with him because he knew what he wanted and he couldn't draw it for you. And he would be so impatient with you if you didn't get it. He had a chair like a director in a studio in Hollywood. He came from Hollywood. He would sit in that chair . . . and have all the people around him: . . . 'Now, move this back. Now do this!' And he would sit there and everyone would run around like a bunch of monkeys. That was the way cars were done when he was here."

His stylists recognized Harley Earl as an exceptional critic of design. Kenneth Coppock, the chief designer for Chevrolet in the 1930s, said, "He was a good one to figure out just what constituted a good design. There aren't many of those. He liked to pick up an idea from one studio and take it into another studio and say, 'Why don't we try it this way?'"

The system Harley Earl created for styling automobiles spread to other auto manufacturers as stylists left

Chevrolet's sales literature of 1940 boosted that this year's cars were "first in quality, performance, appearance, and economy." Appearance had been the work of Harley Earl's styling department. The horizontal layout of the grille was particularly new for the time. Fender skirts were extra-cost items.

Bill Mitchell

William L. Mitchell began his long and distinguished career at General Motors in late 1935. Mitchell was the son of a Buick dealer, could draw well, and loved automobiles, especially the ones built for speed. Perhaps he was predestined to work at General Motors. Thirty-three years later, he succeeded Harley Earl as the head of GM Design.

Mitchell was born in Cleveland, Ohio, on July 2, 1912, but grew up in Greenville, Pennsylvania. Mitchell sketched automobiles as a child, but his parents thought of it as a waste of time. With that in mind, they sent him to Carnegie Institute of Technology in Pittsburg, hoping he would find something more "substantial" to do. Mitchell still found time to pursue his passion for cars. In 1931, he began attending night school in New York at the Art Students League to further his skills as an artist. During the time he attended the school, Mitchell spent his lunch hour in the showrooms along 57th Street where he would gaze upon European automobiles, such as the Hispano-Suiza, Isotta-Fraschini, Mercedes-Benz, and Rolls-Royce.

Even before that, he was hired to work part time as an office boy for Barron Collier agency. Upon graduating high school, he became a full-time employee for the company. There he created the first MG ads in America. The Collier's sons introduced him to sports cars and that led to his interest in road racing. He even joined them in racing and designed the patch logo for the Automobile Racing Club of America (ARCA), which foreshadowed the Sports Car Club of America (SCCA).

In the book *Corvette: A Piece of the Action*, Mitchell wrote, " [I] found out what driving was all about. Those foreign sports cars, they would go like hell over a gravel road. The fun with the car was to almost lose it; I mean to always drive on that narrow edge. No windshield, a cut-down door. It was you and four wheels. You felt every twitch, everything the car was doing. And I drove like crazy."

In the summer of 1935, an insurance agent, Walter Carey, who attended one of the Collier competitions, discovered Bill Mitchell. One of Mitchell's sketches caught his eye, so he introduced himself and asked Mitchell if he had ever thought about designing cars as a profession. Carey was a personal friend of Harley Earl. This meeting led Mitchell to a long career at General Motors. On December 15, he joined General Motors and within one year was made chief designer of the Cadillac Studio. As a sports car enthusiast, Mitchell said he, "devoured every issue of *Autocar*, drooling over the racing paintings of Gordon Crosby, and reading every other foreign journal I could get my hands on, and suffering the strange looks of everyone around Detroit who really didn't know what I was about. Except Harley Earl. He had a feeling for cars."

Harley Earl hired William Mitchell in December 1935. His exceptional talent as a designer resulted in him being placed in charge of the Cadillac Studio six months later. Mitchell was Earl's handpicked successor to the position of VP of GM Design. (Photo Courtesy GM Media Archive)

Harley Earl was very impressed with Mitchell's abilities. Only six months after Mitchell's arrival, Earl put him in charge of the Cadillac studio. There Mitchell sketched the design of what ultimately became the 1938 Sixty Special, a trendsetter with integrated trunk, no running boards, and was 3 inches lower than other Cadillac models. It was Cadillac's bestseller that year. Bill Mitchell joined the U.S. Navy during World War II. Upon his return he joined the Harley Earl Corporation, an industrial design firm. In 1953, he rejoined General Motors as assistant director of styling.

An entire book could be written about Mitchell's career. Some of his most notable contributions include the Corvette Stingray and Buick Riviera. When he took over as Harley Earl's handpicked successor to head GM Design starting on December 1, 1958, Mitchell took the company in a new direction in terms of styling, marked by razor-edge lines. In 1977, upon GM's mandatory retirement age of 65, Bill Mitchell retired, or at least retired from General Motors. He began his own company and continued to draw cars in a studio next to his home. Mitchell passed away on September 12, 1988, in Royal Oak, Michigan.

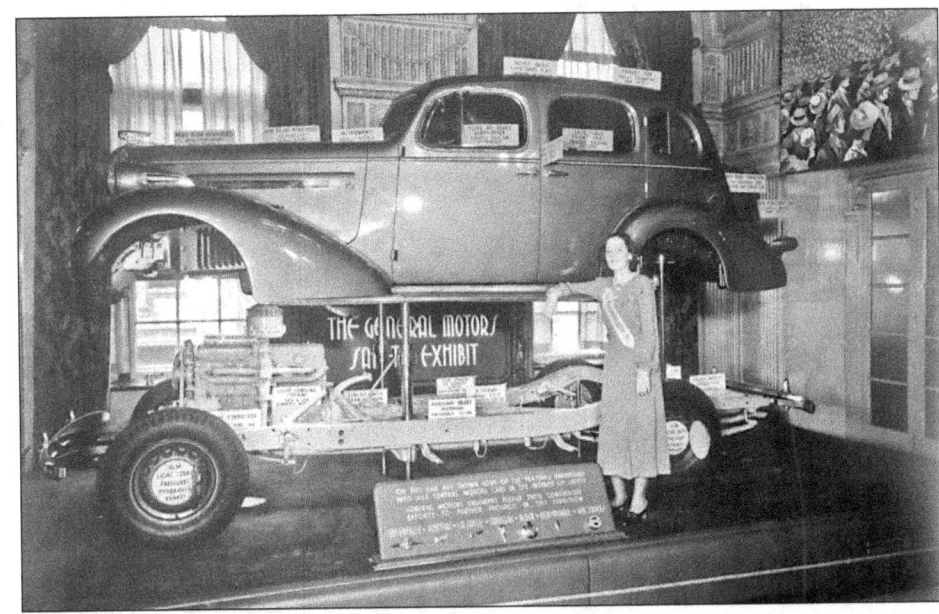

This show car, a 1936 Buick Series 90 Roadmaster, provided views of the various mechanical features of the car. The placard next to the car read, "On this car are shown some of the features engineered into all General Motors cars in the interest of safety." The name "Roadmaster" was new to the model year. (Photo Courtesy GM Media Archive)

A Rare Miss: The "Pregnant" Buick

The 1929 Buick was a flop. Sales dropped from 222,000 for 1928 to 162,000 for 1929, dropping Buick from number three to four in sales. This significantly reduced profits for General Motors because Buick was the top moneymaker for General Motors, even ahead of Chevrolet. Even though Harley Earl accepted responsibility for it, there was plenty of blame to go around. While the miscue was an embarrassing lesson for Earl, it ultimately served him well for the remainder of his long career.

In retrospect, the lines of the 1929 Buick coupes and sedans do not seem particularly out of step with the times, but they were. Because of its bulging beltline (the horizontal part of the body immediately under the side windows), some derisively referred to it as the "Pregnant Buick." Other than the original LaSalle, the earliest bodies Earl designed for General Motors were those for the 1929 Chevrolet, the 1928–1929 Cadillacs, and the 1929 Buick. The first two from this group went through the Fisher Body drafting and engineering processes as intended, but not so for the Buick.

Author Terry Boyce owns this 1940 Buick Model 76C convertible coupe. Running boards were eliminated and bodylines were much like a Cadillac Sixty Special. Sealed beam headlights were also introduced. (Photo Courtesy Terry Boyce)

General Motors to take control of competitors' design departments. For some, it seemed to be the only way to design cars. While Earl could not draw and seldom originated a design, he had an innate feel for line. However, the direction he gave was not precise but instead rather vague. Yet he was able, one way or another, to persuade his stylists to provide the specific direction. When he saw the right shapes he knew it, virtually always. His methods, though, began to fail him in the end, but that is a story reserved for Chapter Twelve.

A Century of Automotive Style provides an excellent account of the 1929 Buick fiasco. According to the authors, Harley Earl said that Fisher changed Art and Colour's design, but others noted the offending body roll originated in Art and Colour. Earl claimed that Fisher's chief engineer had wanted to put a little more hip room in GM's cars and chose Buick to try out the idea. However, any changes had to have been approved by

Chapter Three *The Art and Colour Section*

Cadillac Sixty Special

Cadillac was known as an innovator from its earliest days with advances such as interchangeable parts, electric starter, first 90-degree, V-type, 8-cylinder engine, as well as being a leader in luxury automobiles. That did not matter much in the depths of the Great Depression. Cadillac sales were down, way down. The division was losing money, but so were its competitors. However, Cadillac was in a stronger position to weather the economic storm due to having a giant parent company, General Motors. A number of cost-cutting measures were implemented under the leadership of Nicholas Dreystadt, who moved up through Cadillac before being appointed to the division's top post in late 1934. His emphasis on efficiency was part of his managerial style, and he was known for asking, "If someone else made a part for two dollars, why did ours have to cost three or four?"

Cadillac's Sixty Special began as a model for LaSalle, but it was found to be too expensive for that line. Its low overall height, lack of running boards, and extended, fully integrated trunk were very innovative at the time. Twenty-three-year-old Bill Mitchell was assigned the task of designing this model. (Photo Courtesy Cadillac & LaSalle Club)

Another step in boosting Cadillac's prosperity was the addition of the Series 60, starting in the 1936 model year. It was equipped with the division's new V-8, which was used through 1948. It was less expensive to produce than the previous 353-ci L-head V-8 and was so smooth and quiet it made the V-12 practically obsolete.

Immediately upon taking the reins at Cadillac, Dreystadt noted a $900 price gap had developed between Cadillac's least expensive 1934 model and the LaSalle and acted to have this situation remedied. The Series 60 came into being to fill this market void. Its B-body, which was shared with Oldsmobile, Buick, and LaSalle, sat on a smaller wheelbase chassis of 121 inches, 10 shorter than that of the more upscale Series 70 and Fleetwood Series 80. A smaller displacement V-8 of 322 ci powered the new model. The Series 60 was priced within reach of Buick and Chrysler buyers and sold extremely well upon its release for 1936. In fact, more than half of the Cadillacs sold were a Series 60, and overall sales shot upward by 254 percent over those of 1935!

At about the time the Series 60 made its debut, Harley Earl hired a very talented 23-year-old named William Mitchell. He gave him an assignment to develop a new LaSalle, which in the end was found to be too expensive to be in the LaSalle line. The LaSalle Sixty Special was transformed into a Cadillac. A LaSalle was traditionally sporty, but not Cadillac. The design was a major departure from the styling of the past Cadillacs, so much so management types were concerned that it might be simply too different, even though they had no personal objections to the styling. Cadillac buyers were known to be ultraconservative and this car with its overall height lower than that of any previous Cadillac, no running boards, extended trunk integrated fully into the body, and all four doors hinged in front looked like, as Cadillac's sales director, Don Ahrens, stated, it had come "from a younger designer." It was viewed as an entirely new concept. Earl was convinced the Sixty Special was the right car and he convinced the doubters it was.

The car's double-drop frame with an exceptionally sturdy X-frame along with side rails of reduced depth allowed the car to be 3 inches lower than a 1937 Cadillac. The Sixty Special's use of thin windshield pillar posts allowed for a wider windshield, as well as wider doors. A lack of side trim was seen as a bold move because at the time bright trim was used to make a car appear more expensive; only low-priced cars at the time lacked bright moldings. Its tall chrome-trimmed windows with thin, strong window frames gave a convertible look.

The Sixty Special was ready for the 1938 model year and continued to be produced in its original concept through 1941. For 1942, the model was based upon a stretched version of the Series 62 four-door sedan.

The Sixty Special proved to be a significant car for Cadillac. Its move away from the use of running boards allowed car bodies to extend out to the wheel track, thus creating the six-passenger automobile. It also forced other automakers to respond with specialty models such as Lincoln, with its now classic Continental. The sensational Sixty Special also influenced Packard's Clipper design.

The 1929 Buick was a rare flop done under Harley Earl. It's difficult to understand now, but the closed cars were labeled as the "Pregnant Buick" because of its bulging beltline. Note the slightly arching upper window openings. Earl said Fisher Body changed the design. The fiasco resulted in better communication between departments. (Photo Courtesy GM Media Archive)

Buick's president and sales staff. There is evidence that some changes were made to what was submitted by Earl's department, but exactly what happened will never be known with certainty.

Regardless, the incident showed Fisher's engineers did not particularly like being told how to shape sheet metal. It also revealed Earl did not yet have the degree of power necessary to push his designs through to production. The end result was a couple of important changes in the interaction between Art and Colour, Fisher Body, and the rest of the divisions. Earl insisted that any significant changes made to his department's designs must have his approval. He also hired a body engineer, Vincent D. Kaptur Sr., to work in Art and Colour so he could have the opportunity to know when costs or engineering objections could be an issue well in advance. Kaptur, who previously had worked for Packard for about a dozen years, became a liaison between Art and Colour and Fisher Body. He also soon observed that General Motors was wasting millions of dollars producing completely different bodies with only subtle measurement differences for its car divisions. A body-sharing program offering greater parts interchangeability was instituted in the early 1930s as a result.

Chicago Century of Progress Exhibition

The Great Depression put the brakes on major styling efforts at General Motors, at least for a while. Little more than minor redesigns of emblems and instrument panels accounted for much of the work being performed during the earliest part of the 1930s. However, in 1932, Art and Colour was asked to build something special for the 1933 Chicago Century of Progress Exhibition. The result was the V-16 powered 1933 Cadillac Aerodynamic Coupe, a dream car that was sleek and looked like it was moving just sitting still. It was built on a 149-inch wheelbase Series 452-C chassis.

The Aero Coupe's special styling characteristics included pontoon-like fenders with their sweeping curves uninterrupted by side-mount spares, V-type windshield raked back 35 degrees, chrome-trimmed window edges, chrome beltline molding, a trunk with a built-in spare tire compartment, gas filler built into the top of the taillight, a recessed license plate housing in back, and a fastback roof. Moreover, the roof was all steel at a time when the auto industry did not have the tooling to stamp one-piece all-steel roofs and relied upon rubberized fabric inserts.

Of course, that circumstance soon changed. Despite the advanced styling of the Aerodynamic Coupe, it still had features making it recognizable as a Cadillac, such as its grille.

The fastback roofline of the Aerodynamic Coupe, or "World's Fair Cadillac," as it was then known, perhaps influenced the design of the 1934 Mercedes-Benz 500-K competition model and certainly did serve to inspire Packard's LeBaron-built V-12 coupe of 1934. It also foretold the more streamlined look of the 1934 Cadillacs, which also featured a concealed spare tire in the trunk, a first for a production car. The all-steel roof emerged on the 1935 Cadillac models.

The Aerodynamic Coupe received grand reviews and as a result was put into limited production, with only minor changes, as a custom body listed in the Fleetwood catalog beginning in 1934. Body number one went to the executive vice president of General Motors, William Knudsen. Aero Coupes could be had with a V-8 or V-12 (both on the 146-inch wheelbase chassis) as well as a V-16 (built on a 154-inch wheelbase chassis). The number built over its years of availability, 1934 to 1937, was very small due to the high price; only 20 were built, of which 8 were on the V-12 chassis and just 3 were on the V-16 chassis. The V-8 version cost $5,000, the V-16 around $8,000, and the V-12 somewhere in between. With the newly designed 1938 Cadillacs, the Aero Coupe was terminated. A fastback-style Cadillac would not emerge from Earl's design studio until the advent of the 1941 Series 61.

Styling Gains Status

By 1936, GM's non-automotive divisions had recognized the Art and Colour Section's accomplishments, and as a result an Industrial Design Department was set up within Earl's styling department. GM's Electro-Motive Division benefited greatly from the change. Its stylish locomotives had so many orders there was little need to change them for quite a number of years. Another important work of this Industrial Design Department

Cadillac's avant-garde Aerodynamic Coupe prototype at the 1933 World's Fair led to a production version. Even though built in low numbers, the design very much strengthened the role of Harley Earl's Art and Colour Section in the design of GM's automobiles. The Fleetwood-built car was offered with V-8, V-12, and V-16 power. This example has the latter. (Photo Courtesy GM Media Archive)

was the creation of the Streamliner buses used for the Parade of Progress, a traveling exhibition used to show the latest in scientific and technological advancements at General Motors. (Later, these buses were replaced with the Futurliner. This subject is covered in more detail in Chapter Nine.) Euclid, another division of General Motors, built earth-moving equipment and also sought the expertise of Earl's styling staff.

A Product and Exhibit Studio was also created to design attractive packaging for GM's replacement parts. Styling now had a place in virtually everything General Motors did. Within a span of eight years, Harley Earl, who had begun his career at General Motors wondering how to organize his new department, then fighting for its acceptance, had now been fully acknowledged and was a major power within the company. Indeed, he was made a vice president of General Motors; this first-of-its-kind appointment showed just how important styling had become. Designing things that moved had been reinvented.

Despite moving the wall of resistance put up by other departments, Earl throughout his career at General Motors always had to fight the accounting and engineering departments and even sometimes Harlow "Red" Curtice, after he became president of General Motors. With the unwavering support of Alfred P. Sloan Jr. (president and later chairman of General Motors), he was able to accomplish virtually everything he set out to do. Former GM Design staff member Ken Pickering said to me during a face-to-face meeting, "Earl could not do what he did in today's work environment." Pickering actually witnessed a disagreement over some styling matter between Earl and Harlow Curtice. Earl told Curtice, "Let's see what Mr. Sloan has to say about it." Sloan backed Earl, which immediately ended the matter.

During a telephone interview of the late Homer LaGassey about one decade ago, I was told of a similar incident. Curtice came into the studio and observed a clay mockup of a Buick. Curtice remained partial to Buick even after assuming the presidency of General Motors. Curtice suggested changing the height of the rear bumper. When Harley Earl heard about it, he said something like, "We design the cars around here. I'll take care of it." The bumper stayed put.

Such power in the styling department has not been matched since Harley Earl left in late 1958. Even Bill Mitchell did not quite wield that much influence. Sloan resigned from the chairmanship in 1956, but remained an honorary chairman until his death in 1966. Without backing from someone as powerful as Alfred P. Sloan Jr., Bill Mitchell simply did not have the equivalent of Earl's power throughout the entirety of his career. Such marked the end of what the late designer Chuck Jordan called, "the golden age of the automobile."

The 1937 Oldsmobile benefited from a restyle; its body was shared with the LaSalle. This elegant L-37 Touring Sedan is loaded with extra-cost accessories including fog lights, trim rings, side-mount spares, etc. Production reached a new high for the model year. The letter "L" designated the presence of the 8-cylinder engine and "F" denoted a 6-cylinder car. This L-37 now resides at the Ransom E. Olds Museum in Lansing, Michigan.

CHAPTER 4
THE MODERN CONCEPT CAR

"I want a nice little semi-sports car; a kind of convertible."
– Harley Earl to his designers, "Retrospect: 1938 Buick Y Show Car,"
by Karl Ludvigsen, March 1974 issue of Motor Trend

There was a time when any new car was an experimental or concept car, such as Henry Ford's Quadricycle and Ransom E. Olds' earliest Oldsmobile, in which the powertrain, starting system, steering, and suspension needed to be evaluated. However, as cars became more advanced and more common, any new design was less experimental, having perhaps an engine with new manufacturing methods tested in a car with otherwise proven technology. Then along came Harley Earl, who reinvented the concept car in the late 1930s. At the time, it was simply labeled "experimental." The concept car often exhibits multiple advanced ideas and to be truly accurate, the term should probably be "concepts car."

Buick Y-Job

Harley Earl's Buick Y-Job was a radical car for its time, but not so radical as to be unappealing to the public. It is generally recognized as the first modern concept car thanks to the multiple advanced ideas incorporated into its overall design. In the case of the Y-Job, it was built with advanced styling and advanced mechanical features. Under its hood, however, was merely an improved version of Buick's "Dynaflash" straight-8, which had been in use since 1931.

Harley Earl had the backing of Alfred P. Sloan Jr. Earl had proven himself as a director of styling, so whatever Earl wanted, he typically got. Earl also found Harlow Curtice to

This photo dated May 17, 1940, shows the minor revisions performed to the rear of the Buick Y-Job. The addition of fender skirts and stone guards appear to be the only changes. (Photo Courtesy GM Media Archive)

be one of the more receptive people to his ideas. Curtice became the head of the Buick Division in 1933. Four years later Earl went to Curtice with a proposal for a very different kind of car, the one that became the Y-Job, and that Earl described as a "semi-sports car." The unique name's origin was explained by Vince Kaptur Sr., who was quoted in an article written by Karl Ludvigsen for the March 1974 issue of *Motor Trend*: "We were always working with X-cars, for experimental, and this job was *one step beyond that* [my emphasis]. We just called it the Y-Job."

Kaptur was in charge of the car's body engineering. Charles Chayne (pronounced like chain) became the chief engineer for Buick in 1936 and his skills were put to use on the Y-Job's mechanical systems. As for the styling of the car, Earl put George Snyder in charge of a team, which included Joe Shemansky. Up to that point Snyder headed the Oldsmobile studio. He had an instinctive sense of what Earl wanted, so Snyder was moved over to another studio to focus on advanced design. According to an article by Michael Lamm published in the January/February 1997 issue of *Special Interest Autos*, "Art Moderne, the commercial art form that auto designers borrowed from architecture, was very much in vogue at the time. Snyder incorporated the parallelism, repeated lines, and horizontality of Art Moderne in the Y-Job."

The purpose of the Y-Job was essentially twofold: it was a test of the acceptance of new styling ideas and to serve as Harley Earl's personal car. However, the car's styling led to some engineering issues, which had to be worked through. The special car was also a test-bed for Buick's prototype Dynaflow torque converter transmission, which became an option starting with the 1948 model year. In an article about experimental cars, Earl referred to the Y-Job as "a composite of many ideas" and went on to illustrate the advanced nature of the experimentals by stating they were "ideas, which for sound and logical reasons, couldn't be duplicated in volume in 1938."

The Y-Job also served another purpose: it gave Harley Earl the status he should have had as the chief designer for General Motors. Earl was competitive, so when his contemporaries, Ed Macauley for Packard and Edsel Ford of Ford Motor Company, were out and about in their personal boattail speedsters, Earl had to "make do" with a production car, even if it was modified to suit his taste. Earl, Macauley, and Edsel Ford lived near each other in Grosse Pointe, so Earl frequently saw them driving by in their special cars.

According to an article published in the May 2009 issue of the Cadillac & LaSalle Club's publication, *The Self-Starter*, inspiration for the styling of the Y-Job came as the result of Harley Earl visiting his old stomping grounds at Don Lee's distributorship in 1936. There he saw a 1934

General Motors' Albanita was an experimental car tested in 1933-1934. Chrysler officials who spotted the car going to and from GM's Proving Grounds suspected it might be in production soon; therefore, they reportedly rushed their Airflow into production. The styling of the Albanita was the product of the Art and Colour Section; it is not known who was specifically responsible for it. The grille styling showed up on the 1937 Chevrolet. (Photo Courtesy GM Media Archive)

LaSalle modified with a custom boattail speedster body it received after the car was totaled in an accident. Also there was a similarly styled car built on a 1936 Ford chassis by Frank Kurtis. Afterward, Earl became quite fascinated with the boattail design.

The styling of the Y-Job was spectacular. Allegedly, it impressed Edsel Ford so much he offered Earl a chance to come to work for Ford Motor Company. Earl was soon appointed as vice president in charge of Styling. Whether the two events are truly connected probably cannot be proven.

The frontal appearance of the Y-Job deviated completely from the standard of its time with its horizontal grille layout versus the tall, vertical lines of cars such as the LaSalle. Inspiration for the grille design came from the 1938 Mercedes-Benz W154 Grand Prix race car. It also came from an early look, sometime in late 1937, of the horizontal layout of the 1938 Lincoln Zephyr's divided grille. The Art and Colour stylists had drawn proposals with horizontal grilles in the past, only to have Earl reject the concept. Now, a rare misjudgment by Earl had come back to bite him. The general shape of the Y-Job's grille landed on GM's 1942 and 1946 models. Emphasizing the horizontal grille were the car's hidden headlights, a feature that actually first appeared on the 1936 Cord 810/812. The Y-Job's opened via the headlight switch on the dash while those of the Cord had to be manually cranked open.

Stylists for General Motors had rendered designs with hidden headlights as early as 1933. When the headlight switch was turned on, the horizontally split headlight doors that opened in a fashion much like human eyelids, moved back about 3 inches and the headlights with trim ring moved forward. The headlights fit so well, they appeared to be fixed when exposed. Turning the switch to "off" sent the whole process into reverse.

Snyder designed a "cigar in a ring" hood ornament for the Y-Job, similar to that of LeBaron-bodied Packards of the era. A chromed windsplit molding was placed between this ornament and the slightly V-shaped, two-piece windshield. The car's hood profile was much lower than production cars of that era, and there were no separate hood side panels.

The fender shape flowed back into the door, which was a feature appearing on GM cars starting with the 1942 models. A set of nine horizontal moldings on the front fenders started at the front wheel opening and continued back across the continuation of the fender shape on the door. The nine moldings resumed on the rear fenders. Fender skirts were added (by no later than 1940), which served to lower the car in appearance all the more. Nine bright moldings were attached to the skirts for continuity. As originally built, the front and rear bumpers were somewhat similar to those of the 1941 Buicks, but with a gull-wing shape. These bumpers were replaced after the end of World War II with 1942 Buick units, which wrapped around the fenders, and these are the ones still in place today.

A boattail-shaped rear deck provided additional sports car styling to the Y-Job. A windsplit molding originally chromed but now body color was installed, spanning from immediately behind the cockpit and along the entire centerline of the deck lid. Taillight shape and placement atop the rear fenders gave a preview of the new Cadillac for 1948. Tapered fenders in back were patterned like those of the front. The car's conventional external door handles were replaced with push buttons and finger grips were integrated into the upper doors. When the door button was pushed inward, an electrically activated solenoid released the door latch. If enough electrical power was not available, pushing the button in farther would open the door.

Like many of its exterior styling features, the dash of the Y-Job provided the basis for that of 1942–1948 Buicks. According to author Terry Boyce, the dashboard design was the work of James S. McDaniel. A trio of round housings for all the instrumentation was in front of the driver. In the center was the speedometer, which registered to 120 mph (as originally designed, it registered to 110) along with an odometer and tripmeter; to the left and right were round housings for the amp and water temperature (on left side) and the combo fuel and oil pressure gauges. The radio was placed at the center top and beneath it was the radio speaker.

Today, between the radio and speaker grille is a plaque (that appears to have been installed in the mid-1990s) stating, "Y Job," in red capital letters to the left and, "Joint experimental project of General Motors Styling Section and Buick Motor Division, Project Begun January 1938, First Public Showing December 1939, Presented to Buick Historical Collection July 1951," in white capital letters to the right. Art Deco-style chromed lettering spells out BUICK on the lower portion of the speaker grille. Immediately to the left and right of the speaker grille are buttons that operate the power windows. Another set, marked "U" and "D," operated the electro-hydraulic top. When down, the convertible top was stowed in a well that was covered by a pivoting lid instead of being concealed under a boot.

Incidentally, the sun visors were integrated with the convertible top header bow instead of being affixed to the windshield header. It left a clean appearance with the top down. On the right side of the dash within the glove box door is an electric clock. Lettering and numerals for all instrumentation were done in gold. A small rearview mirror was mounted about midway between the dash and windshield header on the windshield division bar. The door panel design included a contrasting fabric insert originally but was changed to black pleated leather at a later date. Upholstery for the bench seat also had a contrasting cloth insert but was later changed to pleated black leather.

The Y-Job's steel body was mounted upon a 126-inch wheelbase 1938 Buick Century chassis. This was the first year for Buick to have an all–coil spring suspension and a hypoid gear rear axle.

The Buick Y-Job's original steering wheel, monotone dash, and cloth and leather upholstery are shown in this early photograph of the experimental car. (Photo Courtesy GM Media Archive)

As mentioned earlier, an improved Dynaflash engine powered the Y-Job. What appears to have been installed in the Y-Job is a pre-production 1940 Series 50 version displacing 248 ci. When installed in a Century, the straight-8 could propel the model just past the 100 mph or "century" mark, hence the model name. The Dynaflash in the Series 40 Buicks produced 107 hp, up 7 from the previous year thanks to a new domed, light alloy Turbulator piston and a compression increase to 6.15:1 from 5.7:1. A twin, 2-barrel carburetor setup, dubbed Compound Carburetion, went atop the Y-Job's engine. It was very similar to that used for the Series 40 Special for 1941–1942. Compression was bumped up to 7.0:1 and horsepower went up to 125 with the twin-carb engine.

A wheel size of 7 x 13 inches (15- and 16-inch diameters were the norms) dictated the size of the brake drums be smaller than usual. The car was heavy as a result of its steel body and chrome-plated bronze components, so stopping it with smaller than usual brakes offered engineers a challenge. To dissipate heat generated by braking and minimize brake fade, the wheel covers were louvered. An experimental, aircraft-inspired braking system employed pneumatic bellows fed by compressed air from an engine-driven pump rather than wheel cylinders to press the brake linings against the drums. However, while the system worked well on aircraft, it did not on the Y-Job. The bellows could burst and one is known to have done so on at least one occasion. Conventional hydraulic brakes replaced this unreliable setup.

Another experimental system, which produced better results, was the Bendix power steering system. However, Buick's management decided that power steering would prove too expensive to sell profitably. The experimental Bendix unit was then removed from the Y-Job. The car has been said to steer "like a truck" today.

Unlike later concept cars, publicity for the Y-Job was rather light. Some short articles about it appeared in the English magazine *Autocar* as well as in *Popular Mechanics*. There was no round of nationwide auto shows for the Y-Job, although it did appear at the 1940 New York Auto Show wearing a silver paint job at the time rather than its normal black. The car served as Harley Earl's personal transportation for years and he reportedly logged 50,000 miles in it, even though the car's odometer inaccurately reads close to 29,000 miles today. This is because the entire instrument cluster was replaced with 1948 Buick gauges probably in late 1947 when the car received some mechanical freshening.

During its time as Earl's driver, it received yearly repaints in its smooth, glossy black; the car's hand-built bodywork was so good that the mirror-like black finish did not reveal a single imperfection. The car's styling eventually lost its advanced look; most of the ideas it presented were used in production, but that was fully expected to happen. Earl perfectly expressed the fact in an article he penned for *CARS* magazine: "The Y-Job never went into production. It finally was developed and redeveloped out of business. But it served a useful purpose affecting many GM cars now in the hands of customers." At this point, something else was needed to show General Motors remained the leader in styling. Harley Earl put together another team for not one, but two special cars.

GM Le Sabre and Buick XP-300

The Buick Y-Job was a remarkable car for many years, but by about the end of 1946, the ideas it showcased showed little in the futuristic sense. (By this time, GM's 1949 models were in the design stage and the Y-Job's assets had largely been exhausted by then.) This "laboratory on wheels" had served its purpose very well, but the time had come for Harley Earl to begin considering something to replace it, something at least as revolutionary as his Y-Job to show the public General Motors remained at the forefront of automotive design.

In late 1946, Harley Earl discussed his thoughts for a new advanced "laboratory on wheels" with Harlow Curtice, the chief of the Buick Division since 1933. Earl had already long established a good relationship with Curtice, so the effort to convince him of the need for such a car was likely minimal. The two

General Motors has maintained the Buick Y-Job ever since it was built. It is now a part of the GM Heritage Center in Sterling Heights, Michigan.

H-Point to Hard Heel: One Design Criterion

Designing a successful automobile is more than just starting with some pleasing lines on paper. One of a myriad of considerations is the "H-point to hard heel" dimension. Simply put, it is used to ensure the driver is not sitting on the floor. As explained in more detail by retired GM engineer, Ken Pickering, "The 'H-Point' is approximately the hip joint and is the basis for all other measurements. Each of these joints is a center of rotation for the adjacent limb. Headroom is usually as low as 36 inches for the backseat of sports cars, but more like 38 inches and above for sedans. One of the criteria for the package is to have a minimum 'H-point to hard heel,' less for sports cars, more for sedans. This really relates to seat height.

"On the Y-Job, there is an actual depression in the floor below the accelerator pedal, which accommodates the driver's heel in order to meet this desired dimension. I never saw the Y-Job in detail, but I was told that since Earl was so tall and had a long torso, the heel point was actually a cup in the floor to accommodate Earl's heel." The "cup" is, indeed, present and was installed after Earl found his right foot caught on the bottom of the instrument panel when he moved it.

To help designers achieve the optimum H-point to hard heel, a dummy known as "Oscar" was created. Pickering explained to me via email, "I believe 'Oscar' was developed at GM Styling by Ron Roe in Human Factors. This Oscar became the standard for interior dimensions as 'he' was standardized by the SAE. As a result, all manufacturers used Oscar for driver/passenger accommodations. Oscar had a 50 percentile torso and a 90 percentile lower body."

---

agreed the car should be as much an engineering accomplishment as a styling feat. Curtice suggested to Earl that he work with Charles Chayne, Buick's chief engineer since 1936. Discussions between Earl and Chayne ultimately led to not one special car, but rather two: one for Earl's personal use and the other for Buick Engineering.

According to an article about the Le Sabre written by Michael Lamm for the March/April 1997 issue of *Special Interest Autos*, Charles Chayne "agreed rather reluctantly" because he "realized that this project would take up lots of engineering time and would cost much more . . . than the Y-Job."

Building two one-off cars with advanced styling and mechanical systems did result in a significant sum of GM's money being spent. The cost of constructing the Y-Job, $50,000 (equal to approximately $85,000 in 1950 and about $840,000 today) was quite inexpensive measured against the expenditures required for building two even more advanced dream cars about one decade later. The contributions of the Y-Job, though, certainly helped justify the costs of building what ultimately became the GM Le Sabre and the Buick XP-300. The two reportedly cost about $1 million to build, the equivalent of nearly $10 million today.

Chayne wrote an article about the XP-300 for the February 1952 issue of *Motor Trend* in which he explained the purpose and origins of it and the Le Sabre: "We decided that it was time to build a successor to the Y-Job to see if we could better our mark of 'good after ten years' by doing one that would be still fresh and new after fifteen years. We weren't very far before it was clear to us that one car could not possibly contain the things we wanted to try, so we worked out a program for two cars." This was just one of many stories written about these special cars resulting in much free publicity for General Motors, which certainly helped to offset the costs of creating them. The press reports were not just national, but international as well.

The basic designs of each car were established quickly, resulting in other details being settled virtually simultaneously. One of the criteria established for both cars was that an advanced experimental V-8 would power each of them. A couple of matters made this choice a rather easy one.

Earl envisioned short hood/long deck proportions (as on the Y-Job) for the two experimental cars so the relative

This stylist's rendering from early 1949 of a proposed design for the Le Sabre was remarkably close to the final one. (Photo Courtesy Brett Snyder Collection)

A detachable hardtop was provided for the XP-300, even though it was rarely used. This rare photograph shows how the unique car appeared with it in place. (Photo Courtesy Nancy Martin)

compactness of the V-8 fit well with this idea. Furthermore, the V-8 was quickly becoming the industry trend, supplanting the older straight-8 engine. Of course, there was a mandate to create an engineering achievement, so an advanced experimental V-8 was the perfect choice.

In the article he wrote for *Motor Trend*, Chayne explained the design of both cars was dictated primarily by the "decision to build them just as low as possible. Doing this, pretty well forced the cars into being two-passenger convertibles, since with the necessary mechanical parts ahead of and behind the passenger space we would have been forced into an excessively long wheelbase had we attempted to use a second seat." Another important goal of the two projects was that the cars must be "complete in every sense of the word and still be capable of really terrific performance."

Initially dubbed as the XP-8 and XP-9, the two projects later became the Le Sabre and XP-300, respectively. Harlow Curtice formally approved the projects on May 19, 1947, and a newly created studio dubbed Special Automobile Design headed by Ed Glowacke (who came over from the Chevrolet Division) soon went to work on the styling of the Le Sabre. Photographs taken during 1949 show that "Chevrolet" appeared on a simulated license plate attached to the rear of a full-scale clay mockup of the car, and the Chevy "bowtie" insignia was placed on the horn button of the interior mockup. However, the name "Buick" later appeared on the front of the clay model in another mildly altered design, but that is as close as the Le Sabre got to being associated with a specific division of General Motors.

In late 1948, Curtice was promoted, from head of the Buick Division to executive vice president of General Motors, and eventually the decision was made to drop the name Buick and simply give the Le Sabre a GM identity. It was an understandable decision because multiple divisions of General Motors designed its systems, and it was intended as a forecast of all makes of the company's cars for years to come. However, the XP-300 kept its Buick identification. Chayne headed the XP-9 project, but Harley Earl was responsible for its styling.

Harley Earl's fascination with aircraft often served as a source of ideas for styling automobiles. GM's Allison division built the V-1710 engines for the P-38 Lightning (from which the inspiration for tail fins of the 1948 Cadillac originated) and other World War II–era and Korean War–era aircraft. Thus, Earl certainly had the chance to be aware of the newest trends in aviation. Boats also provided ideas for styling automobiles.

Glowacke, an exceptionally gifted stylist, raced cars and boats and was a pilot. He contributed a number of aviation-themed features to the Le Sabre such as the oval grille-like form in front, which was inspired by the air intake in the nose of the new, swept-wing F-86 used by the U.S. Air Force. This grille was actually both decorative and functional as it was in reality a concealed headlight system. The closely set pair of headlights appeared when the headlight switch was set to "on," causing the oval grille to move inward, rotate 180 degrees, and then move outward. The bumper bullets, its gull-wing bumpers, and the car's aircraft-style gauges also were features lifted from various aircraft of the period.

Another remarkable feature of both the Le Sabre and the XP-300 was the tinted wraparound windshield or "Panoramic" windshield in GM parlance. The wraparound windshield for these two cars was a first in the automotive industry. About three decades earlier, Harley Earl had tried to have such a windshield made for one of the custom cars he was building. However, the glassmakers' experiments with bending glass never resulted in anything other than broken glass. He had to settle for a multi-piece windshield with the outer panes angled; that was as close as he could get to such a windshield.

About the time the design of the Le Sabre and XP-300 were underway, GM's glass supplier, Libby-Owens-Ford, finally found a method to shape the glass for Earl after four years of experimentation. Earl was concerned with obtaining the largest field of vision possible while at the same time reaping the benefit of fresh, aircraft-like styling, hence his persistence in the area of acquiring the wraparound windshield. Bending glass to the desired shape was not the only challenge to putting the wraparound windshield into production. Shaping it that way meant the windshield pillar would have to include a "dog leg," which added to costs and engineering considerations

Harlow Curtice: Guiding General Motors in the Golden Age

Harlow Curtice credited his successful career at General Motors to his own guiding principle of, "Do it the hard way. Do it better than it needs to be done."

The man who "did it the hard way" and "better than it needs to be done" was born in Petrieville, Michigan, on August 15, 1893, to Marion and Mary Ellen Curtice. Harlow, however, was raised in nearby Eaton Rapids. While a high-school student, he worked for his father as a bookkeeper during summers before going to Ferris Business College in Big Rapids, from where he graduated in 1914 with an accounting degree. Immediately after graduating he went to Flint, Michigan, to work for the Standard Rule Company, which made steel measuring tapes. However, the company was sold about three months later, leaving Curtice out of a job temporarily. Harlow was soon hired to work as a bookkeeper for the AC Spark Plug Division of General Motors, and within one year he was promoted to comptroller. The young Harlow was ambitious; he learned about the company by speaking to the employees and learning about the equipment used to manufacture the company's products. His motto of "Do it the hard way. Do it better than it needs to be done," was already serving him well.

Curtice left AC Spark Plug to enter the US Army during World War I. Upon his discharge from military service, he resumed working for AC, but as the company's assistant general manager. Six years later (1929), Curtice became the president of AC Spark Plug. Under his leadership, AC not only was profitable, but also grew: this during the time of great economic upheaval known as the Great Depression.

While AC Spark Plug prospered, GM's Buick Division was in trouble. Output of Buick automobiles had dropped to just 17 percent of 1926 levels (266,753 units built), a high point for the division, sending it from third place to sixth in 1933. The Great Depression was only partly to blame; Buick's offerings were simply no longer competitive in the marketplace. Harlow Curtice was made president and general manager of Buick with the hope he could save what was once GM's largest division from being terminated. Harlow quickly ordered new Buicks to be designed and a new model, the Series 40, to be among them. The new cars arrived late in the 1934 model year, but even with the May introduction, Buick sales were about 50 percent higher than those of the previous model year, but it still dropped to eighth place in the industry. The new line appealed to a wider range of buyers and continued to do so for years to come, placing it back into fourth place by 1938 where it stayed until 1942 model year production was stopped due to the United States being forced into World War II.

As America's involvement in World War II appeared to be inevitable, Curtice offered Buick's assembly plants to the National Defense Advisory Committee headed by William S. Knudsen Sr., who served as GM's president from 1937 to 1940, when President Franklin D. Roosevelt asked him to head the committee. By the end of 1940, Knudsen had selected Buick to construct Pratt & Whitney–designed aircraft engines. Buick would also build the Buick-powered M-18 Hellcat tanks for the US Army. With Japan, then Germany declaring war on the United States, automobile production was phased out. Curtice used his skills to manage aircraft engine and tank production as he had automobile production. His efficiency was noticed by the military, and Curtice was offered the rank of General in the US Army, but he declined the offer. Knudsen, incidentally, was commissioned as a Lieutenant General.

Harlow Curtice rose to the presidency of General Motors (1953–1958) after beginning his career with the company's AC Spark Plug division as a bookkeeper in 1914. By the end of the 1933 model year, Curtice was promoted to president and general manager of that division, which was at a low point in sales. He quickly returned Buick to profitability and sales grew immensely under his leadership. (Photo Courtesy GM Media Archive)

With the end of World War II, GM president Charles Wilson offered the position of executive vice president to Harlow Curtice; he declined because he preferred to oversee the conversion of Buick production plants back to automobile production before leaving the division. The offer from Wilson came again in September 1948, and this time it was accepted.

As executive vice president, Curtice was in charge of all staff matters, including distribution, styling, engineering, manufacturing, research, personnel, employee relations, public relations, and business research, thus giving him more authority than anyone who occupied the position before him.

In March 1953, Charles Wilson left General Motors after President Dwight Eisenhower appointed him as secretary of defense. With Wilson's departure, GM's board of directors elected Curtice as the next company president.

As president, Curtice maintained GM's tradition of allowing division chiefs to be largely self-governing. He made an exception, however, with the Allison Division, which built aircraft engines, when it began to falter. During 1953, Curtice ran this division and invested considerable money to efficiently produce a new line of engines.

Another matter occupied Harlow Curtice during the earliest part of his presidency, the strong belief the economy was about to enter into a recession. Rather than slow spending, Curtice announced in February 1954 that General Motors would invest in a $1 billion expansion program in anticipation of the economy soon reviving. The expenditures resulted in capital spending by other companies, which in turn was of great benefit to the economy. General Motors sold approximately five million vehicles in 1955, and as a result became the first corporation to earn $1 billion. Curtice was selected as *Time* magazine's "Man of the Year" for 1955.

During his presidency, Curtice maintained his love for Buick, never driving anything else. He even secretly negotiated a deal with Fisher Body to reduce the cost of Buick bodies below that of others by $25 each.

Harlow Curtice retired from General Motors on August 31, 1958, due to reaching the corporation's mandatory retirement age of 65, although he remained a member of its board of directors.

On November 18, 1959, Harlow Curtice suffered a great tragedy when he accidentally shot and killed retired General Motors vice president Harry W. Anderson while on a duck-hunting trip to St. Anne Island, Ontario. Anderson stood up and then lost his balance slightly, putting him directly in front of Curtice just as the latter was firing his shotgun. The accident overwhelmed Curtice until he died of an apparent heart attack at his home in Flint on November 3, 1962, at the age of 69.

(i.e., strength, designing an acceptable weather seal, etc.). There were manufacturing and installation issues to settle, too. Of course, all of those difficulties were overcome thanks in part to the lessons learned in the construction of the Le Sabre and XP-300. The wraparound windshield, as well as tail fins, quickly became the norm in the auto industry, lasting into the early 1960s.

The long quarter panels sprouted tail fins of similar proportion to those of the 1948 Cadillac, but of larger dimensions. A trio of small, conical taillights was stacked at the end of the blade-like fins. The Le Sabre's deck mimicked the shape of the hood but sloped downward sharply at the rear. Upon its centerline was attached a bright molding (polished stainless steel or chrome-plated), which at its endpoint in back supported the car's radio antenna. The engine's exhaust exited through chrome-plated bumperettes and was a feature that would be applied to Cadillacs in the mid-1950s.

The Le Sabre was extraordinarily low for the day. Its overall height with the top raised stood at just 50 inches and the cowl height as measured from the ground stood at just 36.25 inches. Such figures added to the long list of jaw-dropping traits of Harley Earl's "laboratory on wheels."

As per the directive of Harlow Curtice, engineering aspects of the Le Sabre and the XP-300 were a tour de force. Included among them was an all-aluminum V-8 engine to power each car. The experimental engine was of rather small displacement at just 215.7 ci (3.25 x 3.25-inch bore and stroke), yet provided 335 horsepower, far surpassing 1 horsepower per cubic inch, which was then viewed as a kind of ideal standard. As originally built, the engine of the Le Sabre transmitted its output to a transaxle consisting of a modified Buick Dynaflow (it was soon replaced by a 4-speed Hydra-Matic) connected to a de Dion differential. The XP-300's setup differed. It

Shortly after its completion the 1951 GM Le Sabre was photographed inside the GM Argonaut Building, which housed the studios and offices of the Styling Section as well as this auditorium on the 11th floor. Harley Earl referred to this experimental car as his "laboratory on wheels," and it served him as a daily driver for many years. (Photo Courtesy GM Media Archive)

had a de Dion axle design based on a Daimler-Benz unit used for that company's Grand Prix race cars. In addition, each car's body was constructed of non-standard materials, representing another experimental aspect for these unusual automobiles. Various accessories offered additional advanced concepts, too.

The experimental engine for these XP dream cars presented major challenges for the engineers involved, and it reflected the personal interest of Charles Chayne in advanced European types of the era. (In fact, Chayne owned a Bugatti Type 41 Royale and a Hispano-Suiza J-12.) Ultimately, it required some "out of the box" thinking, especially for the man placed in charge of its design, Joe Turley. Its block and heads were of aluminum (cast for General Motors by Alcoa); complete, the radical engine weighed 550 pounds. The sides of the block extended well below the centerline of the crankshaft and the main bearing caps were cross-bolted for added strength. A chain-driven camshaft was suspended below the intake manifold, which doubled as the engine's valley cover.

Designing the intake manifold required an extra dose of patience and creativity on the part of Turley. After a mockup of the original engine design was crafted and sent to GM Styling for a fit check, Harley Earl suddenly announced the hood line of the Le Sabre was to be lowered 6 inches, meaning the engine as designed would not fit. Turlay's initial thought was that the new specification was unrealistic, but he knew Earl would not withdraw his order. He knew of Earl's power within General Motors. As Ken Pickering, one of the few engineers at Styling, expressed the power of Harley Earl, "Earl's power was legendary. During my time with Fisher Body, one of my associates told me, 'If Earl wants to move the Fisher Building across the street by nightfall, it better be done.'"

After some time analyzing the situation, Turley saw he could reduce the height of the oil pan (and add a windage tray to keep the crank throws from aerating the oil) and substantially decrease the size of the flywheel without sacrificing the required mass by substituting a bronze flywheel for the iron type. (Bronze is much more dense than iron.) Furthermore, placing a set of twin air cleaners to the side rather than on top helped keep the overall height within specs. These changes reduced the overall height of the engine enough to fulfill Harley Earl's command.

A Roots-type supercharger of Detroit Diesel helical three-lobe design and driven by three V-belts was nestled just over the intake manifold. Boost was 18.2 psi. The aluminum pistons certainly had to withstand tremendous forces during hard acceleration.

Wet cylinder liners were centrifugally cast of Ni-Resist iron having a coefficient of expansion closely matching that of the aluminum heads and pistons. (Ni-Resist iron also has a higher resistance to corrosion and a superior wear resistance to cast iron.) The hemispherical combustion chambers had two valves per cylinder. The valves, which were mounted at a 90-degree angle to each other, were filled with sodium for superior heat transfer. The pushrods operated an unusual rocker arm assembly. Those for the intake valves were mounted across the heads in a conventional manner, while those of the exhaust side passed between the cylinder bores, meaning the exhaust

An experimental aluminum V-8 with dual carburetors and a supercharger powered both the GM Le Sabre and the Buick XP-300. (Photo Courtesy GM Media Archive)

Cadillac's Incomparable Designer: Ed Glowacke

Edward E. Glowacke was born in Detroit, Michigan, on April 1, 1921. As a teenager he won multiple awards from the Fisher Body Craftsman's Guild (a national auto design competition sponsored by Fisher Body). In 1939, Glowacke graduated from Cass Technical High School and was soon invited by General Motors to attend its Styling School. Afterward he began his career at General Motors as a beginning designer.

Health issues kept him out of World War II, so during those years he worked at General Motors developing various kinds of camouflage. With the end of the war, he went back to automotive design work; during 1946, he was promoted to chief designer of the Special Auto Studio. Three years later, Ed became the chief of the Chevrolet Studio. Also during this time he performed design work on the advanced Le Sabre. His gullwing bumper design greatly influenced the frontal appearance of Cadillacs in future years.

In 1952, Glowacke was appointed as the chief of the Cadillac Studio. Among the advanced projects he oversaw there was the styling of the 1954 Park Avenue and 1955 Eldorado Brougham, both prototypes of the production version of the Eldorado Brougham released for 1957.

According to former GM Design engineer, Ken Pickering, "Glowacke was the consummate Cadillac designer with immaculate personal attire. Ed lived and breathed Cadillac and demanded those in his studio 'rise to a higher standard.' One day, one of his designers came to work in a shirt that was not up to Ed's standard. So, at noon, Ed gave him $20 (a lot of money in the mid-1950s) and told him to go out and buy a decent shirt.

"One of the reasons the Cadillac models looked so wide in the front end was because Ed said that the front end design gave the car a wide look, but he also 'cheated' the front to look even wider. In the plan view [direct overhead view], the wide point of most cars is at the center pillar and the body narrows slightly as it moves toward the front and toward the rear. Normally, the designer would continue that slight curve into the front end, but Ed interrupted this line coming off the common front door and actually 'bent' it outward slightly. Thus, the line had a break in the plan view, but that was really indistinguishable to most people.

Edward Glowacke began his career with General Motors in 1939. In 1952, Glowacke was placed in charge of GM Styling's Cadillac Studio. He was known for his immaculate attire and high standards for design. Glowacke would likely have succeeded Harley Earl as VP of GM Design had leukemia not taken his life in 1962. (Photo Courtesy GM Media Archive)

"The maximum width legally permitted was 80 inches (and the metal platforms were 80 inches wide in the front view) and Ed made the car front out to the max. Frankly, I do not know if HJE [Harley Earl] ever caught on to this trick, but it was sure effective."

Upon Bill Mitchell's promotion to head GM Design in late 1958, he appointed Glowacke as his assistant, thus Glowacke became the executive in charge of Automotive Design. He held this post until his untimely passing on May 25, 1962.

Those who worked with Ed Glowacke were shocked at the news of his death. Very, very few knew he was that ill because he kept working until almost the end. Upon learning of the diagnosis of leukemia, Ed told only those he had to tell and asked them to keep the matter quiet. He was extremely active as an airplane and glider pilot, diver, pianist, inventor, and more; it was difficult to imagine him succumbing to anything at such an early age.

The October 1996 issue of *Collectible Automobile* included a profile on Ed Glowacke; a number of designers who knew Ed Glowacke and were interviewed for the story used terms such as "gentleman," "soft-spoken," "elegant," and "impeccable in taste" to describe him. As head of the Cadillac Studio, he insisted that everyone dress well to uphold the image

Cadillac's Incomparable Designer: Ed Glowacke CONTINUED

of Cadillac. Glowacke was well known for what we would call his "GQ" fashion sense today. He was a hands-on designer and one of the few who knew how to design a car "from A to Z; exteriors, interiors, the whole shot. Eddie could do it all," said Homer LaGassey, who was one of the stylists interviewed for the *Collectible Automobile* story.

Vintage car enthusiasts would probably know Ed Glowacke as well as they know Harley Earl and Bill Mitchell, if he had lived long enough. He was expected to take over GM Design when Mitchell reached the company's mandatory retirement age of 65 in 1977. Glowacke is best remembered for two design themes of Cadillac, which were used for a number of years, the so-called Dagmar bumpers and the gull-wing bumpers, which he first applied to Harley Earl's Le Sabre.

Tragically, Glowacke died of leukemia before the end of 1962 at the young age of 41. However, he managed to do a lot of living and perform design work on some of GM's more memorable cars, including the 1951 GM Le Sabre, as well as Chevrolets and Cadillacs of the 1950s. If he had lived longer, there certainly would have been many, many more major themes for which he would deserve credit.

Ed Glowacke penned this rendering showing a Cadillac styling proposal in 1948, the first year for Cadillac's trendsetting tail fins. Note the height of the tail fins in this rendering. Four years later he was promoted to head of the Cadillac Studio. (Photo Courtesy GM Media Archive)

rockers ran in a fore and aft layout along the heads and rode on individual minishafts. This arrangement helped to make the engine more compact so as to fit within the rather confined space of the engine compartments of the Le Sabre and the XP-300. Double valvesprings were employed and valveseats were stainless-steel inserts. The experimental engine's hydraulic lifters could function without clatter or bounce up to 6,500 rpm, the redline point.

A pair of aircraft pressure-type Bendix-Eclipse (partly owned by General Motors until 1948) 2-barrel carburetors was fitted to the engines of both cars. Two electric fuel pumps flowed fuel from dual rubberized fuel tanks housed in each quarter panel. The front carburetor ingested premium gasoline until nearly wide-open throttle, at which point progressive linkage and a valve engaged the rear carburetor to receive an atomized spray of methanol, ideal for the engine's 10:1 compression ratio, which was especially high for the time. The compression ratio was beyond any automobile engine then in production. To meet the fuel octane requirement for this engine, aviation gasoline had to be used at least until high-octane gasoline became widely available to the public. Pressing the accelerator pedal to near full travel also activated the supercharger.

To be certain the right fuel went into the correct fuel tank of the Le Sabre, each of its fuel filler doors located on the inner tail fin surface was clearly labeled with embossed letters spelling out "GASOLINE" on the left side and "ALCOHOL" on the right. Each filler cap was integrated into the filler doors. A petcock and overflow tube was used to prevent damage to the paint from spills when filling the fuel tanks.

Choosing aluminum for the radiator eliminated the occurrence of electrolytic corrosion of the cooling passages.

A fuel tank was located within each quarter panel of the Le Sabre. The dual-fuel arrangement consisted of gasoline in the left tank and alcohol in the right one.

Performance was extraordinary for the time; the Le Sabre was reported to have attained a top speed of 138 mph. According to an article published in the December 1951 issue of *Science and Mechanics*, engineers believed another 40 mph could be gained in top speed through revisions to the air cleaner design!

As mentioned earlier, body construction was another experimental aspect of both the Le Sabre and the XP-300. The Le Sabre's body was built of lightweight cast magnesium and aluminum. The front fender valance, cowl, door lock pillars, door skins, and deck lid with ribs cast in place for strength were crafted as single *large* castings of magnesium. As for the Le Sabre, several attempts were generally required to find the correct shape for these panels (which in some areas measure 1/4-inch thick) to obtain perfect alignment. Other than the difficulty of making large cast-magnesium structures (at the time), its surface was more labor intensive to paint because it needed far more preparation than conventional steel; when readied, paint adhesion was fine. The remaining body panels were of aluminum (aluminum honeycomb sandwiched between aluminum sheets for the floor) sourced from and cast by Alcoa.

The Le Sabre frame is a boxed ladder-type frame made of chrome-molybdenum steel. Its front suspension, a parallel double wishbone type, provided superior handling characteristics for the experimental car and is used on today's cars. The A-arms were made of a cast-alloy and the upper A-arm pivot rod was originally imbedded in a solid piece of cylindrically shaped rubber encased in a steel casting. Hydraulic tubular shock absorbers were mounted between the steel casings and the lower A-arms. The setup functioned well for some time until the rubber lost its elasticity. Eventually, Chayne had to replace the setup with torsion bars. The Le Sabre's wheelbase measured 115 inches, which was several inches shorter than the Buick's; it was the same as a Chevrolet.

Although the Buick Division was willing to spend the money necessary for an experimental engine, it was not going to do the same to develop an expensive all-new transaxle. Instead, a de Dion differential was built for the Le Sabre and the XP-300, but each was of a differing design. A de Dion differential is a type of semi-independent suspension with a chassis-mounted differential and driveshafts typically located by various links. It offers a significant reduction in the unsprung weight of the suspension and keeps the wheels parallel under hard use. A transaxle combines the final drive unit with the transmission located between the driving wheels and separates the transmission from the engine, thus moving a significant percentage of the weight toward the rear to help provide the desired weight distribution for a rear-wheel-drive car. As previously mentioned, the Le Sabre was originally equipped with a modified Dynaflow 2-speed automatic transmission, which was soon replaced with an improved Hydra-Matic transmission, something Buick engineers mocked as the "Hydra-jerk" when the original Hydra-Matic was released in 1940 as an exclusive option for Oldsmobiles.

The input shaft of the transaxle in the rear of the chassis drove a generator and hydraulic pump. The hydraulic pump powered four built-in jacks (one at each corner) to raise the car when required; the jacks could be lowered and raised from the cockpit. The 13-inch wheels helped make the car low, but they forced the brake drums to be a smaller diameter than was typical. For adequate braking, the front brakes were composed of double-wide, finned drums 3½-inch wide and 9 inches in diameter, with four brake shoes per drum; in the rear a single set of shoes was employed.

Oil pressure, oil temperature, engine coolant temperature, and electrical function of the 12-volt system were clustered around the base of the steering column. Also included were separate fuel gauges for the gasoline and methanol tanks, an altimeter, a compass, clock, and a digital speedometer. An ultraviolet light caused the instrument faces to glow for nighttime viewing. A console placed between the individual seats contained a chronograph, controls for the radio, and a rain sensor.

The rain sensor would automatically raise the convertible top when left down if a drop of rain struck it. It would activate the entire process of raising the top, latch it to the windshield header, and raise the windows. Earl enjoyed demonstrating this feature.

Leather upholstery was selected to cover the seats and dash of the Le Sabre. Harley Earl made note of the choice in a special brochure produced by GM specifically about the Le Sabre's interior (which even had a sample glued to one page): "I think the best testimony to leather as an upholstery material is embodied in our General Motors laboratory on wheels, Le Sabre. Here is a car composed of experimental alloys, new mechanisms and new designs. Yet its upholstery is fashioned from one of the oldest materials known to man. Frankly, we chose leather for Le Sabre because we could find nothing better for the job. Nothing else matched it for style and durability." The seats were electrically heated via a rheostat control.

Harley Earl liked the look of a clean windshield framing on convertibles. Sun visors were not included on the Le Sabre (or on various other open-type concept cars, as well as the early Corvettes). To that end, he also tended to place a show car's inside rearview mirror on the dash. However, in the case of the Le Sabre something entirely different was crafted for it. Charles Chayne designed a prismatic mirror placed flush into the middle of the dash sill.

Built-in hydraulic jacks at all four points were included in the GM Le Sabre. Easier access to the rear tires was made possible by flip-up fender skirts.

A vast array of instruments provided data to Harley Earl on the state of his Le Sabre. Note the prismatic rear-view mirror located in the center of the dash.

Reportedly the Le Sabre weighed, according to the aforementioned article in *Science and Mechanics*, "something over 3,000 pounds" as a result of using lightweight metals in its construction. Handling was judged as very good. The author of the story stated that the Le Sabre "clings to those curves [of the Milford, Michigan, Proving Grounds] like a magnet, primarily because of the low 6-inch ground clearance," which gave the car a low center of gravity. On the matter of performance the Le Sabre was said to ride "like a confident, smooth-muscled heavyweight, with a feeling of reserve power you can't believe until you drive it."

Details of the XP-300

The XP-300, sometimes referenced as the Phantom while under development, was styled a bit more conventionally than the Le Sabre, but just barely. It was intended as a forecast of styling characteristics of future Buicks. Like the Le Sabre, the XP-300's body was constructed with a non-traditional metal (heat-treated aluminum panels, which were painted "Venus White"), but it did without the use of the more exotic magnesium panels. The XP-300 was structurally quite stiff because its body and frame were welded together.

A concave oval grille was set within a large, encompassing bumper, and this design replaced an earlier proposal composed of a Buick-like "toothy" grille. The combination bumper grille arrangement would later be adapted to other GM cars. This experimental car's hood sloped sharply at its forward end, placing it well below fender height to form a sleek appearance. Upper fenders and hood were integrated to form one piece, which flipped forward for access to the engine compartment. Vertically elongated headlight bezels offered a fresh styling feature, which would be picked up by Buick. The XP-300 had chrome louvers extending down the side from just behind the front wheel openings to across the doors with the fender mounted ones, with the forward one-third of those on the doors serving as engine compartment heat vents. Like the Le Sabre, the XP-300 also had a wraparound windshield, a low overall height, and a simulated jet exhaust nozzle in back. The nozzle shape housed a sealed-beam floodlight-type backup light, and an attached chrome fin running lengthwise atop the centerline concealed the hinges for the side-opening deck lids.

The XP-300 had some mechanical similarities to the Le Sabre but was more complex and, as a result, was less drivable. Its central hydraulic power system was more leak-prone. As a result, it needed constant attention from the system project manager, Lee Furse. It operated the hood, windows, seats, locking devices for cowl vents, jack system, and the doors. The latter had hydraulically operated steel bar locks, which slipped into place like the bolts of a vault door to make the doors very nearly a structural part of the body.

Torsion bars were used in the front suspension of the XP-300 from the start. Other differences between the Le Sabre and the XP-300 included a set of methanol and gasoline fuel tanks mounted behind the seat, a single fan in the engine compartment, coil springs all around, and other suspension and steering component differences. Moreover, the braking system of the XP-300 differed from that of the Le Sabre. The 15-inch wheels of the XP-300 allowed for larger brake drums.

Similar to the Le Sabre, the XP-300 sat on a 116-inch wheelbase versus 115; front track of 59.1 inches versus

Charles Chayne: A Pioneering Engineer

Charles A. Chayne was born on February 6, 1898, in Harrisburg, Pennsylvania. As a child he saw a Brush automobile (manufactured from 1907 to 1913) and the sight of it put Charles on a path to become an engineer. He also became an avid fan of auto racing and a vintage car enthusiast who restored various cars (including the 1931 Bugatti Type 41 Royale he donated to the Henry Ford Museum in 1951) and in 1947, became the president of the Vintage Car Club of America. He was also a strong supporter of the Pebble Beach Concours d'Elegance during its earliest years.

Charles Chayne was the chief engineer for the XP-300 project. He became the chief engineer for Buick in 1936. From 1951 until his retirement in 1963, Chayne was vice president in charge of GM Engineering. (Photo Courtesy GM Media Archive)

Charles Chayne graduated from the Harrisburg Technical High School in 1915, but prior to doing so he received the first of many patents to come for an improvement to airplane engines. He then went on to graduate from the prestigious Massachusetts Institute of Technology (MIT) with a degree in mechanical engineering four years later. Chayne then went to work for the National Advisory Committee for Aeronautics (NACA); this organization was the foundation for the National Aeronautics and Space Administration (NASA), which it became, nearly four decades later. However, he quickly learned that working for the U.S. government in the field of aviation was not for him. He took a teaching job at MIT, where he remained for seven years.

In 1926, Chayne finally fulfilled his desire to work in the automotive industry when he was hired by Lycoming Manufacturing, and then he moved on to Marmon around mid-1927, where he helped develop Marmon's V-16. Soon thereafter, General Motors hired him, and he remained there for the rest of his career. He became Buick's chief engineer in 1936 and stayed in that role into 1951. According to the Buick Club of America's September 2003 issue of *The Buick Bugle*, during this time Chayne acquired many patents on such things as steering linkages, coil spring suspensions, transmission control, temperature regulators, and frames. He led the way for Buick's adoption of all coil springs for 1938. Not all of his ideas were successful. Chayne tried a shortened frame for the 1939 Buicks; he believed the frame could support the load in the rear of the Buick's body but soon learned otherwise. Full-length frames had to be quickly substituted.

For 1941, Chayne's "Compound Carburetion" was released for Buick. After World War II, one of his next major achievements was the release of the Dynaflow automatic transmission (1948), followed by the new 263-ci straight-8 (1950), power steering (1952), and power brakes (1953). Another significant achievement was his design of the experimental Buick XP-300.

For the remainder of his career, from 1951 to his retirement in 1963, Charles Chayne was vice president in charge of GM Engineering. In this capacity, he supervised approximately 2,700 engineers. This was a time in which many major advances in V-8 engine technology were achieved. It was also during these years Chayne worked on the turbine-powered Firebird I and Firebird II concept cars.

During his final years with General Motors, he strongly opposed the design of Chevrolet's first compact car, the Corvair, which was released for the 1960 model year.

Upon his retirement from General Motors, he was active in the old car hobby. In August 1978, he was awarded the Most Elegant Car Award by the Pebble Beach Concours judges for a Hispano-Suiza J-12 he had restored many years earlier. (However, it was by then owned by another collector.) Three months later, Chayne passed away at the age of 80.

The oval bumper-grille concept and oblong headlight bezels are features adapted for GM cars of the 1950s.

The 1951 Buick XP-300 was another concept car built simultaneously with the Le Sabre. This rear view of the clay mockup shows it with its retractable rear window. As originally built, a folding soft top, as well as a detachable hardtop, was provided. Later a conventional soft top with a conventional rear window replaced the original equipment. The boattail shape in back is similar to that of the 1939 Buick Y-Job. (Photo Courtesy GM Media Archive)

58; an equal rear track of 60 inches; ground clearance of 6.6 inches versus 6.0 inches; cowl height of 39.1 inches versus 36.2; and an overall height of 53.4 inches versus 50 for the Le Sabre. However, overall length came up 8.4 inches shorter than the Le Sabre's at 192.5 inches.

Performance testing revealed the XP-300 was rather quick by the standards of the day. Reportedly, Charles Chayne once drove the XP-300 at 140 mph on GM's Milford Proving Grounds test track; another source claimed the car's top speed was just over 120 mph. The time required to travel from 0 to 60 mph was 8 seconds while 100 mph required 21 seconds.

Finely pleated blue leather covered the seats, kick panels, and door panels of the XP-300. The contours of the seats could be adjusted via inflatable bladders controlled with a squeeze-bulb and were adjustable in the fore-aft and vertical directions. A telescoping, 18-inch-diameter steering wheel also offered an additional convenience for the driver. The XP-300's center console held most of the car's gauges, including temperature gauges for the transmission fluid, engine oil, and coolant at the forward end, while controls for the radio and lighting sat in a section of the console between the individual seats. A combination tachometer/speedometer was mounted on the dash directly ahead of the driver's position and a clock, manifold pressure, oil pressure, and fuel gauge were spread across the center of the dash.

As originally configured, the XP-300's soft-top when not in use was folded and stored in a compartment behind the front seat. A hardtop could be affixed as well. A Riviera-type rear window could be raised or lowered as desired with either top. The setup was later removed from the car and a conventional convertible top was installed and retracted into the well where the Riviera-type rear window once was stored. A pivoting lid like that of the Le Sabre concealed the folded top just as it had covered the retracted rear window when it was in place.

Show Time

Of the two cars, the Le Sabre was the first to be revealed to the public. The December 1950 issue of *Life* magazine featured the car using photographs of the mockup.

During February 1951, the XP-300 was shown at the Chicago Auto Show, even though it was not quite finished. Then some months later both the Le Sabre (in July) and the XP-300 (October) were shown together to members of the press at GM's Proving Grounds.

Earl drove the Le Sabre in September at the Watkins Glen race-day parade in front of a crowd of 100,000 thrilled fans and race car drivers. The Le Sabre went to the auto show at the 1951 Canadian National Exhibition in Toronto, where it appeared for a few days. It was then shipped to Belgium before being driven to the Paris Salon, where it drew large, awestruck crowds, so much so that the protective railing surrounding the car was quickly rebuilt to stronger specs!

Both the Le Sabre and XP-300 were among the many displays of the 1953 GM Motorama, a traveling exhibition held at six major cities that year featuring all of GM's products. The Le Sabre was revised somewhat by the time it appeared on this six-city tour. Among the changes were new wheels, deleted fender skirts, and additional air intakes and outlets to fix cooling deficiencies discovered within the engine compartment, as well as the brakes.

Driven

Like the Buick Y-Job had done, the Le Sabre served as Harley Earl's personal transportation on many occasions, and in the process he put about 45,000 miles on the technically and stylistically sophisticated car.

By the time the Le Sabre appeared on the 1953 GM Motorama show tour, it had received some revisions. These included two additional front grilles, engine compartment vents along the front fenders, which were mimicked across the side of the doors, and new wheel discs. The two added grilles and fender vents were intended to relieve the car's tendency to overheat. This photo is dated 1956. (Photo Courtesy GM Media Archive)

The Buick XP-300, which was even more complex, traveled only about 10,400 miles, some of it on the test track and the rest on public roads. Presumably, Charles Chayne drove many of those miles. He demonstrated the car at many SCCA race meetings, such as at Elkhart Lake. The XP-300 remained with the Buick Division for some years before it was sent to Engineering. Chevrolet's chief engineer, Zora Arkus-Duntov, was loaned to Engineering to further improve the car's supercharger.

Influences on Later Design

The influences of the two experimental cars are distinctly different. Although the XP-300 was supposed to foretell the appearance of future Buicks, it had only marginal influence. Its frontal design and upper quarter panel shape were adopted for the 1953–1954 Buicks. As for the Le Sabre, its fin shape in modified form can be seen in the 1953–1954 Pontiacs, 1954 Buicks (except the Skylark), and the 1957 Cadillac. Its gull-wing bumper design showed up on other GM dream cars, as well as production Cadillacs. The Le Sabre's sweeping side trim design appeared on the 1952 and 1953 Buicks. (Its F-86–inspired nose did not make it into production, even though a serious attempt was made to adapt it.)

All-aluminum engines eventually went into production and compression ratios reached and even surpassed those of the experimental cars during the 1960s. The octane ratings for gasoline kept pace with the higher compression ratios, so there was never a need to resort to separate gasoline and methanol systems like those of the Le Sabre and XP-300. While Pontiac produced a transaxle-equipped 1961–1963 Tempest, a more conventional mechanical arrangement for the all-new car was introduced in 1964.

The late GM stylist and VP, Chuck Jordan, explained the impact of the Le Sabre during a telephone interview conducted by me in 2006: "The Le Sabre," said Jordan, "had dramatic proportions and shape. The Le Sabre really knocked us for a loop. It represented Harley Earl's design philosophy and it influenced all of us; it was a very exciting car. We knew we had to go all out." (Jordan was in charge of two GM Motorama vehicles, the 1955 GMC L'Universelle and the 1956 Buick Centurion, and much later, the 1985 Buick Wildcat concept car. He retired from General Motors at the end of 1992.) Jordan learned the value of having a place where a stylist "could design freely and take risks to develop new ideas." Such was the impact of Harley Earl on car design.

At the time of the Le Sabre's introduction, General Motors credited Harley Earl as a "pioneering influence in automotive design . . . Le Sabre is his masterpiece, a super-convertible that is a triumph of designing and engineering genius. It was not produced as a futuristic fad to catch the seasonal fancy of the motoring public. Le Sabre, in essence, is an experimental laboratory on wheels serving as a vehicle for testing out a wide variety of unusual mechanical and styling innovations." It certainly was all it was claimed to be.

Tom Christiansen (standing), Harley Earl's administrative assistant, posed with the LeSabre at the Culver Military Academy in Culver, Indiana. Seated in the car was the commandant of the academy. (Photo Courtesy Karin Christiansen Fowler)

CHAPTER 5
AN AMERICAN SPORTS CAR

"You should have brought a car you could race."
— Briggs Cunningham to Harley Earl at Watkins Glen, September 1951

The creation of the phenomenal Corvette was the brainchild of Harley Earl, who wanted General Motors to produce an American sports car. Sports cars were becoming increasingly popular, but nearly all of them were of European design, such as the MG TD and the Jaguar XK 120, the two most popular sports cars in the United States. However, as popular as these cars were to American enthusiasts, only a little more than 11,000 of new car registrations in 1952 in this country were for sports cars. Because the figure was not necessarily insignificant, the cost of designing and building a sports car to compete with what was already available and to do so for a small niche in the market did not seem practical to most automakers. Nash had entered the sports car market in 1951 with its Healy, hoping to sell just 500 per year. When the car was terminated at the end of the 1954 model year, only 506 had been sold in all. Kaiser agreed to give it a try with the Howard "Dutch" Darrin–designed sports car named Darrin. Production commenced at the end of 1953, but only about 435 found willing and able buyers and the model, too, was terminated. There were other efforts by private parties such as the Muntz Jet from Earl "Mad Man" Muntz and the Edwards from Sterling Edwards, of which only six were built over a six-year period (a four-passenger convertible in 1949 and a different four-passenger car offered from 1953 to 1955). Chrysler Corporation and Ford Motor Company also investigated the sports car market. Dodge built a prototype called the Storm Z-250 but found the costs of production too high to make it marketable; the same fate befell Chrysler's 1955 Falcon. Ultimately, Ford chose to design its 1955 Thunderbird as a sporty boulevard cruiser rather than a true sports car. Even with sales exceeding 15,000 units, Ford Motor Company executives decided the sales were too low to justify continued production and opted to go with a T-Bird with a backseat.

To most Americans, these cars had several undesirable characteristics. Zora Arkus-Duntov told a group at an SAE meeting in 1953 that statistics showed the American public did not want a sports car. But he went on to question if the statistics gave a true picture. He told the group, "As far as the American market is concerned, it is still an unknown quantity since an American sports car catering to American tastes, roads, way of living, and national character has not yet been on the market." He suspected a sports car designed to correspond to the wants of the *American* driver might have a significant following.

First-year production of the Corvette was limited to 300. Shown here is the 300th 1953 Corvette. Like the 299 built before it, the car was painted Polo White and had a Sportsman Red interior.

In September 1951, Harley Earl drove his experimental Le Sabre to the sports car races at Watkins Glen and watched the top European sports cars speed around the track. Briggs Cunningham is reported to have good-naturedly ridiculed Harley's Le Sabre by suggesting to Earl he should have brought a car he could race. Earl said the idea for the Corvette was born while driving the Le Sabre as the pace car for this race. It was a significant turning point in automotive history, although Cunningham's alleged flippant remark perhaps helped to give impetus to the idea.

Thus was born the Opel Passenger Car Development Project. Opel, incidentally, was a name borrowed from GM's German division, so it served to conceal the true nature of the project. Barely more than one year after engineers were shown the plaster mockup of the Corvette, the first three production cars departed the makeshift assembly line in Flint. In late 1952 and early 1953, two prototype show cars were assembled, as well as a "mule" for testing. One of the show cars debuted at the Waldorf-Astoria in New York City, the starting point of the 1953 General Motors Motorama multi-city tour. Many of those who waited in line to see the Corvette, as well as the other show and production cars on display there, indicated a serious interest in buying Chevy's little sports car. Because of this great interest, the go-ahead was given for 250 cars (later increased to 300) to be built prior to the start of the 1954 model year. The first ones rolled off the Flint assembly line on June 30 and the last one on December 24, 1953.

Essentially, the first 300 cars were pilot line cars with various changes made during the run. Even the way the fiberglass body parts were made changed a couple of times. Early cars did not receive the intended wheel covers because the tooling was not quite ready and, therefore, they had to be equipped with the Bel Air type. Because of all the improvements made during 1953, Corvette number 1 and Corvette number 300 were not exactly alike, even though at a glance they appeared identical. As time went by, forming and assembly techniques improved so the last of the 300 1953s were better than the first ones. By 1954, the bodies were of sufficient quality that colors other than Polo White were offered.

Fiberglass was initially seen as an expedient means of constructing a few prototype Corvettes and, in fact, the production versions were planned to have conventional steel bodies. The Corvette assuredly would have been a steel-bodied car but for the research conducted with developing more and more uses for fiberglass. The material was used extensively as covers for aircraft radar antennae systems because it would not interfere with transmission and reception. Then someone had the idea that perhaps fiberglass could be used to build an automobile body. As early as 1944, Owens-Corning worked with industrialist Henry Kaiser in building experimental glass-reinforced plastic (GRP) bodies for automobiles. Kaiser ultimately went on to build his automobiles with steel with the exception of the Kaiser Darrin sports car.

Road test reports regarding the 1953 Corvette were generally favorable, and this generated interest, but the cars were in short supply. The first 300 cars were all built at Flint and were offered to VIPs (such as actor John Wayne) or retained by General Motors for further testing. When interested members of the general public discovered that they could not simply go to the local dealership to purchase one, they began to lose interest in the car. Several of the early prospects had to be called before Chevy found a buyer for a Corvette. Moreover, the lack of roll-up windows and other conveniences made the car somewhat of a disappointment to many of the VIP owners.

The Corvette was not quite up to the expectations of the American driver. Quality control was another

Paired fins were conservative compared to those of a Cadillac. A 150-hp "Blue Flame Special," a modified version of the one used in other Chevy cars, powered all 1953 Corvettes. A full set of gauges and a signal-seeking AM radio (the latter ostensibly an option) was included on all 1953 Corvettes.

problem with the cars. Fiberglass technology was at a rudimentary level at that time. Panels were often thin and fragile. In addition, panel fitment was generally poor and stress cracks appeared fairly quickly. Chevrolet's engineers worked with the Molded Fiberglass Company (MFG) in developing the fiberglass bodies. Some of the earliest research took place in the basement of the home of the founder, Robert Morrison. General Motors and its supplier experimented to determine the correct thickness of fiberglass for a part and the correct ratio of resin and hardener. In the end, General Motors contracted with MFG to supply fiberglass components for the Corvette beginning in 1954, and the company continues to do so today.

The price tag of $3,490 was certainly on the high side. And, even though that was the official base price, in reality, the so-called optional AM-radio and heater were mandatory equipment. The base price was $3,734. At the end of the 1953 model year, more than 180 of the 300 Vettes assembled remained unsold. At the time, this did not alarm General Motors because so many of the cars were being used for special dealer displays to draw people into showrooms.

Those who owned a 1953 Corvette at least had a car with great styling and decent performance. All were Polo White with a Sportsman Red interior. The 6-cylinder engine received a number of upgrades to improve its performance, including a trio of Carter YF side-draft carburetors, aluminum intake, higher lift camshaft with aluminum timing gear, increased compression ratio, and dual exhausts. Modifications pushed the output from 115 hp to 150. The suspension was composed of as many standard parts as possible, but included a larger diameter stabilizer bar, special front coil springs, 16:1 steering ratio, and four-leaf springs in back. Weight distribution with driver, passenger, full fuel tank, and luggage worked out to about 50/50; empty it was 53/47. The center of gravity was low, just 18 inches above the ground.

Motor Trend judged the Corvette to be "an exciting car to drive" but noted it would "barely nose out an average [Buick] Century on an unobstructed freeway." The Vette's top speed was found to be approximately 108 mph. One serious downside was its handling characteristics. Road testers for *Motor Life* reported, "When we tried to break it loose at high speed on a rather severe corner the Corvette . . . showed a definite unwillingness to tuck back in."

Today, the 1953 Corvette is simply judged on its rarity as well as its great styling, as it has been for many years now. The longtime popularity of the 1953 Corvette has resulted in about half of the 300 built still remaining in existence.

Designing the Original Corvette

Harley Earl's interest in producing a sports car coincided with the refinement of what was then a still relatively new material (glass-reinforced plastic or GRP), which soon became very important to the Corvette project, as well as for the construction of dozens of later dream cars shown at the GM Motorama (see Chapter Eight). One of the earliest uses for GRP was for aircraft radomes during World War II. After the war, aircraft were built with an increasingly greater number of fiberglass pieces. Civilian uses included storage tanks, pipes, laminates, and sports gear.

The Glasspar Corporation, which manufactured fiberglass boats, was experimenting with the material; it built a prototype fiberglass sports car, the Alembic I, which was evaluated by GM officials. Howard "Dutch" Darrin had been working with the material to build a sports car for Kaiser. His Darrin was revealed to the public in 1952, which was about the time that work started on the Corvette project. But even Dutch Darrin's car was not the first to be built of GRP. As early as 1944, Owens-Corning was working with Henry Kaiser in developing GRP bodies for automobiles. With the Korean War underway and certain metals being rationed, automakers began investigating alternative materials. After an article arranged by US Rubber about the new material appeared in a February issue of *Life* magazine, a Chevrolet production engineer called the company to learn more. Technicians from the Mishawaka, Indiana, plant went to Detroit to show how a mold could be made from a fender to make an identical part from fiberglass. GM Styling and Chevrolet Engineering immediately began experimenting with GRP.

Harley Earl was impressed with the Alembic I; he was also impressed with the rakish 1949 Willys Jeepster, a vehicle modified from the Jeep Station Wagon by Brooks Stevens, an independent industrial designer.

Cadillac's chief engineer at the time, Ed Cole, was also enthusiastic about sports cars. Earl and Cole knew any GM sports car had to be inexpensive, thus it had to use as many off-the-shelf components as possible. The price target was set at $1,850, about the cost of a 1952 Chevy sedan. However, the price for the production car would ultimately be twice that of the original goal. Such cost constraints dictated the use of the Chevrolet 6-cylinder, Powerglide transmission, and the existing Chevrolet chassis in modified form. Proposed, but ultimately not made available by Chevrolet, was a McCulloch supercharger, although, McCulloch Motors Corporation offered the setup as an aftermarket kit.

With enthusiasm for the "Opel" gaining momentum, design work began in a small, enclosed area of the ninth floor of the GM Building where the main Body Development Studio was located. Earl placed stylist Robert McLean, a graduate of Cal Tech and a sports car enthusiast, in charge of the car's styling. According to Karl Ludvigsen's book, *Corvette: America's Star-Spangled Sports Car*, McLean was to perform the general layout. The standard practice was to start a layout from the firewall and work fore and aft to locate the wheels, engine, and passengers. Instead, McLean began with "the rear axle centerline and started constructing the car from the back to the front." When other stylists saw what he was doing, they collectively told him his method was "impossible." McLean proved them wrong. He brought the seats as close as he reasonably could to the rear wheelhouses and then drew the occupants seated low and stretched out in the traditional sports car arrangement.

From there McLean located the dash line and placed the 6-cylinder engine and gearbox back as much as possible, something considered revolutionary at the time as it was 3 inches lower and 7 inches more rearward than the then-current Chevrolet. The arrangement helped with achieving as close as possible the desired 50/50 weight distribution. Lowering the drivetrain lowered the center of gravity, which made for better handling. With all of this done, he was able to establish the centerline for the front wheels and, in so doing, arrived at the Corvette's 102-inch wheelbase, the same as that of the Jaguar XK-120. General Motors purchased at least one XK-120 for dismantling to study its design. McLean's drawing was then converted into a full-scale, detailed, white-on-black profile drawing by Bill Bloch. Upon completion Harley Earl viewed it and questioned McLean about the engine placement. "Is that how the Jaguar and MG are?" to which McLean confirmed with a simple, "Yes, sir." Harley Earl accepted the design. McLean proceeded to refine the styling for the prototype to be unveiled at the first venue of the 1953 GM Motorama, the Waldorf-Astoria.

The exposed spare tire of the Jeepster was a styling feature originally included in the early stages of the Corvette's styling. Another proposal placed the spare in a recess atop the deck lid. Ultimately, the spare was placed in a well under a panel in the trunk floor. Harley Earl gave the Corvette its wraparound windshield, as showcased on his Le Sabre. Another Le Sabre feature passed on to the Corvette (one that had been passed on to the Le Sabre from the Y-Job) was the concealed folding top. Earl originally wanted transparent covers over the recessed headlights blending with the shape of the front fenders. In the end, the so-called "fencing mask" grilles were applied. Joe Schemansky was charged with the car's interior styling, consisting of bucket seats and a symmetrical dash layout with centrally located instrumentation.

Upon seeing the completed full-scale plaster model of the Corvette in April 1952, Ed Cole is said to have "literally jumped up and down" and gave it his full support. Amazingly, the time to bring the car from a paper proposal, to the mockup stages, and then finally to a functional prototype was accomplished in only about eight months. The production version changed very little visually from the appearance of the prototype show cars. A small reduction in the thickness of the fiberglass used for the body resulted in a lighter car. Also, going to a two-piece (upper and lower) body made the production process easier and also meant the resulting seam down the side needed a molding to cover it.

The weaknesses of the Corvette in the eyes of American sports car enthusiasts would be discovered soon; matters such as metal-edged, snap-in plexiglass side curtains rather than roll-up windows, less than ideal instrumentation placement, and of course the powertrain, along with other issues, would almost put an end to the Corvette before many were built.

1954: Unrealistic Expectations

Expectations were high at the start of 1954 Corvette production. The forecast was to increase production of the Corvette to 10,000 units per year, but sales were slow, forcing a drastic cut in production, which in the end amounted to only 3,640. Of those, more than 1,100 (one source stated in excess of 1,500) remained unsold at the end of the model year. Incidentally, 15 of the cars were built on the last days of 1953, sometimes resulting in an erroneous report of 315 of the 1953 models being built.

Changes made for the 1954 were few; the biggest was in where it was assembled after those first 15 cars were built. Production moved from Flint to St. Louis. The

Additional colors became available for the Corvettes of 1954. However, black was limited to a few (some say four while others say six) of the cars built reportedly for executives and for auto shows. (Photo Courtesy Wayne Ellwood)

earliest 1954s had few visible alterations. The canvas top and frame color were changed from black to tan, so with the top in the up position, a 1954 Corvette (painted Polo White) could easily be distinguished from a 1953. About 80 percent of the 1954 Corvettes were painted Polo White with a Sportsman Red interior, but a few other color choices were offered and included Pennant Blue with a tan interior (approximately 300 in this color) and Sportsman Red with a Sportsman Red interior (approximately 100 in this color). A few Corvettes (four or six, depending upon the source) were painted black with a Sportsman Red interior, but they were reportedly built for GM executives and for the auto show circuit. Some owners of 1954 Corvettes report that the original color of their cars were shades not listed in official Chevrolet brochures. Some paint bulletins listed metallic green and metallic bronze as additional colors for the Corvette that year.

Partway through the production run, the approximately 2-inch-long exhaust extensions installed on the previous Corvettes were replaced with longer units. Customer complaints about exhaust gases staining the surrounding paint and even entering the passenger compartment led to the change. With the top up, side curtains in place, and the vent window open a little, the spent gases could enter the car because of a low-pressure area created as the Corvette moved through the air. As a result, the extension was made about 6 inches long, was capped at the back, and a baffle directed exhaust downward through a slot. This eliminated the annoying exhaust being pulled into the passenger compartment and minimized the staining of the paint in back.

Another running change was the replacement of the two-handle hood release, which was replaced with a single-handle mechanism. Fuel and brake lines were relocated inboard of the right side frame rail, the chock control was moved from the right to the left of the steering column for convenience of operation, and the horsepower was increased by 5 to 155 by means of an improved camshaft. Partway into the model year, the three side-draft carburetors became filtered by twin air cleaners, instead of three air cleaners. Some cars had a chrome-plated rocker arm cover and/or a chrome-plated ignition shield.

The officially listed price was $3,498, which kept much of the youth market, the primary target market, from purchasing a 1954 Corvette. Chevrolet decided to lower the advertised price to $2,774 to boost sales, but there was a catch: the only transmission offered, the Powerglide, was listed as an option, as were windshield wipers and the heater. In the end, the price tag actually totaled $3,254.10. Many potential buyers were put off by the deception in pricing. Another contributing factor to the poor sales was dealer attitude; some dealers had doubts about trying to sell a "plastic" car that seated only two people. They did not have anyone skilled in repairing fiberglass either so servicing a wrecked Corvette presented a problem. Many Chevy dealers were doing well selling conventional Bel Airs, Two-Tens, and station wagons and saw no need to complicate matters by promoting the unusual Corvette.

The Corvette probably would have been discontinued at this point if Ford Motor Company had not released its new Thunderbird, which landed on dealer lots in September 1954. The rivalry between Chevrolet and Ford played a role in saving Harley Earl's sports car from being terminated. Zora Arkus-Duntov also played an important role. Chevrolet's legendary engineer and sports car enthusiast wrote a now-famous letter dated October 15, 1954, to engineers Ed Cole and Maurice Olley, stating, "By the looks of it, the Corvette is on its way out. I would like to say the following: Dropping the car now will have adverse effect internally and externally. It is an admission of failure. Failure of aggressive thinking in the eyes of the organization, failure to develop a saleable product in the eyes of the outside world . . . Ford enters the field with the Thunderbird, a car of the same class as the Corvette. If Ford makes success where we failed, it may hurt. We will leave an opening in which it can hit at will. 'Ford out-engineered, outsold, or ran Chevrolet's pride and joy off the market.'" Evidently the letter was well received.

1955: Finally a V-8, but Almost Too Little Too Late

Just as for 1954, the 1955 model Corvettes received extremely few styling updates, although some significant updates were proposed. The money for alterations was extremely limited, so these proposals were rejected for

Harvest Gold with a dark green top was one of five color schemes offered for 1955. This was also the first year for Corvette to have a V-8. Despite having the new small-block, only 700 Corvettes were built for this model year.

production. In the end, the updates amounted to new paint color choices, vinyl-coated canvas top material, tubeless tires, electric windshield wipers, improved body construction, and the inclusion of an anodized gold "V" over the lowercase "v" of the Chevrolet script mounted on the sides of the front fenders; the big "V" signified the presence of a V-8. However, for most of 1955, the 2-speed Powerglide was the only transmission to be had. Base price was $2,909 for the V-8 cars, of which most were, while the few sixes were listed again for $2,774.

An early Corvette was modified to illustrate styling changes proposed for the 1955 model year. It was known as SO (shop order) 2151. Among the ideas presented were a Ferrari-like egg crate grille, fin inside the headlight bezels, hood scoop, engine compartment cooling vents behind the front wheels, and a 1954 Corvair rear treatment. All of these ideas were ultimately rejected as unjustifiable due to cost considerations in combination with the poor sales of the sports car. This car was refitted with stock components (the vents on the side of the front fenders were left in place) and apparently sold. It surfaced in the early 1980s on a used car lot in Northern California. At last report it was being restored to the appearance it had as SO 2151 by an enthusiast in Indiana.

Color choices for the Corvette were altered for 1955. Pennant Blue was carried over until about the middle of the model year then was replaced by Harvest Gold with a medium green, pale yellow interior and a dark green top. Other color schemes offered were Corvette Copper with a dark beige interior and beige top, Gypsy Red (different than Sportsman Red) with a light beige interior, red saddle stitching, tan carpeting and a beige top, plus Polo White with a red interior and a white top. Nearly half of the cars were Polo White; only 15 were Corvette Copper; 45 were Pennant Blue; 120 were painted Harvest Gold; and 180 were sprayed Gypsy Red.

During 1954, one of the 1953 Corvettes retained by Chevrolet Engineering was fitted with an experimental version of Chevrolet's 265-ci small-block. Many miles of testing revealed there were no major problems with a V-8 installation in the Corvette and, in fact, the modifications needed to make the engine fit were minor. Furthermore, Mauri Rose, a three-time winner of the Indianapolis 500 and Chevrolet engineer, had a 1954 Corvette fitted with a prototype V-8. As an experimental Chevrolet, it received an "EX" designation; in this case it was EX-87. Once Rose had completed his tests, EX-87 was turned over to Duntov in late 1955, for high-speed driving at Daytona.

The Corvette V-8 of course made use of the new Chevrolet small-block (detailed in Chapter Six), but received

An early Corvette was modified into a 1955 styling prototype illustrating mildly differing features. Note the concave grille, engine compartment vents, and the differing headlight treatments with a "shark fin" over the headlight (inset) demonstrated on the passenger side of the car. Also note the hood scoop (inset). (Photos Courtesy GM Media Archive)

The "1955" styling car offered this design for the rear that was based upon the Corvair shown at the 1954 GM Motorama. This car left General Motors with mostly stock components and was pictured as it sat on a California used car lot in the 1980s in volume two of Noland Adams' five-volume set, Corvette: American Legend. (Photo Courtesy GM Media Archive)

Light yellow upholstery with dark green upper dash, upper door panels, and carpet was the only color scheme offered with the Harvest Gold exterior paint color.

The 265 V-8 small-block arrived for the 1955 model year. All but a half-dozen or so of the 700 1955 Corvettes built had this engine; the rest were equipped with the Blue Flame 6.

an 8.0:1 compression ratio, a hotter cam, and a Rochester 4-barrel carburetor; in this form it provided 195 hp at 5,000 rpm and torque of 260 ft-lbs at 3,000 rpm. Redline was 6,500 rpm. With the lighter V-8, weight distribution changed to 52/48. Acceleration and top speed improved substantially with 0 to 60 mph requiring only 8.5 seconds while top speed was near 120 mph. Despite the extra two cylinders, fuel mileage actually went up by 2 to 3 mpg as compared to the 6-cylinder Corvettes.

Late in the 1955 model year, Chevrolet released a Saginaw 3-speed manual transmission for use in the Corvette, but only about 75 Corvettes received it. Nearly every one of the 700 Corvettes of the 1955 model year was powered with the new V-8. Reportedly, at least six to as many as ten of the 700 cars were assembled with leftover Blue Flame Six components and, indeed, a few of the 6-cylinder cars still exist. Incidentally, the 6-cylinder cars retained a 6-volt electrical system while those with the V-8 received a 12-volt system.

The paltry 700-car production must have embarrassed some of GM's upper management. It was a failure in their view. Why did the Corvette almost fail to continue beyond 1955? While the lack of simple conveniences such as roll-up windows, no 4-speed transmission, and some handling problems appear to answer the question, the bottom line is that General Motors just did not understand what the car needed to be. According to the book, *Corvette: America's Star-Spangled Sports Car, a Complete History*, by Karl Ludvigsen, Ed Cole admitted as much: "We really didn't know what we wanted. We had no real feeling of the market. Was Corvette for the boulevard driver, or the sports car tiger? We weren't quite sure. But we loved that car. We weren't going to let go." There was a group within Chevrolet who resisted the pressure from higher up to suspend the production of the Corvette.

1956: Corvette on Life Support

After extremely slow sales became evident during the 1955 model year, Chevrolet's management was ready to put an end to building its fiberglass sports car and try to forget it ever existed. However, Zora Arkus-Duntov, Ed Cole, and others were not about to abandon the project. With the support and skills of these key people within General Motors, the Corvette began to mature into a true sports car competitive in racing events. There were rumors of Corvette's demise in the automotive press, but someone at *Motor Trend* must have had an inside track on acquiring the facts; its editors boldly stated "a very hot version" with a detachable hardtop and roll-up windows was on the way. The writer was, indeed, correct.

The small-block V-8 was bored out to 283 ci and could be had with twin, 4-barrel carburetors (a $172.20 option on the Corvette), which boosted output to 225

The Corvette underwent its first restyle for 1956. A new upholstery design was included in the freshened sports car. This Venetian Red example on display at an auto show was equipped with the extra-cost detachable hardtop. (Photo Courtesy Cecil Burdick, via Josh Burdick)

hp at 5,600 rpm. Also available was the Duntov cam, for a cost of $188.30, which was available only for the twin-carb engine; it added another 15 hp at the same 5,600 rpm. Compression was boosted to 9.25:1 from 8.0:1. Still, there was no 4-speed transmission this year. The close-ratio 3-speed, however, was standard issue while the Powerglide was an extra-cost option adding $188.50 to the base price of $3,467. Most buyers, though, did not opt for the automatic. Performance with the 225-hp engine was impressive with a 0-60–mph sprint taking only 7.5 seconds while the quarter mile could be run in 15.9 seconds at a terminal speed of 91 mph according to a road test published in the May 1956 issue of *Sports Car Illustrated*.

The author of the report, Karl Ludvigsen, declared, "In my opinion, the Corvette as it stands is fully as much a dual-purpose machine as the stock Jaguar, Triumph, or Austin-Healey. Without qualification, General Motors is now building a sports car." The base engine topped with a 4-barrel carburetor offered 210 hp at 5,600 rpm. Writer Tom McCahill, in his unique style, noted in the December 1956 issue of *Mechanix Illustrated*, "The Chevrolet Corvette in 1956 astounded more sports car purists with its terrific speed and acceleration than Briggs Cunningham would if he entered Sebring in a rowboat."

Another important factor in converting the Corvette into a genuine sports car was its chassis refinements. Duntov tested a 1955 version to find the flaws in the car's handling. In an article he wrote for *Auto Age*, he stated, "The target was to attain such handling characteristics that the driver of some ability could get really high performance safely. The main objects of suspension changes were: increase of high-speed stability, consistency in response to the steering wheel over a wide range of lateral acceleration and speeds, and improvement of power transmission on turns (that is, reduction of unloading of inside rear wheel)."

To achieve these goals, shims were installed between the front crossmember and the frame to increase the caster angle to two degrees and to alter the angle of the central steering idler arm so that the roll oversteer geometry was removed from the front suspension. Also, changing the rear spring hangers so the slant of the springs was less abrupt decreased the roll understeer at the rear. Duntov noted in his article, "The car goes where it is pointed, and does so without hesitation. On turns taken hard, it does not plow or skid, but gets into a drift. If the right amount of power is fed, the drift can be maintained without danger of the rear end getting presumptuous and assuming the position of the front." The 11-inch drum brakes were also improved through the use of linings more resistant to fade.

The close ratio 3-speed transmission (2.2:1 in first, 1.31:1 in second gear, and 1:1 in third) was driven by a 10.5-inch clutch with 12 heat-treated coil springs that replaced the previous diaphragm-spring unit. New internal components included the clutch shaft gear, counterbalance gears, and a new second gear.

A new rear axle very much like the passenger version came with a 3.55:1 ratio in standard form; manually shifted Corvettes could be equipped with the 3.27:1 ratio as an extra-cost option.

Chevrolet took the Corvette racing and came away with some image-enhancing results for its sports car. In late December 1955, three Corvettes were shipped to Florida. One was a 1953 model equipped with a 1956 powertrain. Another was a 1955 model (with its body from EX-87) also with a 1956 powertrain. The other was assembled using the body from the 1956 prototype and was powered with a small-block enlarged to 307 ci and equipped with the Duntov cam. After constant weather delays, the Daytona Speed Weeks events finally got underway. Duntov drove the 1956 car to a two-way average of 150.583 mph! John Fitch and Betty Skelton drove the other two cars. Fitch was then known as America's best road-racing driver and Skelton had set a number of racing as well as aviation records. Fitch drove his car in the top speed trials, achieving a first with 145.543 mph to set a record as the fastest production car while Skelton came in second with 137.733 mph.

In April, Dr. Dick Thompson drove a Chevrolet-prepared Corvette at the Pebble Beach races, where he drove to a first-in-class victory and a second-place finish overall. Brake problems near the end of the race allowed a 300SL to overtake Thompson. Chevrolet advertising promoted this success by boldly proclaiming that, "The

One of the show cars at the 1954 GM Motorama was a Corvette modified with features that were finally available with the 1956 model: an optional detachable hardtop, roll-up windows, and waffle-patterned upholstery. (Photo Courtesy GM Media Archive)

1956 Corvette is proving, in open competition, that it is America's only genuine production sports car." In March, four factory-backed Corvettes were raced at the Sebring 12-Hour Sports Car Grand Prix of Endurance. Two of the cars completed the grueling race, finishing 9th and 15th, they were among only 24 of the 60 cars that started the race to complete it. The race revealed the Corvette still needed some more work in the area of braking, at least for a tight road course such as Sebring. Its solid axle rather than independent rear suspension also showed itself to be less than ideal on such a course.

Of more concern to owners who were not racing their Corvettes (at least not in officially sanctioned events) was the matter of comfort. A power-operated soft top was now available (costing $107.60), but in making room for the mechanism, interior space was reduced. In the aforementioned article by Tom McCahill, he wrote, "If Chevy had adopted the adjustable steering wheel of its closest competitor, the comfort and safety factors would have shot way up. As it is, the steering column cannot be moved in or out to fit the driver. Tie this up with shallow, small seats and you have a car that is suitable for men on the smallish side only." Regardless of its drawbacks, the Corvette was earning respect.

Styling and Options Revised

Styling was significantly altered for the first time since the Corvette became available. Bob Caderet with the Chevrolet Studio was assigned to the 1956 Corvette project. He was responsible for the frontal styling and the wheel covers with a simulated knock-off spinner. Interestingly, the wheel covers continued to be used through the 1962 model year, the final one for the C1 generation platform. Harley Earl wanted to retain the grille shell and grille teeth, so they were carried forward. However, the recessed headlights with the "fencing mask" grilles were replaced with a headlight installation based upon the design of the 1954 Mercedes-Benz 300SL coupe.

General Motors purchased a new 300SL and brought it to the styling studio. In fact, General Motors purchased an example of every new car, domestic and foreign, for study. Its hood bumps, which the stylists labeled windsplits, were also carried over into the styling of the new Corvette. However, there was a functional purpose for it on the 300SL. One was needed for clearance of the 6-cylinder's single overhead camshaft cover while the other served for cosmetic symmetry.

A new set of wraparound front bumpers was also included as part of the styling updates. The cowl-mounted scoops included on the original 1953 Corvette prototype were included in the 1956 design, although they were not functional. Carl Renner, also of the Chevrolet Studio, designed the side coves; it was a trait included on three of the 1955 concept cars (Chevrolet Biscayne, LaSalle II Roadster, and LaSalle II Sedan) shown at that year's GM Motorama. The side coves helped to provide the Corvette with a unique appearance.

In back, the jet-pod taillights with mini fins were replaced with lights recessed into the quarter panels. The recessed rear license plate "shadow box" was filled in and the plate mount relocated to beneath the bumper. Exhausts exited through an opening within the vertical bumperettes at the ends of the quarters. Not long after 1956 production commenced, an extra molding was added to the forward edge of the optional hardtop.

Corvette owners finally had the chance to have roll-up windows as well as a detachable hardtop. A soft top was standard while the hardtop option added $215.20 to the base price. However, buyers could choose to exchange the soft top for the hardtop at no additional charge. Those who opted for the hardtop found rearward visibility to be much better than that afforded by the soft top. Other options included power windows priced at $64.60, Signal-Seeking radio for $198.90, and heater for $123.65.

Bob Bartholomew of the interior studio crafted a mildly revised instrument panel. A new steering wheel was included, as were new door panels and waffle-patterned

Each side of this 1956 Corvette mockup shows alternative ideas for side cove design. Note the exhaust outlet in the lower rear of the quarter panel of the passenger side and the mid-level location on the other. Both were rejected for production. (Photos Courtesy GM Media Archive)

upholstery. The latter two were based upon those seen on the Corvette show cars with the prototype detachable hardtop shown at the 1954 auto shows, including the GM Motorama. Furthermore, the passenger seat was now adjustable in the fore and aft direction.

Color choices were updated again and included Arctic Blue, Aztec Copper, Cascade Green, Polo White, Onyx Black, and Venetian Red. However, the presence of side coves provided an opportunity for various two-tone schemes at a cost of $19. Soft tops were offered in beige or white with all paint colors with the exception of Onyx Black, which could be had with a black or white top.

Production for the 1956 Corvette totaled 3,467 units, nearly five times 1955's output. Unlike 1954, when nearly one-third of the 3,640 Corvettes built remained unsold at the end of the year, there remained few, if any, unsold cars at the end of the 1956 model year. Furthermore, the 1956 Corvettes had only an eight-month sales year instead of the more typical 11 months. No doubt more Corvettes would have been sold that model year had there been more time to do so. Most likely, potential buyers turned to the 1957s. Dealers found the Corvette to be boosting showroom traffic. Chevrolet now had a performance image that was attracting buyers, not just to the Corvette, but to the big cars also. The 1956 model year was a turning point for the Corvette.

The SR-2

The Sebring Racer (SR) Corvette was built to resolve a rather awkward situation. One of the sons of a certain GM vice president chose to drive a Ferrari instead of a Corvette. That just did not look good. The Ferrari driver was Jerry Earl and as the reader by now has likely guessed, the GM VP was Harley Earl. To remedy the problem, Harley told Jerry he would build a Corvette especially for him if he would give up the Ferrari. That Corvette had to be especially sporting for the deal to work and it was. In the end, two SR-2 race cars were built. A third with only the styling attributes of the race cars was assembled for Harlow Curtice, GM's president. Curtice's car was mainly for show, and he certainly did not drive it to work.

Harley Earl oversaw the styling of the SR-2. A 1956 Corvette, serial number E56S002522, built on May 21, was secured for the conversion. It was stripped of its paint and hardware; its body was then separated from its chassis. By mid-June, the first SR-2 was completed, including even having its Sports Car Club of America assigned number, 144, painted on its sides.

During that three-week period, the Corvette was transformed into a full race car with modifications that included a new lightweight, extended nose, a set of windscreens, functional air scoops to cool the rear brakes, an added central rear fin, modified taillights faired in with the quarter panel, and added optional heavy-duty components (shocks, stabilizer bars, springs, brakes) to the chassis. Also installed was a set of magnesium wheels with knock-off hubs. The body was painted a light metallic blue, evidently a favorite shade of Earl's.

The second SR-2, built for Bill Mitchell, differed in having a headrest with a fairing similar to that of the EX-87 Corvette, a large nose emblem (similar to that of the later production 1958 Corvette), and was painted red. Adding the fairing in back resulted in having to hinge the trunk to open backward. Earl liked the look of the fairing and added the feature to the original SR-2. Both of the racing SR-2s still exist. The original car at the time of this writing is being offered for sale for nearly $6.9 million. The third SR-2, the one built for Harlow Curtice, was the only one of the type built to be street driven. It was equipped with the following options: heater, AM Signal-Seeking radio, parking brake alarm, courtesy lights, windshield washers, whitewall tires, power windows, and power soft top. This car also still exists and is in a private collection. It is the most original of the three and at last report had accumulated 48,000 miles.

The first of three SR-2s (SR for Sebring Racer) was built for Jerry Earl, son of Harley Earl. Jerry Earl was driving a Ferrari, which was not viewed as an appropriate choice for the son of the head of GM Design. A Corvette built for competition in Sports Car Club of America races was viewed as a much better alternative. Chevy engineer "Mac" MacKichan (passenger seat) and GM Styling engineer Ken Pickering (standing at far right) posed with the new SR-2. (Photo Courtesy GM Media Archive)

The second of three SR-2s was built for Bill Mitchell, who loved sports car racing. Other than the color, his car differed from the original SR-2 in having a faired-in headrest, a feature similar to that of the Jaguar D-Type. A faired-in headrest was later added to the original SR-2. Paul O'Shea and Pete Lovely drove this car to a 16th place finish at Sebring in 1957. (Photo Courtesy Gene Bussian)

Bill Mitchell (seated in car) fitted his SR-2 with rear fender skirts and smooth-disc wheel covers for improved airflow over the car. (Photo Courtesy GM Media Archive)

The SR-2 built for Harlow Curtice was much more suitable for the street than the other two versions. (Photo Courtesy GM Media Archive)

1957: Corvette Gets More Respect

The 1956 Corvette was good, but the 1957 was better. Production climbed to a new high point of 6,339. The 283-ci small-block combined with the availability of a Borg-Warner 4-speed transmission later in the model year and a fuel-injection unit developed by GM's Rochester Division made the Corvette an even bigger hit with enthusiasts.

The FI Ramjet engine came in two states of tune for the street; the milder version provided 250 hp at 4,800 rpm and the other 283 hp–1 horsepower per cubic inch at 6,200 rpm. In fact, the stated horsepower was an advertising gimmick, as true output was at 290 hp. Torque specs were 305 ft-lbs at 3,800 rpm and 290 ft-lbs at 4,400 rpm, respectively. Compression ratios, respectively, were 9.5:1 and 10.5:1. Regardless of the output, the price tag was high at $484.20, which was an approximately 15 percent premium over the base price of $3,176. A racing version was also offered, costing $726.30. The Corvette included a column-mounted tachometer and a cold-air induction system, and only 43 were built with the option.

Also offered was a competition suspension at a price of $780.10, which gave the buyer heavy-duty springs, a thicker front anti-sway bar, limited-slip axle, larger piston shock absorbers with firmer valving, a faster steering ratio that reduced turns lock-to-lock from 3.7 to 2.9,

This 1957 Corvette was ordered with the 270-hp 2 x 4-barrel carburetor option and 4-speed transmission. Over half of the 6,339 Corvettes built that year had either the 245- or 270-hp dual 4-barrel 283s. The two-tone color scheme of Venetian Red with the Shoreline Beige side cove was an option.

The waffle-patterned upholstery of the 1957 Corvette was carried over from 1956. Beige and red was the only color scheme offered with the Venetian Red exterior color. Note the 4-speed shifter.

The twin, 4-barrel engine was introduced for 1956, but on the smaller 265 V-8. Shown here is the 1957 version of the 283.

and ceramic-metallic brake linings with finned ventilated drums. A total of 51 cars were built with this option.

The 4-speed was ready for sale starting April 9. It was a close-ratio type with ratios of 2.2:1 in first, 1.66:1 in second, 1.31:1 in third, and 1:1 in fourth. Because of its late introduction, only 664 of the 1957 models received the 4-speed. An optional "Posi-Traction" limited-slip rear end was offered in four final drive ratios.

Performance of the Corvette with the fuel-injected engine was impressive. In a road test report in the June 1957 issue of *Motor Life*, a 283-horsepower test car sprinted from 0 to 60 mph in just 6.35 seconds with a 3-speed manual transmission and 3.54:1 rear end. The *Road & Track* staff found that with the 4-speed attached to the 283 FI engine, the 0-60–mph time improved to 5.7 seconds and also found the standing-start quarter-mile required only 14.3 seconds, reaching 96 mph in the process. Top speed was stated as 132 mph. In total, 1,040 Corvettes were purchased with a fuel-injection engine, about 16 percent of total production.

In addition to the "fuelie," the Corvette could also be had again with dual-quad carburetion. The twin fours offered some advantages over the exotic fuel-injection setup: less expensive and less maintenance.

Fuel-injection proved somewhat troublesome; fuel nozzles clogged with dirt deposits and also absorbed heat, causing rough idling. This time the 2 x 4-barrel setup was offered in two versions offering 245 hp at 5,800 rpm and 270 hp at 4,800 rpm. As before, a single 4-barrel version (220 hp at 4,800 rpm) was standard issue and the Powerglide remained an option. A total of 3,666 buyers opted for one of the dual-carburetor engines, nearly 58 percent of the year's production.

Styling revisions were almost non-existent this time. "Fuel Injection" script with an emblem of crossed-flags

Betty Skelton had an early 1957 Corvette modified by Styling for her in gold with a white leather interior plus other touches, like crossed flags in the coves accompanied by a "Chevrolet" script. Skelton, who was an accomplished aerobatic pilot and the women's land speed record holder in 1956, served as a spokesperson for Chevrolet. (Photo Courtesy GM Media Archive)

1957 Corvette Super Sport Show Car

A 1956 Corvette was modified into a show car (Shop Order 90181) for the 1957 auto show circuit. It received a new serial number designating it as a 1957 model. External changes to the car included a set of bubble windscreens that replaced the wraparound windshield. This required modification to the cowl and upper dash. An air scoop resembling those of the SR-2s was mounted in the rear of each side cove, which was painted contrasting silver. "Fuel Injection" script was also attached in the fender portion of the cove. A wide racing stripe flanked by thin stripes in blue ran lengthwise along the centerline of the show car. Special tires with a narrow band white sidewall were also installed.

Changes to the interior were more extensive. Upholstery, door panels (similar to what appeared on the then-upcoming 1958 Impala), carpeting, dash, steering wheel, and even the foot pedals were altered. Courtesy lights were mounted in the door panel armrests and additional gauges were installed along the dash.

According to a 1959 newspaper article about the car becoming owned by an Albuquerque, New Mexico, dealer, the cost to modify the car amounted to $18,000. The work was completed in December 1956

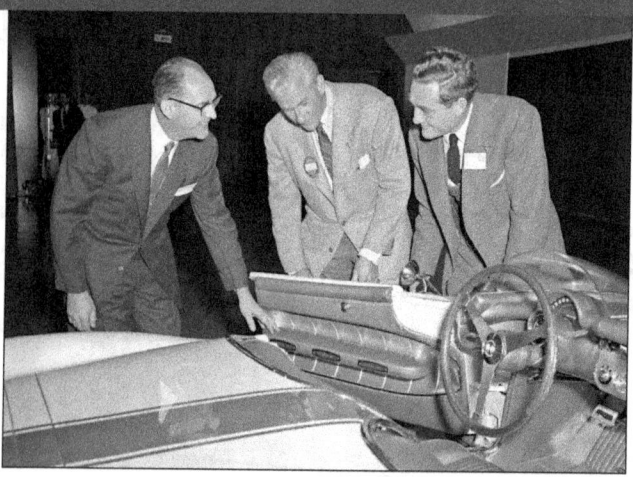

Among the features of the 1957 Corvette Super Sport show car is a special steering wheel, unique door panels with red lights in the armrests, custom floor covering, and textured metal pedals. Appearing on the far right is entrepreneur and sportsman Briggs Cunningham. (Photo Courtesy GM Media Archive)

and the first showing took place the following month at the New York Auto Show. It was also exhibited at the Chicago Auto Show; the remainder of the venues where the Super Sport was exhibited is not known. This car still exists and is in a private collection.

The white and silver-blue 1957 Corvette Super Sport (actually built from a 1956 model) was created for the auto show circuit. It featured twin bubble windscreens, scoops in the rear cove area, thinly white-stripped tires, and a modified interior. This car, incidentally, still exists in a private collection. (Photo Courtesy GM Media Archive)

Carl Renner of the Chevrolet Studio penned this full-size rendering of a proposed 1957 Corvette. It was based upon the styling of the 1955 GM LaSalle II Roadster concept car displayed at the GM Motorama. (Photo Courtesy GM Media Archive)

appeared on the side coves and the script was mounted on the deck lid when equipped with the FI engine. Color choices were unchanged with the exception of the addition of Inca Silver, which was rarely ordered.

1958–1959

The 1958 Corvette received a significant facelift. However, at one point a C2 generation Corvette was being proposed for introduction as a 1958. It was based largely upon, of all things, an *Oldsmobile* dream car known as the Golden Rocket. The Golden Rocket featured a split rear windshield with a sloping roofline and modest fins. In the end the split backlight would have to wait for 1963 when the C2 was finally introduced and after 1955, no production Corvette would have tail fins. The Golden Rocket design was dropped due to a lack of manpower to complete the engineering chores; efforts had to be focused on the new Impala for 1958, as well as a new truck line also for 1958.

Other than the wraparound windshield, one feature from the Golden Rocket–inspired proposal made it onto the 1958 Corvette: its quad-headlight layout. The setup splits low- and high-beam functions into individual seamed-beam units. These became legal in all states, so auto manufacturers took advantage of the additional styling concepts offered by the arrangement. A chromed bezel surrounded the headlights; trailing behind the bezel was a bright metal molding, which flowed along the fender top terminating at almost the windshield post. The grille from the past years continued to be used, but flanking it were non-functional air inlets split horizontally by thin wraparound bumpers. A new nose emblem larger in size than the previous one was set just behind the grille opening and the leading edge of the hood. Windsplits still appeared on the hood, but in between was a set of 18 simulated louvers, a one-year-only feature. Another set of windsplits, but as bright moldings rather than formed into the fiberglass skin, ran along the deck lid; as with the fake hood louvers, this was also a one-time feature.

As with the previous two model years, the taillights were faired into the quarter panels. Thin wraparound rear bumpers were designed with an oval opening for the exhausts. Bumpers this time were attached to the frame rather than the body, thus they actually provided some protective function. Side coves also continued to be applied, but this time simulated air outlets were placed at the front of the coves immediately behind the front wheels. Three thin horizontal moldings extended several inches behind the fake outlets.

This latest revision of the first-generation Corvette resulted in a heavier looking car because it was larger, 3 inches wider, 10 inches longer, and about 200 pounds heavier. Not all of the weight gain was simply due the larger dimensions. Improvements to the fiberglass and additional support along the rocker panels also contributed to extra pounds.

A more user-friendly instrument panel was crafted for the newest Corvette. Instrumentation was grouped directly ahead of the driver's position and included a 6,000-rpm tachometer, but with the fuel-injected engine,

The 1956 Oldsmobile Golden Rocket showed the general design of proposed second generation Corvette for release as a 1958 model. However, the original C2 was canceled due to cost and other issues. (Photo Courtesy GM Media Archive)

The Corvette SS Race Car

Zora Arkus-Duntov lobbied General Motors for the construction of a Corvette race car. He knew that one properly built could bring favorable publicity for the Corvettes built for the street. Duntov had witnessed the impact the Porsche 550 Spyder had on sales of the typical Porsche and the racing version of the Mercedes-Benz 300SL's impact on Mercedes-Benz. In September 1953, Duntov spoke to a group of SAE members in Lansing, Michigan, on the topic of the sports car. He noted, "Even if the vast majority of sports car buyers do not intend to race them, and most likely will never drive flat out, the potential performance of the car, or the recognized and publicized performance of its sister (the racing sports car), is of primordial value to its owner. The owner of such a car can peacefully let everybody pass him, still feeling like the proud king of the road, his ego and pride of ownership being inflated by racing glory."

According to *Corvette: America's Star Spangled Sports Car*, by Karl Ludvigsen, "Duntov's philosophy was given added credibility by the 1956 Sebring event. Watching the race, it didn't take Ed Cole long to realize that no modified version of the stock Corvette would ever be able to challenge for the outright lead against the specialized sports-racing cars such as Jaguars and Ferraris, which were the chief protagonists that year. He came to the realization that a special Corvette would be needed, one that bore the same pace-setting relationship to the stock Corvette as the Corvette itself did for the Chevrolet production models."

Harley Earl evidently saw the matter the same way. Earl acquired a D-Type Jaguar that had been driven to a third-place finish at Sebring in 1956. Soon after that race, the car's engine was damaged beyond repair and was removed. Styling took in the Jaguar, which was minus an engine, and that was just fine. Earl said he wanted a Corvette engine installed, the steering converted from right-hand drive to left-hand, the body modified extensively to make it resemble a Corvette, then he would race it as an experimental Corvette. Engineers found fitting a Corvette engine onto the D-Type Jag chassis to be problematic. Chevrolet's chief engineer, Harry Barr, contacted Duntov regarding the matter. Duntov expressed his reservations about the swap and ultimately determined there were serious problems with doing so. He proceeded to sketch a new chassis for a racing Corvette, which was soon accepted. The Jag went back to its former owner and the XP-64 Corvette SS was born.

Clare "Mac" MacKichan was in charge of the body design work done at Styling. The D-Type Jaguar heavily influenced its shape. A tube-type chassis was crafted weighing 180 pounds and was based upon that of the Mercedes-Benz 300SL for expediency; little time was available to develop the tubular space frame originally planned by Duntov. The first car, built for show, needed to be completed in time to be shown

Zora Arkus-Duntov lobbied General Motors for the construction of this Corvette SS racecar. He knew that one properly built could bring favorable publicity for the Corvettes built for the street. The car was raced at Sebring and was driven by John Fitch and Piero Taruffi. There had been little time for testing to find its weaknesses, thus it did not finish the race due to a broken rear axle. In 1959, Zora Arkus-Duntov demonstrated it at the opening of the new Daytona Speedway, where it reached 155 mph on the high banks. (Photo Courtesy Gene Bussian)

at the New York Auto Show, which was scheduled to open on December 8, 1956, a date just six months away. The front suspension was given non-parallel control arms linked by coil spring-surrounded shock absorbers to provide excellent cornering stability and positive control. Inboard rear brakes, a feature seldom found on American cars, were installed on the SS. The cast-iron drums were power-assisted with two separate systems operated by a single brake pedal. A de Dion-type axle was chosen in back.

A 283-ci Corvette engine with fuel injection and aluminum cylinder heads powered the SS, but horsepower was boosted a bit to 315 hp at 6,800 rpm.

The first XP-64 was built simply as a non-functional show car. Three additional fully functional cars were intended to follow it. All of them had bodies constructed from sheet magnesium and exhaust systems of titanium. Cast-magnesium wheels with knock-off hubs for quick tire changes were also included. These cars were designed to be lightweight to help achieve a high horsepower-to-weight ratio. A "mule" test car was built with a fiberglass body, as was another fiberglass body for wind-tunnel testing. With manpower and time in impossibly short supply, the order for three racing cars was cut to one.

As originally proposed, the body had rounded well openings and a tail fin jutting from the circular cross-section headrest (which concealed a roll bar). In the end the wheel openings were partially enclosed and the fin was eliminated. The grille helped give the car an instantly recognizable Corvette identity. Side coves also provided another Corvette link. A competition windscreen was part of the design, but an auxiliary plastic canopy was also included to abide by the SCCA rule requiring sports cars to have a top. The final product was a work of art. Performance was excellent, but the car's first outing at Sebring came to a rather quick end due to overheating, erratic braking from the rear brakes, and improperly installed bushings for the chassis.

All of that was fixable. However, the AMA agreement to ban factory-sponsored racing put an end to the Corvette SS project. All components of the SS were ordered scrapped, except the car itself. A couple of years later, Duntov drove the SS on the newly opened Daytona Speedway at a speed of 155 mph. He then tested it at GM's Mesa, Arizona, Proving Grounds where he reached 183 mph. Even without the AMA ban on factory racing promotion, the SS would have soon been disqualified from competition. A rule change cut the allowed maximum engine displacement to 3 liters (approximately 183 ci), which was well below that of the Corvette SS.

For 1958, the Corvette featured fresh styling, although it was still on the original first-generation chassis. Among the new styling features was the use of quad headlights, a new trend in the auto industry.

an 8,000-rpm tach was installed. The passenger side of the dash was deeply curved. Spanning the area was a grab bar to help a passenger maintain his or her position during high-performance driving. A center console housed the clock as well as the optional radio and controls for the optional heater. Upholstery and door panel patterns were also new.

Chevrolet advertising claimed its 1958 sports car was the "Sweetest Two-Seater Going," but the new exterior styling was not widely accepted; however, the highly revised interior was much appreciated by buyers. Despite the somewhat tepid response to the car's external appearance, sales still reached a new high of 9,168 units, and this result was achieved during a recession year in

Clare "Mac" MacKichan: Designer of Dream Cars

Clare MacKichan was born in Applegate, Michigan, on March 10, 1918. He earned a Bachelor of Science degree in mechanical engineering from the University of Michigan in 1937 and went to work as an apprentice designer for GM Styling in April 1939.

At the start of World War II, MacKichan left General Motors for defense assignments, but came back in 1943 to work at Fisher Body Division as a project engineer. Four years later he returned to GM Styling as a senior designer. MacKichan became chief of the Chevrolet Studio in 1951, a position he held for 11 years. He was deeply involved in the designs of the first-generation Corvettes, the Corvette-based dream cars for the 1954 GM Motorama, and the 1955-1957 Chevrolets. He treasured his role in the development of the Corvette and even decorated his office with Corvette parts that had been discarded.

In 1962, he was appointed to head GM's West German subsidiary, Adam Opel A.G., where he led the development of the Opel GT. MacKichan returned to the United States five years later after being named executive director in charge of advanced automotive engineering and international

Clare "Mac" MacKichan became chief of the Chevrolet Studio in 1951, a position he held for 11 years. (Photo Courtesy GM Media Archive)

design. In August 1977, he was named director of engineering for GM Design, and then nearly one year later became special assistant to vice president of GM Design, Chuck Jordan. MacKichan retired from General Motors in 1978. In 2011, in recognition of his major contributions to the Corvette, Clare "Mac" MacKichan was posthumously inducted into the Corvette Hall of Fame.

---

which overall sales were substantially down for all auto manufacturers. This was the first time the Corvette was profitable for Chevrolet.

Color choices numbered eight this time and were composed of (in order from least to most ordered) Inca Silver, Panama Yellow, Tuxedo Black, Regal Turquoise, Signet Red, Charcoal metallic, Silver Blue, and Snowcrest White. Two-tone paint was again offered for an extra $16.15 over the $3,591 base price. About three out of eight of the Corvettes built for 1958 had the two-tone paint option.

Other options offered included the 250- or 290-hp fuel-injected 283, the 245- and 270-hp engine with dual fours, 4-speed transmission, Powerglide, Posi-Traction, heavy-duty brakes and suspension, power top, power windows, and Signal-Seeking AM radio. Well over half of the total Corvette production for 1958 had one of the optional engines.

Styling changes were minimal for 1959. The hood and deck lid had the most obvious changes. Color choices totaled seven and were (in order of least to most ordered) Classic Cream, Crown Sapphire, Inca Silver, Frost Blue, Roman Red, and Tuxedo Black. Sintered metallic brake linings, which reduced brake fade, were added as an option for $26.90, but found only 333 buyers out of the total production of 9,670 Corvettes produced. A very practical option was a set of sun visors ($10.80); while the uncluttered windshield frame looked good, no sun visors proved to be an inconvenience when driving into the sun. Wheel color was changed from silver to black for 1959. Base price climbed to $3,875.

Engine choices remained unchanged, but orders for one of the fuel-injected types fell sharply from 1,511 the previous year to 920, while orders for one of the twin-four setups stayed at close to the same pace.

Finally, in 1960, production of the Corvette surpassed the 10,000 mark. For 1962, the final version of the first generation Corvette brought to Chevrolet a total of 14,531 orders for its fiberglass sports car. After a decade, the Corvette was receiving recognition as the American sports car envisioned by Harley Earl in 1951. This only happened because of the efforts of Bill Mitchell, Zora Arkus-Duntov, and Ed Cole, who all had a passion for the Corvette. Earl's sports car entered its seventh generation in 2014 and is more popular than ever.

TRI-FIVE CHEVROLETS

CHAPTER 6

"We tried to put a little Cadillac design in this new [1957] Chevrolet."
— Harley Earl

During the early 1950s, Chevrolet managers recognized their car had an image problem. The cars were known as very reliable but were thought of as a bit too stodgy. Stodginess was not at all attractive to the growing youth market of the time. The situation was not unique to Chevrolet, or even to General Motors; companion, Pontiac, was in the same predicament as was competitor, Chrysler Corporation. This is not to say that Chevrolet was in immediate trouble, but no one with the division wanted to wait until the condition became critical. In fact, Chevrolet was staying ahead of its archrival, Ford, as it had for almost every model year since 1927. The gap was narrowing, though.

From 1949 to 1954 Chevrolet built approximately 7.5 million cars with Ford trailing by as much as 40 percent in calendar year production through 1951, at which point the sales gap had narrowed to about a 25 percent difference. By 1954, the margin was razor-thin. In plain numbers, Ford actually bested Chevrolet by a little more than 15,000 cars in model year production, but in terms of calendar year production Chevrolet topped Ford by fewer than 20,000 units.

Ford had also already beaten Chevrolet in the matter of the V-8 engine by offering its Y-block overhead-valve engine in Ford passenger cars starting with the 1954 model year. Even Studebaker was offering a V-8. Within General Motors itself, only Chevrolet and Pontiac were without one. Fortunately for General Motors, Chevy had already taken action to reverse the trend in sales with the planning for all-new and exciting 1955 models, which began in late 1951.

This fiberglass mockup shows the 1955 Chevrolet in an advanced state of styling. However, a grille design similar to that of 1954 was still under consideration. It was ultimately replaced with a Ferrari-inspired grille late in the design phase. Note the wraparound windshield. The glass area increased greatly with the 1955 models. A four-door sedan, for example, had 3,528 square inches of glass area, providing excellent all-around visibility. (Photo Courtesy GM Media Archive)

Styling the 1955 Chevrolet

During the early stages of styling the 1955 Chevys, a great number of sketches were made depicting various ideas. Soon thereafter, as the story goes, the stylists began to give Earl more attractive designs.

The process of styling the Chevrolet began in GM's Argonaut Building in downtown Detroit under Charles Stebbins in what was known as the body develoment room on the 9th floor, one floor beneath the Chevrolet Studio. (At the time, General Motors divided its bodies into groups, and certain brands were assigned specific bodies. Chevrolet and Pontiac were shared by the A-body. The B-body was for Oldsmobile and lower-series Buicks;

This hardtop design was proposed in the latter part of 1954 and probably originated in the Body Development Studio. Note the angled windshield posts and the wraparound rear windshield. The overall length of the roof was a few inches shorter than a production type as well. (Photo Courtesy GM Media Archive)

upper-series Buicks and Cadillacs shared the C-body. Stebbins was charged with determining the basic specifications and general shape of the new car. Meanwhile, Clare "Mac" MacKichan, head of the Chevrolet Studio, had overall responsibility for the exterior and interior. Of course, overseeing all of this activity was Harley Earl, who maintained constant contact with both men.

Various styling ideas were pursued. Not too surprisingly, the first approach, which seemed promising at the start, had to be rejected as other aspects of the car evolved. This approach pursued the idea of having the hood line low between the front fenders. The fender line would continue into the front door, where it would subtly dip at the A-pillar (windshield post) then the bodyline continued straight back. As the engine design progressed, it simply became too high to fit under the low hood, leading, of course, to a higher hood line, which in turn caused the fender height to be raised to maintain the recessed hood. This forced the dip to be much greater than in its previous form, resulting in an awkward appearance. The changed height of the hood and fenders also altered the proportions of the car, giving it a tall, narrow look. Finally, the recessed hood concept was abandoned and was essentially raised to fender height. The fender line continued almost through the door then dipped near the C-pillar just as on other GM passenger cars. Wagon models lacked this dip.

The idea for a Ferrari-inspired grille arrived late in the process. Prior designs for the grille were modifications of that used for 1953 and 1954, none of which suited Harley Earl. During his annual trip to the European auto shows in the fall of 1953, he particularly noticed the egg-crate grille of the Ferrari and decided it was just what the new Chevrolet needed.

When the 1955s debuted one year later, however, the public was not quite sure what to think about the Chevrolet. That grille was just so "foreign." Sales were initially slow, so much so that company president Harlow Curtice called Chevrolet general manager Thomas Keating and Chevrolet chief engineer Ed Cole into his office to discuss the problem. Soon a full-width grille was designed as a mid-year replacement. It proved unnecessary. Soon, the public fully accepted the Ferrari-like grille and sales took off. The revised grille waited for the 1956 Chevrolets.

The Hot One

"Here's Chevrolet's new show car styling at its beautiful best," proclaimed the sales literature promoting the new 1955 models. Some promotional material featured the phrase, "Motoramic Chevrolet." The best known of all the slogans is "The Hot One." The boasts were substantive. The wraparound, or Sweep-Sight, windshield, planned from the start of the styling process for the 1955 models, was a styling touch lifted from the GM Le Sabre and Buick XP-300. Both cars were completed in 1951 and included in the 1953 GM Motorama show circuit. However, a series of limited-production cars of 1953 (the Cadillac Eldorado, Buick Skylark, Oldsmobile Fiesta, and the Corvette) received this windshield first. (By the 1955 model year, General Motors had the wraparound windshield as a standard feature for all passenger-car lines.)

This gadget-laden 1955 Bel Air convertible is one of 41,292 built for the model year. Among the dealer accessories and factory options are grille guard, outside rear-view mirror, radio, wire wheel covers, fuel-filler door guard, and Continental Wheel Carrier. Powering the Gypsy Red and Shoreline Beige car is a 265 V-8 with Powerglide. This car scored 998 points out of a possible 1,000 at the 2011 International Chevy Classics show held in Springfield, Missouri. (Photo Courtesy Eckler's Chevy Classics *magazine and Colin Date, Editor)*

This Onyx Black 1955 Bel Air convertible is outfitted with wheel covers, spotlight, outside rear-view mirrors, fender skirts, and chromed exhaust tips.

In addition, the 1955 Chevrolet line had a twin-cowl dash and instrument panel very similar to that of the Corvette, a car that first appeared in prototype form at the 1953 GM Motorama. A decorative panel had 987 "Chevy bowties," the official logo for the division, cut into it. The idea for this feature may have evolved from an external rear panel included on the 1954 Chevrolet Corvair shown during that year's GM Motorama. Additionally, the "Coloramic" interior was offered in various color-coordinated two-tone patterns for the Bel Air and Two-Ten series; seats for these models also had chromed moldings along the seat edges.

The car *appeared* lower, longer, and wider. In reality, the look was partly an illusion; the car was indeed lower (about 6 inches for wagons and more than 2 inches for other models), but was around 1-inch *shorter* and 1-inch *narrower*. The lower height in combination with a hood line nearly flush with the top of the front fenders helped in obtaining the desired effect. Flush rear fenders were a first for Chevrolet; at last, it fully departed from the 1940s-era look.

One brochure stated the 1955 Chevrolet offered "a new concept in low-cost motoring . . . a low-cost car that looks, performs, and rides like the finest on the road." Those who wrote Chevrolet's advertising also said the car was "for the young in spirit," which was certainly accurate. What ultimately emerged from the studio bore a youthful look that had great attraction to Chevy buyers not only for its styling, but also its new, powerful V-8. Compared to a 1950 Chevrolet, the 1955s were a rocket ship. A 1950 model, equipped with Powerglide, required 27 seconds to go from 0 to 60 mph; with a 3-speed manual the time dropped by 7 seconds. A V-8 equipped 1955 Chevy cut that time in half (to 9.7 seconds).

More Than Skin Deep

The significance of the 1955 Chevys went much further than skin deep. Under the fresh new styling were important engineering upgrades to the suspension, and most important, an all-new optional small-block V-8 displacing 265 ci. It offered performance not previously experienced in a Chevrolet. This engine actually formed the basis of Chevrolet engines that would be in use for more than four decades.

Chevrolet's new engine went from drawing board to tooling within four months through the efforts of the Chevrolet division's engineering team of about 2,900 personnel. Edward N. Cole, the newly appointed chief engineer, led the group; he replaced Edward Kelley who had developed the crankshaft used in Chevrolet's Stovebolt Six, which dated back to 1929. Kelley, at the suggestion of Cole, was moved over to head the manufacturing side of the upcoming V-8. Work on the V-8 began under Kelley, but progress was not at a fast enough pace. Kelley, even though highly competent, was stuck in the past. In May 1952, GM asked Ed Cole to head the effort. Among the 2,900 people Cole had working under him was Frank Winchell, who contributed much to the design of the small-block. He later became VP of the Engineering staff at the GM Tech Center.

Cole believed new manufacturing methods would provide needed cost-savings to General Motors. He also understood the engine block and crankshaft would have to be as compact as possible. An illustration of his cost-cutting approach and, to a minor degree, a weight-saving measure as well was the design of the intake manifold for the new V-8. Other than distributing fuel to the cylinders, it also doubled as the valley pan, thus replacing the stamped-steel unit used in other engines.

Ed Cole's team created a modern V-8 weighing 488 pounds, 40 less than Chevy's in-line 6-cylinder. Dubbed the Turbo-Fire, it featured hollow pushrods, independent stamped-metal rocker arms, fully water-jacketed ports, aluminum pistons, pressed forged-steel crankshaft, and a splash lubrication system. The hollow pushrods allowed for oil flow to the fulcrum ball surface and valve stem; as a result, oil passages in the head were no longer needed. The design of the rocker arm assembly permitted lower reciprocating mass, which in turn brought a higher maximum attainable RPM.

Turbo-Fire's fully water-jacketed ports and aluminum pistons provided improved heat dissipation and new forging techniques resulted in a relatively short crankshaft, and thus less vibration. Its splash lubrication system eliminated the need for expensive oil feeder lines. Furthermore, the new block casting technique delivered much higher precision cylinder bores. It also dissipated heat better than the old 6-cylinder, meaning it did not require as large a radiator, thus reducing weight and materials. The fresh design offered a high-performance engine in a form, which was economically practical to mass-produce. As a $99 option, it was chosen by 43 percent of the people who purchased a new 1955 Chevrolet.

As one would expect, Chevrolet boldly advertised its new Turbo-Fire 265 V-8 and described it as "a milestone in automotive history." For 1955, this "milestone" engine could be had with either a 2-barrel or the Power-Pack 4-barrel carburetor with respective horsepower ratings of 162 at 4,400 rpm and 180 at 4,600 rpm. The Power-Pack also came with dual exhausts (except in station wagons).

Other appointments made by Cole included Ellis J. "Jim" Premo to take charge of body development and Maurice Olley as director of research and development. Olley was recognized as one of the most knowledgeable of suspension engineers; he came to General Motors from Rolls Royce in 1930. Incidentally, working under Olley, starting about mid-1953, was Zora Arkus-Duntov.

Cole certainly had the right people working under him. He believed in efficiency and was very much against having any unnecessary weight in an automobile. (He was something of a maverick in this regard because at the time heavy weight in a car was for whatever reason perceived as somehow better.) His philosophy was passed along to those he appointed to take charge of the various components making up the new Chevrolet. In the end, 151 pounds was shaved off the previous Chevrolet, 99 of it in the chassis. Major body panels interchanged with Pontiac, and that resulted in reduced tooling and manufacturing costs.

One other important point about Ed Cole's leadership in the creation of the 1955 Chevrolets was his excellent relationship with Harley Earl. Earl and engineers many times did not see eye-to-eye, so this was an exceptional situation. Cole firmly believed the new car had to look good as well as perform well, an attitude that served General Motors very well.

The Lineup

The 1955 season began with Chevrolet offering 14 models; in February, the sporty two-door Nomad wagon was added, followed by the Two-Ten Sport Coupe (a hardtop) in June.

The interior of the new Nomad two-door station wagon was richly appointed with waffle-patterned vinyl upholstery and chromed headliner bows. This photograph shows the interior of the prototype. (Photo Courtesy GM Media Archive)

The Nomad design was based upon the 1954 Corvette-based Nomad shown throughout the 1954 GM Motorama. Its roof design was modified as needed to fit the wider Bel Air body. This publicity photo taken by GM Photographic shows an early 1955 Nomad painted Cashmere Blue and India Ivory. (Photo Courtesy GM Media Archive)

Of course, the top-of-the-line series was the Bel Air, which made its debut five years earlier. This series comprised a two-door hardtop, two- and four-door sedan, Beauville four-door station wagon, as well as a Beauville convertible. The Nomad was also positioned under the Bel Air umbrella. Prices ranged from a low of $1,888 (6-cylinder two-door sedan) to $2,571 (Nomad with V-8).

Standard equipment was composed of a 123-hp 6-cylinder engine with a 3-speed manual column-shifted transmission, anodized gold Bel Air script, front and rear windshield reveals, stainless steel moldings for the front fenders, upper beltline, along with quarter panel and sash moldings. The horizontal component of the quarter panel trim had a white-painted insert. The design of the side trim on the quarters made possible various optional two-tone paint schemes not offered for the lower-series Chevrolets. Richer fabrics combined with vinyl upholstery, along with full carpeting, chrome-plated moldings on the seat side shields, glove box light, armrests on all doors, cigarette lighter, and ash receptacle were also included. The interior for the convertible was upholstered in full vinyl.

The next step down was the Two-Ten series composed of two- and four-door sedans, a two-door Del Ray Club Coupe, two-door Sport Coupe (a hardtop), and Handyman two-door station wagon, and the Townsman four-door station wagon. This mid-range series had prices ranging from $1,725 (Two-Ten two-door sedan with a six) to $2,226 (Townsman with V-8). Not surprisingly, the Two-Ten was a little less flashy than a Bel Air. It lacked the moldings on the front fenders and across the headliner. Furthermore, the horizontal component of the quarter panel moldings was narrower than that of the Bel Air and did not have a painted insert. There was no slanted sash molding between this molding and the rear bumper ends either. A rubber mat covered the floor rather than carpeting. Upholstery was cloth. The exception was the Del Ray Club Coupe, for which a grid-patterned vinyl covered the seats.

At the bottom was the economical One-Fifty series offered as a three-passenger two-door Utility Sedan (no backseat), a six-passenger two-door sedan, and the Handyman two-door station wagon. Prices ran from a low of $1,593 (a 6-cylinder Utility Sedan) to $2,129 (Handyman with V-8). The plain-Jane One-Fifty had the least brightwork on its body sides of all the models with only a chromed Chevrolet script decorating the front fenders. Its interior was quite austere; even armrests were deleted. Upholstery was of patterned cloth and vinyl.

Standard axle ratios were 3.70:1 with manual transmission, 4.11:1 with overdrive, and 3.55:1 with Powerglide.

Options and Accessories

The list of optional equipment and dealer-installed accessories was extensive. Other than the 162-hp V-8 ($99.00) and Powerglide ($178.35), one of the more significant extra-cost items, which could be specified by the buyer for the first time in a Chevrolet, was air-conditioning. Developed by GM's Harrison division, the system was compact enough to fit under the hood. Earlier units in other models were so large they had to be placed within the trunk compartment. The option was very expensive, however, at $565, so it was not commonly ordered. It was offered for any V-8 equipped Chevrolet except the convertible.

Two-tone paint (Navajo Tan and India Ivory) is among the options on this 1955 Two-Ten two-door sedan with 34,000 actual miles. It also has the optional 265 2-barrel coupled to the standard 3-speed manual transmission. With production of nearly a quarter-million units, it was the third most purchased Chevy passenger car for the model year.

Nylon-faced fabric, ripple-weave Gabardine, and leather-grained vinyl upholstery was standard on the Two-Ten sedan models. Note the radio delete plate on this original car.

A plethora of accessories were offered to buyers of a 1955 Chevrolet. Seen here are the Autronic Eye automatic headlight dimmer, traffic light viewer, compass (largely hidden by steering wheel), floor mat, and tissue dispenser. (Photo Courtesy Eckler's Chevy Classics *magazine and Colin Date, Editor)*

All-vinyl upholstery was standard for Bel Air convertibles; the power seat and power windows were extra-cost options. (Photo Courtesy Eckler's Chevy Classics *magazine and Colin Date, Editor)*

Other available options included a Power-Pack 180-hp engine ($59.20 in addition to the $99 charge for the base V-8), overdrive ($107.60), power front seat and windows ($145.30), power steering ($91.50), power brakes ($37.70), tinted glass ($32.30), and push-button radio with antenna ($84.50), or a Signal Seeker radio ($105.00). A large number of two-tone paint schemes were offered for the Bel Air and Two-Ten lines, something made possible because of the body-side trim, which provided a break between the colors.

Among the dealer-installed accessories were the Continental Wheel Carrier, tissue dispenser, compass, dash-mounted traffic light viewer, spotlight, wire-type wheel covers, and a rain sensor for lifting the convertible top when the car was parked and rain began to fall. However, it was not as sophisticated as the one on Harley Earl's Le Sabre. It did not raise the windows nor could the device lock the top to the header. Furthermore, if the top were lowered as per the instructions, the rear window would need to be unzipped. Also, the boot had to be left uninstalled. Surprisingly, this accessory was reportedly exclusive to the Chevrolets. Incidentally, Ford also offered the accessory (it may have been from the same vendor) and had the same drawbacks. The rain sensor kit was not among the more popular accessories purchased. Both Ford and Chevy dropped this accessory after 1955.

A Sales Success

With several great selling points to offer ranging from great new styling, to a new V-8, to success on NASCAR speedways, the 1955 Chevrolet line-up sold very well; about 1.8 million were ordered despite the early mechanical issues with the 265. By comparison, Ford sold less than 1.5 million copies of its freshly restyled cars. The four-door sedan sold in the greatest numbers in both the Bel Air (345,372 sold) and Two-Ten Series (317,724 sold) while the two-door sedan was the top seller in the One-Fifty series (29,898). Convertible sales increased tremendously (a little more than double the number sold the previous model year) with 41,292 units finding willing and able buyers. Station wagon sales in the Bel Air series were impressive. The Beauville brought 82,303 sales to Chevrolet; it was about 10 times the number sold of the 1954 Bel Air Townsman. The Nomad was certainly not a top seller at 8,386 sales, but it brought additional publicity as well as extra showroom traffic to Chevrolet dealerships.

In regard to the successful redesign, Chevrolet's general sales manager at the time, William E. Fish, stated he had never seen a study claiming that styling was an extremely important consideration for purchasing a car, but added, "We know it's true."

Incidentally, 102 Chevrolets were given away in "Chevrolet's $330,000 Miracle Mile Prize Contest. Winners were selected based on giving the correct answers to four simple questions about the 1955 Chevys and on writing in 25 words or less why they would want to own one of the cars. The same number of $1,000 US savings bonds was given away as the second-place award.

Early in the model year, Chevrolet assembled the 50-millionth General Motors automobile, a milestone reserved for a Bel Air two-door hardtop. It was painted gold on all surfaces and had several hundred gold-plated components, including the bumpers, grille, and even the

General Motors' 50-millionth car, a 1955 Bel Air Sport Coupe, occupied a turntable at that year's GM Motorama. The special car was painted gold and adorned with hundreds of gold-plated components, including bumpers, grille, door handles, interior hardware, and even the shock absorbers! Note the Neptune Green and India Ivory Bel Air Sedan with the see-through hood. It promoted the new air-conditioning system contained entirely under the hood. (Photo Courtesy GM Media Archive)

shock absorbers! Another milestone was the construction of Chevrolet's 32-millionth automobile, a Bel Air convertible.

For 1956, Chevrolet ads proclaimed, "The Hot One is Even Hotter!" It was.

1956

Updates to mark the 1956 Chevrolets were mild, yet distinctive. The grille originally designed as a mid-year replacement for the initially slow-selling 1955 models became one of several updates for the 1956 models. Other alterations included revised bumper guards, hood ornament, wheel covers, body-side trim, rear wheel opening

Sales of the Bel Air convertible stayed steady for the 1956 model year. They accounted for 41,268 sales, a figure only 24 units short of the number produced for 1955. (Photo Courtesy GM Media Archive)

Clare "Mac" MacKichan (conversing with a stylist) was deeply involved in the designs of the first generation Corvettes, the Corvette-based dream cars for the 1954 GM Motorama, and the 1955–1957 Chevrolets. Note the upholstery samples on the desk in the foreground. (Photo Courtesy GM Media Archive)

shape, and taillights. Inside were new upholstery patterns, hidden fuel filler, door panels, and a differently textured appliqué (without the bowtie emblems) for the dash. The series lineup remained the same as it was for 1955, but the Two-Ten and Bel Air series received some additional offerings. Both now included a four-door hardtop dubbed the Sport Sedan and a nine-passenger Beauville station wagon.

Chevrolet achieved a milestone when the 35-millionth Chevrolet, a Bel Air Sport Coupe, rolled off the assembly line in this model year.

Improved Performance

While a 1955 Chevrolet with the Power-Pack engine could run 0 to 60 mph in 9.7 seconds, the new 205-hp version could make the same run in only 8.9 seconds. The

A concave grille and stacked lighting was considered as possible updates for the 1956 Chevrolet as shown in this mid-1954 photograph. Not clearly seen in this view, the rear bumper design was similar to that used later for the 1957 Buick. Note the bumper with fin-like grille guards and "bullets." (Photo Courtesy GM Media Archive)

An Executive Coupe was proposed for the 1956 Chevy lineup but was ultimately rejected for production. (Photo Courtesy GM Media Archive)

This photograph taken in January 1955 shows a roof treatment that was under consideration for 1956, according to GM Media Archive records. It is very similar to one on a 1955 model also shown in this chapter. Unlike the earlier proposal, the windshield posts are vertical as on a production car and the quarter windows are somewhat larger. (Photo Courtesy GM Media Archive)

A milestone was observed during the 1956 model year; the 35-millionth Chevrolet, a Bel Air Sport Coupe, was built. It was among the 128,362 built for the model year. (Photo Courtesy GM Media Archive)

This 1956 Bel Air convertible without its standard side trim was modified for an executive's wife. Styling often designed cars with special trim and interiors for various executives or their families, as well as VIPs. (Photo Courtesy GM Media Archive)

comparison, though, is somewhat misleading without explaining that the axle ratios varied between the cars, which were evaluated. The 1955 model that was tested had the 4.11:1 axle ratio while the 1956 had the 3.70:1 ratio. The standing quarter-mile time also improved to 16.6 seconds, which was also eight-tenths of a second better than the 1955 Chevy. If the same axle ratio had been used for both cars, the times for the 1956 Chevrolet would have been better.

Writer Tom McCahill noted that the 1956 Chevrolet was the "best performance buy in the world" and that "it would whiz by a Duesenberg like Haley's Comet."

Sales Results

Sales for 1956 were down and not just for Chevrolet, but this is explained in part by the fact, "The industry had offered some unusually attractive cars in 1955, and peddled an enormous amount of them through relaxed credit terms, in effect borrowing from future (1956) sales," according to *The Hot One: Chevrolet 1955–1957* by Pat Chappell. (Often the second-year run, in other words a lightly retouched version of a completely restyled or fully redesigned model does not sell as well as the first anyway.) Chevrolet still ruled the *low-priced market* with a 44.4 percent share and overall held a 27.9 percent share of the automobile market. Total sales were nearly 1.6 million units. Of those, 669,064 were Bel Airs.

Four-door sedans sold in the highest numbers; the Two-Ten accounted for 283,325 sales and the Bel Air version totaled 269,798. The lowest-selling model was again the Nomad with only 7,886 finding buyers. The One-Fifty Utility Coupe was the second lowest seller at

The Sport Sedan was a new model to the Bel Air (as well as the Two-Ten) lineup for 1956. A total of 103,602 were sold. (Photo Courtesy Phil Aubrey)

Hiding the fuel filler was in vogue throughout the 1950s. Generally, it was hidden behind the driver's side taillight as seen on this 1956 Bel Air Sport Sedan. (Photo Courtesy Phil Aubrey)

9,879 units sold. Sales of the Beauville wagon were down drastically, nearly cut in half, with only 13,279 being sold in spite of its increased passenger capacity. However, convertible production was almost exactly equal to that of 1955 at 41,268, just two-dozen units under that of 1955. The newly offered Bel Air Sport Sedan brought 103,602 sales, which almost equaled the sales figure for the Bel Air two-door sedan (104,849).

Even though the 1957 models were the hottest of the so-called Tri-Five Chevys, sales continued to slip.

1957

Styling changes for 1957 were much more extensive this time, but were not quite as successful, judging by the result of the perpetual sales competition between Chevrolet and Ford. Ford offered a newly designed car for 1957, which at the time had about as many admirers as those of the Chevrolet. The decades-long popularity of the 1957 Chevy did not begin until about 1960. Up front was an entirely new bumper, redesigned grille, different headlight bezels incorporating blacked-out grilles for interior ventilation (increasing airflow into the passenger compartment by 22 percent over the previous system), and twin windsplit hood ornaments.

At the back, greatly altered body-side trim stood out, and included on the Bel Air series, a large, ribbed, brushed-aluminum insert along the quarter panel that

The dual-carb version of Chevy's small-block debuted for 1956 and was carried forward for 1957 when the V-8 was enlarged from 265 ci to 283. (Photo Courtesy Eckler's Chevy Classics *magazine and Colin Date, Editor)*

This 1957 Bel Air convertible scored 999 points out of a possible 1,000 at the 2014 Classic Chevy Convention. The owner purchased the car in 1974 and collected parts for the next 30 years. It is equipped with the dual-quad 283 and is loaded with factory accessories, including bumper guards, outside rear-view mirror, spinner wheel covers, spotlight, dual rear aerials, Continental Wheel Carrier, traffic light viewer, compass, and radiator bug screen. (Photos Courtesy Eckler's Chevy Classics *magazine and Colin Date, Editor)*

was reshaped. The new body-side moldings dictated a more basic two-tone scheme with the roof one color and the lower body another. Other details restyled included the wheel covers, taillights, and emblems. Bel Airs with a V-8 had an anodized gold "V" emblem attached to the hood and deck lid. Also, the mesh grille was finished in anodized gold. Inside were updated upholstery patterns, door panels, dash, and steering wheel.

There were significant mechanical changes, as well. The small-block engine was bored out to displace 283 ci; the 265 2-barrel was also offered for the passenger-car line. It was offered in six states of tune this year including one with fuel-injection induction. Transmission choices increased by one with the addition of another automatic transmission.

Styling the 1955–1957: An Eyewitness Account

After working at Fisher Body Trim as an engineer, Ken Pickering joined GM Styling in October 1952. He was introduced to Harley Earl by Bunkie Knudsen, thus "opening the door" to GM Styling. On his first day, he had a chance to have an early look at the styling for the 1955 Chevrolet. He also witnessed the work done on subsequent updates for 1956 and 1957 versions. As he recalls, "On this, my first day at GM Styling in 1952, I was given a tour of the facility at 465 West Milwaukee (Detroit) where we occupied floors 8 through 11. The 11th floor housed the Executive Offices and the Auditorium. When we entered the Auditorium, the beauty of the two fiberglass models on display, a 1955 Chevrolet Sedan and an absolutely gorgeous 1955 Chevrolet Hardtop Coupe, just blew me away. The Coupe was shown in Gray and Salmon two-tone exterior and interior and it was unforgettable.

"The Chevrolet Studio team, who had created this 1955 model, consisted of Clare MacKichan (chief designer), Joe Schemansky (assistant chief designer), Hans Hertia (studio engineer), and Jack Parks (chief modeler). Bob Caderet was a designer and Bill Tochman, a blackboard man. I also believe Bob Dieboll assisted Parks in modeling. (Dieboll later created and sculpted the rear end of the 1958 Chevrolet while the designers were at lunch.)

"The 1955 Chevrolet featured a Ferrari-type center grille design, and this proved to be the weak point from a customer standpoint, as they did not relate to the heritage of Ferrari.

"Shortly before the introduction of this 1955 model, Ed Cole, who I believe was Chevrolet's chief engineer, called MacKichan from Geneva, Switzerland, and said he must have a new front-end design for the 1956 model. Since this show is in the spring, this was probably March 1954 . . . Cole must have seen some . . . models that caused him to make this move.

"Mac and his staff did a remarkable job of designing this new front end in record time: new hood, front fenders, grille, bumpers, and lights. Mac said later, 'We extended the nose of the hood ornament 13 inches.' Although that was an exaggeration, Mac was trying to make the front visually longer. [Actual overall length increased 1.9 inches.] The 1955 Chevrolet front is what I would call a negative arrangement, as the grille section is somewhat depressed in the front-end design. However, the 1956 front is a more positive arrangement because the grille and fenders project.

"After release from Styling, the model was in production in nine months, unheard of today. The 1956 model was an immediate success in the marketplace.

"As designing for the 1957 model year came into focus, there was an eerie concern at GM Styling [by now actually renamed GM Design]. Ford would have an all-new model for 1957, and Chevrolet would not be all new until 1958. How could a face-lifted 1957 Chevrolet compete with an all-new 1957 Ford?

"By this time, I had moved from the Experimental Engineering Department (where we did the engineering for the Motorama models) to staff assistant to Bob Lauer, director of engineering. In this position, I was privy to all of the high-level meetings, including those of Harley Earl, the legendary vice president of styling for General Motors.

"By this time, Styling had moved from the location on Milwaukee in Detroit to a new, state-of-the-art facility in the GM Technical Center in Warren, Michigan. I distinctly remember the showing of the 1957 fiberglass model to Chevrolet management on the stage of the domed auditorium. As Harley Earl walked around the model, he said in his stuttering voice, "We d-d-decided to put a little bit of C-C-Cadillac in this Chevrolet." We all thought Earl and Mac had done the best they could with a carryover body, but none of us at that meeting had any idea of the icon that had been created."

For 1957, the Two-Ten (as well as the Bel Air) series continued to offer the Sport Sedan body introduced the previous model year. It accounted for 16,178 sales. The Two-Ten was the mid-level series in the Chevrolet lineup.

The two-door Nomad was in its final year of availability in 1957. It was never expected to be a high-volume seller, but rather an attention-getter to increase traffic to dealerships where people would generally purchase one of the more affordable four-door wagons. This Dusk Rose and India Ivory Nomad is one of 6,103 built, which represents the lowest output of the three model years this wagon was offered.

Turboglide

A new automatic transmission called Turboglide made its debut for 1957. This transmission was a constant torque, continuously variable automatic transmission similar to Buick's Flight-Pitch Dynaflow. It consisted of three separate turbines, multiple disc clutches, and an accelerator-controlled dual-pitch stator. It was intended as an improvement over the Powerglide's somewhat lackluster performance. It was noted for its smoothness, but unfortunately, at the time, its aluminum case was prone to cracking, thus giving it a bad reputation. All the bugs in the design were not fully resolved until the 1961 model year. By then, the public's lack of confidence in it could not be reversed, so it was dropped at the end of that model year.

Higher Performing Small-Blocks

Six versions of the 283 V-8 were offered for 1957. With the 2-barrel carburetor and 8.5:1 compression, the base V-8 provided 185 hp at 4,600 rpm, 5 more than the Power-Pack 4-barrel version offered for model year 1955. The next step up was the Power-Pack engine, again with a 4-barrel and dual exhaust, it provided 220 hp at 4,800 rpm and required premium fuel due to its 9.5:1 compression ratio. A dual 4-barrel pumped out 245 hp at 5,000 rpm as well as a maximum of 300 ft-lbs of torque at 3,800 rpm. Another twin-four type pumped out 270 hp at 6,000 rpm; it was a competition version with mechanical lifters. Finally, two fuel-injected 283s were also available. One developed 250 hp at 5,000 rpm with a 9.5:1 compression ratio while the other was rated at 283 hp at 6,200 rpm with a 10.5:1 compression ratio and mechanical lifters. The torque rating of the latter was 290 ft-lbs at 4,400 rpm. The "fuelie" engines were expensive options; both were priced at $484.20. Approximately 1,500 of the 1957 Chevrolet passenger cars are believed to have been built with one of the fuel-injected engines.

The Sales Race

While Chevrolet was putting up a good fight in NASCAR, but coming up a bit short with 21 wins against Ford's 26, the all-important sales race also came up short. At the start of the 1957 model year, company president Harlow Curtice saw demand for auto production increasing. At the National Automobile Show in New York City held in December 1956, Curtice announced in a speech that he expected the domestic market for cars and trucks would reach about 6.5 million and 900,000 units, respectively. Indeed, while production was up, the actual combined results fell 200,000 short of the total of 7.4 million cars and trucks predicted by Curtice.

Market share for General Motors dropped from 52.8 percent to 46.1 percent, with the losses going to Ford and Chrysler. Chevrolet lost ground, too. Its market share fell 3 percent to 24.9 with Ford increasing 1.2 percent to 24.9, even with Chevy. Chrysler had the greatest gains, 7.8 percent to 10.7, due to the spectacular styles from the company that year. When Curtice was asked by *Time* magazine why sales of Chevrolet and other GM cars were not as good as predicted, he replied that "static styling" and "present management" were responsible. Such remarks were unimaginable in past years.

Ford sold about 170,000 more cars than Chevrolet. There was no single reason for the outcome, but one reason was Ford's well-accepted, newly styled line of cars, along with an improved version of its Y-block V-8. However, as time moved on, the 1957 Chevrolet gained in popularity, first as used cars in the early 1960s and finally as iconic collectibles in the present.

TAIL FINS, CHROME, GADGETS AND MORE!

CHAPTER 7

"The requirements of creative automotive styling are almost as numerous as they are demanding. Truly successful automotive styling, then, must be pleasing to the creator, gratifying to the engineer, and inspiring to the motorist, a rare and magic meeting of beauty, practicality, and popularity."

– Harley Earl, 1954 Cadillac sales brochure

With the resumption of automobile manufacturing following the end of World War II, the manufacturers released lightly restyled versions of the 1942 models. The pent-up demand for new cars made unnecessary all-new designs for a while. Cadillac was first among the GM divisions to offer all-new cars; the other divisions' new cars came along for the 1949 model year.

The truly new post-war cars would offer buyers (and future car collectors) a wide array of exciting automobiles (lower, longer, and wider) with high-performance V-8s, advanced styling features inspired by modern aircraft such as wraparound windshields and fins, as well as bright colors, two-tone paint options, and new body styles, with General Motors leading the way.

Chevrolet

During the first few years after the end of the war, Chevrolet sales took up where they left off. Rival Ford, however, soon caught up, thus challenging Chevrolet's supremacy in the market.

Chevrolet: 1946–1948

Chevy's 1946–1948 models were barely distinguishable from each other. Two series were again offered: Stylemaster (the economy offerings) and the Fleetline. Not too surprisingly, the Stylemaster was the best selling in 1946; however, that changed for 1947 and 1948 when the Fleetline Aerosedan, a two-door fastback, drew the most buyers.

With the last 1948 Chevrolet to leave the assembly line, the pre–World War II era cars finally came to an end. All-new, more sophisticated cars were on the way for 1949.

A 1948 Chevrolet Fleetmaster convertible served as the pace car for that year's Indianapolis 500. Its color combination consisted of a Dove Gray body with a red interior and black convertible top.

Chevrolet: 1949–1954

Buyers flocked to Chevrolet dealerships to buy the redesigned 1949 models. Even though sales soared to more than 947,000 units, the total fell well short of Ford's sales, which were in excess of 1.1 million cars. Ford, however, also began offering an all-new car, and started its 1949 model year much earlier in June 1948. Chevrolet did not launch its until later, in January.

Chevy's new cars offered fully integrated front fenders and rounded rear decks (on Styleline models). Inside was new, too, with instruments clustered in a circular pod over the steering column.

The 1949 Bel Air two-door hardtop prototype displayed at GM's Transportation Unlimited auto show gave a preview of what was in store for Chevrolet with the 1950 model year. During 1949, Buick and Cadillac introduced the two-door hardtop body style. The other divisions added the hardtop the following year. To be accurate, the style was referred to as a "hardtop convertible" because the design gave the look of a convertible with its top raised and windows lowered. The B-pillar (middle post on non–station wagon bodies) of the hardtop was terminated at the beltline. To make up for the lost body rigidity, the frame had to be strengthened.

A Bel Air offered more than a new body style. The interior consisted of leather and pile-cord fabric, a step up from lower level Chevrolets, and bright metal strips across the headliner, which simulated convertible top bows.

The hardtop design was another major success for General Motors and Harley Earl's styling department. For 1950, the Bel Air brought 74,634 sales to Chevrolet. Its impact was felt by the competition, thus forcing the other companies to release competing models. Ford finally caught up in 1951 with the introduction of its Victoria after making do with a two-door sedan dubbed Crestliner, which wore a fabric-covered roof, special side trim, and two-tone paint. The Victoria outsold the Bel Air by nearly 7,000 units that model year, even though the Bel Air had more than 103,000 sales. Nevertheless, Chevrolet's overall production stayed ahead of Ford's.

Chevrolet's 1951 model year updates included fully integrated rear fenders. This allowed designers to do away with the bolt-on fenders and the fender welt. A new grille with outboard parking lights gave these cars an illusion of greater width.

Model year 1952 marked the last of the Fleetline fastback series. Sales had begun to decrease as buyers found the hardtop more desirable. The Fleetline, in its final year of production, was offered only as a two-door sedan.

Starting with 1953, Chevrolet used new model designations and added a new series as well. At the bottom was the economical One Fifty/Special followed by the

The 1954 Bel Air convertible brought 19,383 sales for the model year. This was the last time Chevrolet relied solely upon its straight-6 and was also the last for this body design. The time for major changes had come, as indicated by the increasing competition from rival Ford. (Photo Courtesy Lydia Juras Boiles)

In 1949, the top three divisions in the hierarchy of General Motors received two-door hardtop models. The hardtop came to the other two divisions the next model year. Chevrolet's was labeled, "Bel Air." GM's hardtop body style was a trendsetter and it continued to be used into the 1970s.

Not everyone found the flashier offerings of Chevrolet to meet their particular needs. This 1954 Chevy One-Fifty Utility Sedan was built for traveling salesmen and for fleet service. The back seat was deleted to make room for whatever needed to be carried. The example shown here is a low-mileage car still equipped with its original tires, however, the suspension has been lowered about 1 inch.

This 1958 Chevrolet Del Ray must have been ordered new by a hot rodder. It is equipped with the 315-hp 348 3 x 2-barrel and a 4-speed transmission. Until recently, enthusiasts believed Chevy did not offer a 4-speed in its big cars until 1959. The economy model Utility Sedan had fixed quarter windows, no passenger-side sun visor, and no armrests. (Photo Courtesy Phil Aubrey)

Two Ten/Deluxe and the Two Forty/Bel Air. This was the only year in which the Two Ten offered a convertible; it also offered a hardtop, but it was dropped, too, only to return again for 1955. Bel Air offerings were expanded to also include a two-door sedan, four-door sedan, and a convertible. A new grille with three vertical blades and parking lights in round housings at the far ends updated the look of the 1953s.

The 1954s received another new grille, this time with five vertical blades and oblong parking lights. An eight-passenger station wagon was also added to the Bel Air line, as was a Del Ray Club Coupe to the Two Ten series.

Meanwhile, during these years Chrysler's sales took a nosedive due to lackluster styling. It lost its number-two spot to Ford in 1949. Styling was a major consideration in the purchase of a car, and corporate chairman Kaufman T. Keller was more concerned about sufficient headroom for a man to wear his hat inside a Chrysler product. The result was a boxy-looking car with generally little eye appeal. The solution to the problem was the appointment of a former GM designer, Virgil Exner, to head Chrysler's styling department. Sales began an upward climb under his direction. The 1957 models, incidentally, would have a big impact on General Motors, a story told in Chapter Twelve.

Chevrolet: 1958

All new styling, a new chassis, and a new V-8 were among the upgrades offered with the 1958 Chevrolet lineup. The chassis received a newly developed Safety-Girder X-frame and a four coil-spring suspension, as well as optional air suspension. To make up for the lack of strengthening side rails, the cowl, floor pan, and rocker panels were beefier. The result was a lower floor pan and a cushier ride than in the past. The extra-cost air suspension (referred to as Level Air in Chevrolet literature) was similar to the version used on the Eldorado Brougham and it proved to be just as leak-prone. Luckily, few were ordered with the trouble-plagued system and the examples so equipped were in most instances refitted with conventional coil springs.

Also new to the lineup was the Impala; it displaced the Bel Air as the top-of-the-line model; it was actually included in the Bel Air series, thus technically it was a Bel Air Impala. The name "Executive Coupe" was proposed at the start, but ultimately Impala was chosen to convey the image of grace and speed and when equipped with one of the high output V-8s, the Impala was reasonably quick. As for the grace or elegance aspect, the Impala lived up to the image by having some of the styling attributes of a Cadillac, fancy interiors with tri-tone upholstery and plenty of chrome, plus a list of optional equipment that included power steering, power brakes, power windows, power seat, tinted glass, air-conditioning, padded dash, two-tone paint, radio, and so on. The first-year Impala was available only in two forms, as a two-door hardtop and as a convertible. However, a Southern California dealer did offer an Impala trim package to spice up a Bel Air four-door. The Impala was more than fancier trim; its sheet metal was unique to the model from the cowl back. The simulated air vents on the quarter panels and roof were specific to the Impala as well.

Under the hood of full-size Chevrolet cars was any one of several engines carried over from 1957 with

This Onyx Black Impala convertible is equipped with the 315-hp 348 with 3-speed transmission and Posi-Traction, a rarely ordered combination in the drop-top model. Other equipment on it includes spinner wheel covers, license plate frames, spotlight, fender skirts, and dual aerials.

Exclusive to the Bel Air Impala were triple lights in back with the center serving for backup. Such an arrangement helped to give the impression of a more expensive car. Bob Dieboll, an asistant clay modeler, was responsible for the taillight arrangement and quarter panel loop around them. No one else had developed a suitable design; Dieboll did it during the lunch hour when everyone else had left!

some mild modifications, or one of the new 348s. The former examples include the Blue-Flame straight six, a 185-hp Turbo-Fire 283 2-V, and the Super Turbo-Fire 283 4-barrel. Both the Blue-Flame and Super Turbo-Fire received an output boost, although the 235 six went from 140 hp at 4,200 rpm to 145 hp, while the Super Turbo-Fire increased from 220 hp at 4,800 rpm to 230 hp at the same revs. Also, the 250-hp (at 5,000 rpm) Ram-Jet fuel-injected 283 was retained, although in an improved form. The fuel-injection equipment received upgrades that increased reliability. Its high price tag resulted in very few 1958s being ordered with the Ram-Jet setup.

A new engine made big news. Offered in three states of tune, it displaced 348 ci. These 348s were the Turbo-Thrust with a 4-barrel carb, a Super Turbo-Thrust with a trio of 2-barrel carburetors, and a higher compression tri-carb type with a hotter cam. Their respective output ratings were 250 hp at 4,400 rpm with 9.5:1 compression, 280 hp at 4,800 rpm with the same fuel-air mixture squeeze, and 315 hp at a rather high-winding 5,600 rpm and 11.1:1 compression. The 315-hp engine was not available until about the last quarter of the model year. The hottest-performing 348 developed its extra gallop from a Duntov cam, solid lifters, and, of course, the trio of Rochester 2-barrel carburetors.

In order to transfer the power to the pavement, several transmission choices were offered. A 3-speed manual was standard issue with any engine. A 3-speed manual with overdrive and a Powerglide automatic were options for the carburetor-inducted 283s; a Corvette version of this 2-speed automatic could be ordered with the fuel-injected engine. The Super Turbo-Fire, Ram-Jet, and Turbo-Thrust could be had with a close-ratio 3-speed while the Super Turbo-Thrust came with only the close-ratio 3-speed. The Turboglide automatic, introduced in 1957, was yet another transmission choice for Turbo-Thrust powered cars. Recent research by Vintage Chevrolet Club of America member, Phil Aubrey, has revealed that a 4-speed for the big Chevys arrived at about the middle of the model year. Somehow the 4-speed (listed as RPO code 685) failed to arouse much notice; therefore, very few were ordered.

Chevrolet Styling

Design work for the 1958 Chevrolets commenced in June 1955 with a meeting between Clare MacKichan of the Chevrolet Studio and Paul Gillan of the Pontiac Studio (since Pontiac would share the body), along with the GM body design committee. As was the norm, trim helped to differentiate each series of the 1958 Chevrolet lineup: Del Ray, Biscayne, and the Bel Air. However, the Impala component of the Bel Air series stood apart from the rest, not only for its exterior moldings and high-grade interior, but also because from behind the cowl, it had sheet metal not shared with the other series, not even a Bel Air.

Common to all series of Chevys was the front end being equipped with quad headlights, a setup that had become legal in all states only months before the 1958s became available. The frontal styling was a complete departure from the previous Chevrolets, even though early design proposals made use of some past ideas. One grille proposal was based upon that of the 1956 Corvette Impala dream car shown at that year's GM Motorama. The "toothy" grille was much like that of a Corvette's. It was reportedly judged as too costly to produce for the big

The mid-level Biscayne nameplate replaced the Two-Ten for 1958. Shown is the four-door sedan, one of the four offerings in the series, which also included a two-door sedan, six-passenger station wagon, and a nine-passenger station wagon.

Chevrolets. Still another design kept the 1957 Chevy's bumper, but with a different grille insert. The engine nacelles of two U.S. Air Force bombers, the B-47 and the new B-52, inspired the parking light shape.

All members of the Bel Air series had a 1954 Fiat V-8 coupe inspired body-side spear and all series had gull-wing fenders. In back, all but the Impala had twin pods for tail and backup lights; Impalas received individual lights consisting of a pair of taillights with a backup light in between them. More lights suggested a more expensive car. Centered at the rear of the Impala hardtop roof was a Mercedes-Benz Gullwing–inspired simulated air extractor vent. Ahead of the rear wheels on the quarter panels was a "pitchfork" molding simulating a vent.

Ed Donaldson, the head of the Chevrolet Interior Studio, designed the Impala's interior. It featured a unique, two-spoke competition-styled steering wheel with an Impala medallion on its hub. Also exclusive to the Impala was vinyl upholstery with tri-tone, horizontal-striped cloth inserts, along with color-keyed door panels adorned with brushed aluminum and a red light at the end of the armrests to warn oncoming traffic at night when the door of a parked car was open. (Parallel parking was common in those days.)

The purpose of the Impala was to break out of the low-price market to enter the lower end of the medium price market. It met this goal successfully as indicated by the number of Impalas built for 1958: 125,480 hardtops and 55,989 convertibles. These figures accounted for 15 percent of Chevrolet's total output of cars and pushed them into a market share of 30 percent for the first time, an impressive outcome in a year that experienced an economic recession. Overall sales figures vary depending upon the source, but *Automotive News* reported a total of 1,249,485 Chevrolets (including the Corvette) were built. The recession hurt Chevy's sales, but those of Ford and Plymouth were impacted much more. Chevy's market share increased to nearly 29.6 percent. Not all of GM's 1958 models would be this successful, but at least Chevrolet had the right look.

Pontiac: From Reliable Family Car to Driving Excitement

Pontiacs for 1946–1948 were similar to the Chevrolets with similar body styles. However, they were easily distinguished from the entry-level Chevy because of their additional length and the "silver streaks" design cue across the center of the hood (popular since 1935). Moreover, the 1949 Pontiac Catalina two-door hardtop prototype also signaled that the body style would soon be available; it arrived for the 1950 model year.

This 1949 Pontiac Streamliner 8 sedan prototype has a grille a little closer to that of a 1950. Parking lights also differ from the final product. (Photo Courtesy GM Media Archive)

Even with a hardtop in the lineup and the Dual-Range Hydra-Matic Drive, which was offered starting with the 1952s, Pontiac's sales were in decline. Sales were becoming so poor that there was some discussion of terminating the division altogether. While the cars were viewed as dependable and durable transportation due to promoting them that way, they lacked the sort of image needed to win over young car buyers. Quite frankly, they were boring cars to the youth market. A new engine, the V-8, was thought to be the answer to changing the downward direction of Pontiac sales. Until then, the Pontiac Division did the best it could. The 1953s were

The 1951 Pontiacs differed in only minor details from the 1950 models. This Chieftain Super Deluxe 8 Catalina has two-tone paint accentuating its hardtop body style. Its wraparound rear windshield was less expensive to form as a three-piece unit. The Pontiac shared its A-body with Chevrolet, even though its 120-inch wheelbase was 5 inches longer than the Chevy's.

This full-size rendering depicts a proposal for a 1952 Pontiac Jubilee. Note its use of side trim to create an interesting two-tone scheme. No information was available on this proposal through GM Media Archive. However, previously the name "Jubilee" was used for a Canadian Pontiac show car. (Photo Courtesy GM Media Archive)

Styling Accomplishments and Manufacturing Challenges

Harley Earl's styling team could generate the styles people wanted, but actually building them presented challenges. Some insight into one aspect of manufacturing the cars is in the book, *Setting the Pace: Oldsmobile's First 100 Years* written by Helen Earley and James Walkinshaw. In GM's building 78, Oldsmobile performed its chrome-plating in addition to that for Buick. In 1954, operations had problems keeping up with the "ever larger, chromier bumpers" of the day. Methods and Plant Layout supervisor, Bob Russell said, "It seemed to me in all the time I was around that plant, the bumper you wanted, you couldn't find. Most of the ones you found had dings."

A replacement building was needed and became available as the Korean War wound down; the jet engine assembly building provided the space needed at that point. However, to outfit it with state-of-the-art equipment was going to cost about $16 million. Too expensive, said management, and only $14 million was allocated for the project. The $2 million cut resulted in a "power and free" conveyer system that gave constant problems. A power and free conveyer can be thought of as a train track system with multiple trains moving independently, starting and stopping, and changing tracks as necessary. In this case the bumper handling racks were automatically being moved anywhere they were needed. As explained in *Setting the Pace*, "With conveyer tracks stacked upon conveyers in the plant's overhead space, this was a Rube Goldberg contraption prone to frequent breakdowns. 'Economizing' the system to meet budget limits only made things worse."

One of the plant superintendents, Bob Scott, stated, "I never worked so many 16 to 18 hour days as I did when we tried to start that thing. I spent 12 to 15 hours on the second deck over the plating room when we were trying to get the conveyers and stuff to work. It was all new electronic stuff [run from] an office over the plating plant. Stuff just wasn't coordinated. That was the first massive conveyer system around. Once in a while somebody would push the wrong button and we'd drop 18 [bumpers] in the [plating] tank. That's quite a mess." The problems took considerable time to solve. Even so, Olds produced nearly 589,000 cars in 1955.

An all-new Pontiac arrived for 1955. Included in the new styling was a massive bumper and grille combination, as well as a wraparound windshield. Its body was shared with that of the Chevrolet. This Bolero Red Star Chief Catalina is equipped with the extra-cost lighted hood ornament and fender skirts. Wheel covers were standard issue for all Star Chiefs.

substantially updated with a 122-inch wheelbase for all models (a 2-inch increase), a one-piece windshield, wraparound rear windshield, and a new instrument panel.

The Delayed V-8 Finally Arrives

Under Arnold Lenz, Pontiac's general manager, Pontiac had started a V-8 program. He was well aware of the need for Pontiac to produce a V-8. The 6-cylinder, in use since 1933, had served as long as it could. Tragically, Lenz was killed in an auto accident before he could lead the project to conclusion. As early as 1953, the Pontiac frames had been designed to accommodate the new V-8.

The program continued albeit a bit slowly, but for 1955, Pontiac had its first V-8, which displaced 287 ci. It offered much-improved performance over the old six and initially came in two states of tune, depending upon the transmission behind it. With the 3-speed synchromesh and a compression ratio of 7.4:1, it was rated at 174 hp at 4,400 rpm. When bolted to the Hydra-Matic, compression was 8.0:1 and output was listed as 180 hp at 4,600 rpm. Around mid-year, a 4-barrel "power pack" was released, boosting maximum horsepower to 200 at 4,800 rpm.

For 1956, Pontiac V-8's performance increased. An enlarged displacement to 317 ci and a compression increase pushed horsepower upward by more than 10 percent. Two lines of V-8s were offered, the Chieftain rated at 192 hp with the synchromesh and 205 with the Hydra-Matic, as well as the Star Chief V-8 rated at 216 with synchromesh and 227 hp with the H-M. In March, an even higher performing V-8 was made available known as the "NASCAR" engine. It differed in having a 10:1 compression ratio, higher performance camshaft, and twin Rochester 4-barrel carburetors. Its official rating was 285 hp at 5,100 rpm.

Styling

The newly styled 1955 Pontiacs were given a massive, divided combination bumper-grille, a hood lowered to about even with the tops of the fenders, and a wraparound windshield. Split, twin "silver streak" moldings ran lengthwise across the hood, a feature that was forecasted by those of the 1954 Bonneville Special dream car shown at the GM Motorama. Like the Chevrolet with which it shared its body, the Pontiac also had a beltline dip. In back was a matching set of silver streak moldings atop the crown of the very modest tail fins. Other than the silver streak theme, the only other vestige of the 1953–1954 Pontiacs was the shape of the tail fins.

The 1956s were updated with a new combination bumper-grille and revised side trim. Very colorful two-tone paint combinations were offered for both the 1955 and 1956 model years.

Despite the styling and V-8, Pontiac's image problem lingered. In fact, sales of Oldsmobiles and even Buicks (cars with significantly higher prices than the Pontiac) were much better.

Canadian-built Pontiacs were more closely aligned with the U.S. Chevrolets, but they had unique model names. They used the Chevrolet engine as well as its shorter chassis. The coral and gray two-tone paint was a Chevrolet combination offered in the United States. This beautiful Canadian Pontiac is a 1955 Laurentian two-door hardtop. (Photo Courtesy Bill Rathgeber)

Chapter Seven: Tail Fins, Chrome, Gadgets and More!

Pontiac also received its version of a sporty two-door station wagon akin to Chevrolet's Nomad. The Safari, like the Nomad, had its roof design based upon the Corvette-based 1954 Chevrolet Nomad dream car. Paul Gillan of the Pontiac Studio was given responsibility for the Safari design. Production was low throughout its three-year run. (Photo Courtesy David McGee Collection)

This is where Pontiac's styling for 1957 stood until Bunkie Knudsen was promoted to general manager of the division. He ordered a redesign of the bodyside trim as well as the removal of the silver streak hood moldings, which he said "looked like suspenders." Note the wheel cover design, which resembles that of a 1957 Olds 98 Starfire. (Photo Courtesy GM Media Archive)

The styling of the limited-production Bonneville convertible was nearly locked-up when this photo was taken in October 1956. Note the simulated oil cooler on the front fender, a feature similar to that of the 1954 Pontiac Bonneville Special dream car exhibited at the GM Motorama. The feature, in the end, was deleted from the production model. (Photo Courtesy GM Media Archive)

Notable Achievements

At the Bonneville Salt Flats in Utah in 1956, a stock sedan ran for 24 hours at an average speed of 118.375 mph to establish a new record for the time. Further publicity came via famed race car driver Ab Jenkins when he drove another 1956 model to a speed of 126.65 mph. Pontiac advertising was quick to take advantage of the achievement by advertising that, "You can own an optionally powered 285-hp Pontiac just like Ab's!"

Two other notable milestones occurred at Pontiac this model year. On August 3, 1956, Pontiac built its three-millionth car, a Star Chief Catalina two-door hardtop. Also, the last two-door Safari station wagon left the assembly line; just like its Nomad cousin, it had served its purpose of giving General Motors publicity and increasing showroom traffic. The name would later be used on a four-door wagon.

Moving Ahead

Harlow Curtice promoted Semon "Bunkie" Knudsen to general manager of Pontiac after Robert Critchfield decided to take an early retirement at age 61. The appointment went into effect on July 1, 1956. (Bunkie's father, William, was the president of General Motors from 1937 to 1940.) Curtice told him to go visit the Pontiac Studio before doing anything else. Upon his inspection, Knudsen did not approve of everything he saw regarding the 1957 Pontiacs, a design that had been finalized some time earlier. He recognized they were still out of step with the younger buyers. "You can sell an old man a young man's car, but you can never sell a young man an old man's car," he once said.

The silver streak hood moldings were still there, something he considered old-fashioned. To him they looked like "suspenders." They had to go, even though the tooling was already made. He said in an interview some years later, "We had to get rid of that 'Indian concept.' No reflection on the American Indian, but old Chief Pontiac had been associated in the public mind with a prosaic family toting sedan from the time Pontiacs were first built." Knudsen also ordered that the side trim be redesigned to look something like a guided missile. Guided missiles were making news at the time, so Knudsen believed there should be something missile-like incorporated into the car's styling. One might suspect Harley Earl was not at all pleased with the orders to perform last-minute changes to a design he had already approved. However, Knudsen and Earl were good friends, so Earl likely was not especially offended.

About two months into his work as general manager, Knudsen appointed Elliot "Pete" Estes as the new chief engineer and John Z. DeLorean as director of advanced engineering.

The Limited-Production Bonneville

The next step in Pontiac's makeover was a special model to gain publicity and increase showroom traffic. This model was built in very limited numbers, but it represented the direction Pontiac was heading, building excitement. The limited-production car took its name from the aforementioned 1954 Motorama show car. Only 630 of the 1957 Bonnevilles were built (all convertibles) and were initially intended for dealer use and demonstration. All were equipped with a fuel-injected 347 V-8 delivering 310 hp at 4,800 rpm, along with every major option Pontiac offered: automatic transmission, power brakes, power steering, power seat, power windows, "Wonderbar" radio with power antenna, and power top. Nearly all of the cars were painted white. Lower series cars could not be ordered with the fuel-injected engine, thus the FI engine was exclusive to the Bonneville.

Tri-Power Makes Its Mark

At the same time the Bonneville was announced on December 2, 1956, a three-deuce carburetor setup labeled "Tri-Power" was also announced. In February 1957, a fleet of Pontiacs with the new Tri-Power setup set class records winning in acceleration, standing mile, and flying mile events at Daytona's Speedweek time trials. A Pontiac was also driven to victory the following week in the 160-mile NASCAR late-model convertible race held at Daytona Beach and marked the first time the average speed exceeded 100 mph (101.541 mph).

Sales Down Again

The record-setting sales of the 1955 models far exceeded those of the disastrous 1954 model year, but Pontiac's market share did not increase nearly as much as expected, a situation resulting from the 1.7 million more cars sold overall for the model year. The lightly restyled 1956s brought fewer sales. As for 1957, the sales for Pontiac tumbled again, down about 70,000 units from those of 1956. Seemingly nothing could be done to make the public consistently excited about owning a Pontiac. Higher prices (8 to 10 percent) did not help either. That attitude would not change until the 1959 model year.

Pontiac: 1958

The 1958 Pontiacs were advertised as having "big car" styling probably because of their lower and longer body design. Quad headlight arrangements were in vogue now, so of course, the Pontiacs were so equipped; indeed, even quad taillights were included at the end points of the "jet pod" rear fenders. The Super Chief, Star Chief, and Bonneville had trim rings around the taillight assemblies as standard issue. Only the entry-level Pontiac Chieftain was without them. Once again, the guided missile served as inspiration for the missile-like body side trim on these cars, although there were variations depending upon the model. A concave section along the rear fenders served as a placement for a contrasting paint color.

The Bonneville was now a full series with a two-door hardtop also available. Outwardly, it was identifiable with the name Bonneville appearing on the hood in chromed, block letters, as well as with anodized gold script on the front fenders. Four chevrons on the lower front fender behind the wheel openings and a ribbed half-cylinder at the front of the concave section of the rear fenders

Nearly all of the 630 Pontiac Bonneville convertibles built for 1957 were painted Kenya Ivory with only the body-side molding insert and top color differing in color. The inserts were generally red and the top white, unlike this particular car seen at the 2012 Pontiac-Oakland Club International Convention. The special model was loaded with nearly every option offered.

The Bonneville became a regular production model for 1958. A two-door hardtop was offered, as well as a convertible.

were unique to the model. Carpeting like that of the Star Chief, dubbed "Stardust" carpeting, was also included. The fancy name was the result of the metallic flecks embedded in it. Other features included a deluxe steering wheel, wheel covers, and special upholstery. A bench seat was standard, but bucket seats were an extra-cost option. A Bonneville convertible was chosen as the pace car for that year's Indy 500.

General Motors celebrated its 50th anniversary in 1958. One of the ways in which the occasion was noted was the release in November 1957 of a "Golden Jubilee" package consisting of special ornamentation and paint scheme (paint code "Z"). Very few cars had the option,

This 1958 Bonneville convertible was custom fitted with a leopard-skin interior by GM Design. Presumably it was used as a show car. Bucket seats were an option. (Photo Courtesy GM Media Archive)

though, and most, if not all, were Star Chief Custom four-door sedans.

At the end of the model year, sales amounted to 217,303 units, enough for a 5.1 percent market share. However, this total was approximately 117,000 lower than that of 1957. Certainly the economic recession combined with further price increases (4 to 7 percent) were at least partly to blame.

Fuel Injection and Tri-Power for 1958

The fuel-injected engine was now available on all models, but its high price of about $500 kept it out of reach of most buyers. More economical was the Tri-Power option consisting of three, Rochester 2-barrel carburetors. The latter offered 300 hp at 4,600 rpm, whereas the expensive fuel-injected engine offered only a little more, 310 hp at 4,800 rpm. Road test reports revealed the Tri-Power offered 0-60–mph times of only 7.6 seconds.

For the third model year in a row, Pontiac made an even higher level of performance available. The Tempest 395-A engine was available with two NASCAR–certified option packages. The first option package, PK, included a 4-barrel carburetor, 10.5:1 compression ratio, a higher-lift cam, and output specified as 315 hp. It was priced at $233 for the Star Chief and Bonneville series and $254 for other models. The second, PM, differed by using the Tri-Power setup. It was $320 when ordered for a Star Chef or Bonneville and $331 on others.

Oldsmobile

Once pent-up demand was met for new cars following the end of the war, Oldsmobile became more

Like the other GM passenger car divisions, in 1946, Oldsmobile took up where it left off in 1942. The first post-war cars had a much less complicated grille design. (Photo Courtesy Bill Kinsella; Illustration Courtesy David Temple Archives)

popular than ever. It was thanks to styling and mechanical innovations enthusiastically embrace by the public.

Oldsmobile: 1946–1948

Oldsmobile entered the post–World War II years much the same as it was when production of cars ceased in February 1942, although it had transformed from the "Oldsmobile Motor Works," the name it had since being founded by Ransom E. Olds in 1897, to the "Oldsmobile Division of General Motors." As expressed in an article published in the April 2002 issue of *Collectible Automobile* magazine, "Oldsmobile rolled into the 1940s with access to all of GM's styling innovations, a choice of engines, and one special technical advancement. Hydra-Matic gave Olds a leg up on the competition in the years surrounding World War II. Middle-class families snapped them up."

Oldsmobile was first to offer the Hydra-Matic automatic transmission. It was an extremely popular option costing $57; about half of the 1940 models were equipped with it. Cadillac, incidentally, did not acquire the Hydra-Matic until the following model year.

The 1946 models were styled under Oldsmobile Studio chief Edmund Anderson, who had done the design work on the 1941s from which the 1946s had evolved. A few hand-built Oldsmobiles appeared in mid-1945; the cars were displayed at Olds' corporate headquarters in Lansing, Michigan, and at various auto shows. Full-scale production commenced on October 15. Updates included a four-bar grille turned down at the ends and revised side trim. Model lineup was composed of four series: Special 66 with a 119-inch wheelbase, Dynamic Cruiser 76 and 78 with a 125-inch wheelbase, and the Custom Cruiser riding on a 127-inch wheelbase. The numerical portion of the nomenclature broke down into the series number and the number of engine cylinders; hence the Special 66 was a Series 60 with a 6-cylinder engine and so on. A new hood emblem, hood ornament, and minor trim alterations defined the 1947 models. An 8-cylinder Special, the "68," was also added to the line.

Model year 1948 again brought only slight updates for all but the top-of-the-line model now dubbed Futuramic 98. It marked the start of a short-lived trend in which the 98 would feature new styling one year ahead of the lower level Oldsmobiles. After 1951, the "98" was marketed as

The 1948 Oldsmobile Ninety-Eight shown sitting in a San Antonio dealership showroom featured unique styling that would be used on all 1949 models. Oldsmobile used this "year ahead styling" a few more times for its top-of-the-line series. Banners in background promoted the Hydra-Matic automatic transmission. (Photo Courtesy the University of Texas at San Antonio, UTSA Libraries Special Collections, Institute of Texan Cultures)

the "Ninety-Eight," but will be referenced here as the 98. Released in early 1949, the new Futuramic 98 made use of Cadillac's new C-body. The lower series cars were all now labeled as a Dynamic.

Oldsmobile 88: A Rocket for the Road and Track

For 1949, Oldsmobile released its 90-degree 303-ci Rocket V-8. It almost did not happen. Unknown to Olds engineers who had started its V-8 program in 1946, Cadillac had been working since 1936 on a replacement for its L-head engine. When Cadillac officials learned of Oldsmobile's engineers developing a V-8, they were determined not to have their modern V-8 overshadowed by Olds. Cadillac's management raised objections and as a result GM's corporate management cut off funding for further development of the Olds 90-degree V-8. Olds' chief engineer, along with engineer Elliot "Pete" Estes and division head Sherrod Skinner, skirted the matter by looking at other configurations such as 60- and 70-degree V-8s requiring balance shafts to make them run smoothly. Once again seeking funds from the corporate brass, they took the results of the studies to Charles Wilson, president of General Motors in March 1947. About one month later, the Executive Committee allocated funding to build a new Olds V-8. At that point, work ceased on other engines and resumed on the 90-degree engine, and it was ready for the start of the 1949 model year.

The 1950 Oldsmobile 98 featured styling that did not appear on the rest of the Olds lineup until the following year. This beautiful Garnet Maroon convertible is equipped with the extra-cost wire wheel covers and a very rare see-through hood used by dealers. (Photo Courtesy Tom Burns)

With the launch of the 1949 model year, all Oldsmobiles (now reduced to just a Series 76 and 98) had the same styling forecasted by that of the 1948 Olds 98. Initially, the Rocket V-8 was to be available only in the top-line model, but testing by chief engineer Jack Wolfram (reportedly on orders from Sherrod Skinner) found exceptional performance was available when the engine was installed in the Chevrolet-sized Olds Series 76. After some resistance to the idea, the engine became available in the Olds A-body (shared with Chevrolet and Pontiac) cars, thus was born the "88," a monogram that would become quite famous in a short time. The concept of placing the highest output engine in the lightweight body was not a new one; Buick had done the same with its 1936–1942 Century.

Some professional competition drivers in NASCAR quickly discovered the 88s and put them across the finish line the first six times out of the nine in the late-model division races held in 1949. An 88 convertible served as the official pace car for that year's Indianapolis 500, too. Performance was helping to sell the Oldsmobiles, especially the 88. Sales of the 88, pardon the pun, took off like a rocket and led to a 43 percent increase in overall orders compared to 1948. The 88 was also the division's best seller, but it took some sales away from the more profitable 98.

This original rendering of a 1949 Olds Futuramic Ninety-Eight convertible reveals the minor styling changes made, which include an around-the-world emblem on the hood and air scoops under the headlights. More significant was the arrival of a modern V-8. (Bob Najjar Collection)

The outcomes of NASCAR races for 1950 and 1951 were 10 first-place finishes out of 19 events and 20 out of 41 events, respectively. Oldsmobile's V-8 stayed popular partly as a result, so much so that the 6-cylinder was dropped entirely for 1951 and the model lineup was changed to 88, Super 88, and 98. The former, incidentally, was dropped late in the model year. As for the latter, it again featured year-ahead styling. Also notable for the year is that Jack Wolfram moved up to Oldsmobile's general manager.

As the model years advanced, the Oldsmobiles became heavier, and therefore, were much less suitable for NASCAR competition. Even so, the 88s remained very popular with the public.

For 1953, the Super 88 series shared the body of the Buick Special and the bottom-rung Deluxe 88 had the basic 1952 body shells.

In subsequent years, two-tone paint schemes became an integral part of styling with body-side trim designed to give the buyer many choices of color arrangements. In 1955, Oldsmobile offered 89 two-tone color combinations, which no doubt helped contribute to a record-setting year; the former record was broken eight months into the model year. For the following year, the

This dealer see-through hood allowed showroom visitors to see Olds' new Rocket V-8, which was all the rage. At the same time, they were able to view the graceful lines of the car without the interruption of a raised hood. (Photo Courtesy Tammy Reed)

This Crest Blue 1950 Olds Ninety-Eight convertible is one of only 3,925 built for the model year. Not surprisingly, it was the highest priced model in the Olds line at $2,615. For comparison, most Buick Supers were substantially lower in price. (Photo Courtesy Nick Pagani)

Harley Earl, GM vice president in charge of Styling, had many cars built for his use or his wife's use. This 1950 Olds Ninety-Eight has a number of special styling touches not offered to ordinary customers, such as special interior including door panels with rocket pattern, special body-side moldings with the model identification highlighted with paint, upper chrome door "saddle" moldings, special rocker panel moldings, Fleetwood script on trunk, etc. (Photos Courtesy GM Media Archive)

A 1952 Oldsmobile 88 Holiday was posed with a US Navy F3D-1 Skyknight for this publicity photo. The car is accessorized with an outside sun visor, spotlight, and white sidewall tires. (Photo Courtesy San Diego Air and Space Museum Library & Archives)

A four-door hardtop arrived in the Olds line for 1955. Like the two-door version, it wore the Holiday label. It was offered in all trim levels: 88, Super 88, and 98 Starfire. (Photo Courtesy Hampton Wyatt)

An array of Oldsmobiles of various styles were on exhibit at this 1957 auto show, including a 98 Starfire convertible, a Super 88 two-door sedan, and a Super 88 convertible. On the turntable are a solid white (including wheelwells) show car and a Super 88 Fiesta station wagon with two-tone paint. In the far background behind the Super 88 convertible is a four-door hardtop painted Platinum Mist. (Photo Courtesy GM Media Archive)

New styling was offered with the 1957 Oldsmobile lineup. However, the three-piece backlight and the new styling in general were not especially well liked by the public. This Victoria White 88 Holiday Coupe two-door hardtop is equipped with the optional 300-hp J2 engine, consisting of a trio of 2-barrel carburetors, 10:1 compression ratio, and high-performance cam.

side trim was altered but still made possible some outstanding paint schemes, which increased to include 184 recommended two-tone combinations.

As with the other four passenger-car divisions of General Motors, Oldsmobiles received a major redesign for 1957. The new, more rounded sheet metal gave the cars a lower, longer, and wider look. They were, indeed, about 5 inches longer. Windshield posts were also swept back more. An accent stripe was included in a recess of the molding starting along the door and sweeping down and back along the quarter panel on all 88s and 98s. Where the molding began depended on the model. On 98s it began at the vent window post, while on 88s it began near the door handle at about the notch in the beltline. Two-tone paint remained an option of course, and a contrasting accent stripe made a three-tone scheme possible.

The three-piece back window, dubbed the Twin Strut Rear Window, was a somewhat controversial feature of these Oldsmobiles. It was a shared feature with some Buicks and one taken from the 1954 Pontiac Strato Streak concept car. Two vertical struts painted body color, and with a ridge that continued across the roof, separated the rear windshield into three pieces. Some complained the feature interfered with rearward visibility, but mostly those complaining simply did not like the style.

All Oldsmobiles were now subtitled as Golden Rockets to celebrate the division's upcoming 50th anniversary. The name "Fiesta" was also brought back for Oldsmobile's first station wagon offerings since 1950. Three versions were available: 88 four-door sedan, 88 four-door hardtop, and Super 88 four-door hardtop.

Performance was still a strong selling point, even though the approximately 250-pound weight increase negated to some degree the extra horsepower offered by the larger 371 "Rocket T-400." Olds made available a tri-carburetor setup with progressive linkage; the option was labeled as the J2. There were two types: one for normal driving (offering 300 hp at 4,600 rpm) costing $83 and the other really intended for racing (312 hp). With a price of $385, not many of the 312-hp cars showed up on the street. The package included thinner head gaskets for the engine, which bumped the compression ratio to 10:1. A hotter camshaft was also included in the racing version.

The April 1957 *Motor Trend* road test report on a J2-powered Olds 98 revealed that a 0-60–mph sprint required only 9.4 seconds. An impressive time considering the 98 weighed approximately 300 pounds more than the 88 and Super 88. Well-broken-in J2s could propel the car roughly one-half second faster than that. For comparison, a 1956 Super 88 tested by Tom McCahill handled 0 to 60 in 10.8 seconds; the increased ci combined with the J2 option made a tremendous difference in performance for 1957.

In NASCAR Grand National competition, Lee Petty won four events with his J2-powered Olds sponsored by Air Lift Corporation, while his son Richard joined him

The 1957 Olds V-8 received a larger bore, raising displacement to 371 ci. Dubbed the Rocket T-400, it supplied 277 hp at 4,400 rpm. However, even more output was offered by the J2 version as shown here: 300 hp at 4,600 rpm. The option cost only $83. It is bolted to a Jetaway Hydra-Matic transmission.

A specially prepared, J2-powered Super 88 Holiday Coupe served as the official pace car for the 1957 Pike's Peak Hill Climb. (Photo Courtesy GM Media Archive)

This stunning 1958 Olds 98 convertible is painted Mountain Haze, one of 17 single-tone colors offered for the model year. Note the matching paint accents on the wheel covers and the extra-cost fender skirts. Only 5,605 of this model were built. (Photo Courtesy Magnus Karlsson, Bilsport Classic Sweden)

on the tracks also driving a J2 car. Oldsmobiles achieved only five Grand National wins that year and the division dropped out of factory-backed competition afterward. However, partway through the year, NASCAR's rule-making committee decreed that multiple carburetor setups would no longer be allowed in its races. Even so, the J2 option remained available through 1958.

Oldsmobiles had a new-looking body for 1958, but the inner structure from 1957 was retained. The new look did away with what had become recognizable Oldsmobile themes and was not well received by the public. Writing for *Car Life*, Jim Whipple wrote, "If we had come on last year's Olds and the new one side-by-side and had no way of knowing which was the 'new and improved' car, we would have unhesitatingly picked the '57," but added that, "A well-designed and well-built automobile lies beneath the baroque festoons of chromium and stainless-steel trim."

There was, indeed, plenty of chrome and stainless steel on the 1958 Olds. Judged by the eyes of the time, the applications of body moldings were incongruous, or as expressed in a story on the 1957–1958 Oldsmobiles in the February 1994 issue of *Collectible Automobile*, "The forward and rearward trim looked completely unrelated, as if they'd been designed by separate committees, neither of which knew what the other was doing."

In front, a missile-shaped outline was formed by the stainless trim, which joined the heavy chrome frame of the paired headlights and swept back to a point across the front door. In back was a set of four "speed lines" below which was another missile-shape stamped into the sheet metal. The grille was similar to that of the 1958 Pontiac's. Chromed block letters across the front of the tall hood spelled out OLDSMOBILE. The author of the previously mentioned *Collectible Automobile* magazine recalled seeing one in which the disgruntled owner removed the "I" and rearranged the letters to spell SLOB MODEL! While many found the styling questionable, Oldsmobile sold enough cars in the recession-plagued model year to move up to fourth place and a notch ahead of Buick.

The four-door hardtop Fiesta Holiday station wagon was carried forward from 1957, but it was in its final year of availability; only the four-door sedan would be offered the following model year. This Marlin Blue and Alaskan White Super 88 version was one of 27,521 built. It was the most popular of the Fiesta wagons offered in both the 88 and Super 88 series. (Photo Courtesy Bill Stewart)

The 98 Starfire

Among the displays visitors to the 1953 GM Motorama were able see was an Oldsmobile dream car dubbed "Starfire." The low-slung car featured a bright two-tone interior and a wraparound or "Panoramic" windshield. While that version did not go into production, those features did appear on Oldsmobiles the following year, and the Starfire label would be used for an especially flashy convertible in the top-shelf 98 series. By the way, the dream car's oval bumper-grille combo appeared on Oldsmobiles for 1955.

Art Ross moved up to chief of the Oldsmobile Studio in early 1947 and remained there until about the time Bill Mitchell replaced Harley Earl as VP of GM Design. Under him, the redesigned 1954 Oldsmobiles were styled. Reportedly, Harlow Curtice thought the earliest proposals for 1954 kept too much from 1953. In the end, grilles were very mildly updated and bullet-shaped taillights continued to be used, but much of the rest was noticeably altered. Of course, the Panoramic windshield brought forth a completely new cowl and dash.

The limited-production Fiesta (detailed later in this chapter) was dropped but replaced with a more economical-to-build Starfire, the sole convertible offering of the Series 98 line. It was introduced after the January 20 start of the 1954 model year, along with the Deluxe 88 and the 98 Deluxe Holiday. ("Holiday" signified a hardtop model.) The 98 was instantly distinguishable from the 88s due to its unique side trim, longer overall length and wheelbase, as well as its teardrop-shaped rear wheel openings.

Standard equipment for all 98s included the highest output 324 Rocket (185 hp at 4,000 rpm), padded instrument panel, parking brake warning light, courtesy light package, wheel covers, rocker panel molding, deck lid ornamentation, windshield washer, deluxe steering wheel and horn ring, plus nylon and leather upholstery. The Starfire added saddle-stitched, patterned, hand-buffed leather, hydraulically operated windows, and two-way power seats. A total of 6,800 Starfires were built for this model year.

Updates for 1955 included a new oval bumper-grille, but the oval parking lights with a horizontal bar in between were carried forward. Side moldings were also changed. The Starfire was a little less distinctive this time as it shared its side trim design with the Super 88, and teardrop-shaped rear wheel openings were applied to all models. Sales of the Starfire were much stronger with 9,149 being built. Late in the model year, Olds built its five-millionth car, a 98 Holiday sedan.

A new divided grille, redesigned parking lights, and revised side trim were among the changes for 1956. The 98 series continued to use an exclusive wheelbase of 126 inches, 4 more than that of any 88, and the Starfire remained the convertible offering in that line. Power steering was added to the standard equipment list of the 98 this year. Sales of the 98 drop-top fell back somewhat to 8,581 units.

All 98 models were labeled Starfires for 1957, thus there were two- and four-door hardtop Starfires, a four-door sedan Starfire, as well as a convertible version.

Sales of the Starfire remained nearly the same as for 1956, at 8,278. With the end of the 1957 model year came the last use of the Starfire nameplate, although it emerged again for 1961. Overall sales for Olds were

Glen Green and Polar White was one of several dozen two-tone paint options offered for the 1955 Oldsmobile line. All 1955 models received a new combination bumper-grille with a "floating" horizontal bar with OLDSMOBILE block letters in the space above it. The pictured car is a 98 Starfire convertible, which sold new for $3,276. (Photo Courtesy Jim Jordan)

enough to maintain its fifth-place spot, but on much lower volume. Two reasons for this were an economic recession that began in mid-1957 (its full effects were not felt until the next year) and buyers were now turning away from big, flashy cars and toward more conservative, economical cars, such as American Motors' Rambler, as well as foreign imports like Volkswagen.

Buick

Like Oldsmobile, Buick offered some memorable, trend-setting designs once truly new post-war versions entered the marketplace. Among the hallmarks were portholes and the hardtop body style.

Buick: 1946–1948

The 1942 model Buick Roadmaster and Special, which shared the new C-body with the Cadillac Series 62 and Sixty Special and Oldsmobile 98, emerged little changed when production resumed in October 1945. The design with its horizontal grille and front fenders sweeping across the front door had been patterned after Harley Earl's remarkable Buick Y-Job. On the Roadmaster the fenders, called "airfoil" front fenders, swept all the way back to the rear fenders. Little changed the following model year.

The 1948 models were supposed to be new and were even tooled for production, but in the end they were not.

When the 1949 models went into production, the Special series continued to use the styling that dated back to 1942, while the higher series cars were restyled.

The Original 1948 Buick: Canceled

Harley Earl had a close relationship with Alfred Sloan and a track record of successfully styling GM's cars, so he usually had his way when disagreements with Harlow Curtice materialized. Those disagreements seem to have been not exactly uncommon in later years. However, Curtice prevailed regarding the 1948 Buicks, according to an article written by Richard H. Stout and published in the fall 1998 *Automotive History Review*. Stout was an apprentice designer at GM Styling in 1947. According to him, in Curtice's evaluation the proposed 1948 Buick front end was not "sufficiently Buick." As he wrote, "Curtice and his staff had tried to learn to like this front, but in the end it didn't work. Buick management, especially Curtice, was adamant about keeping Buick in character. Year after year, mechanically and stylewise, they maintained strong consistency. The 'Buick Look' was sacred." According to Stout, the design reminded Curtice of the failed Airflow built by Chrysler Corp. about a decade earlier; it was judged as simply too rounded.

The idea was abandoned. Instead, one of the most famous grilles replaced it and in one form or another stayed in use through 1954. A newly designed Buick with an acceptable front end had to wait until 1949.

Buick Acquires Portholes, a Hardtop and More

Harley Earl strongly believed each line of cars should have an identity. In other words, a Chevrolet should easily be recognized as a Chevrolet, a Buick as a Buick, and so forth. Part of that approach was giving each line of cars a distinctive "face." For Buick starting in 1942, it received a "toothy" vertical-bar grille that would stay in use in various forms through 1954. More enduring were portholes and the "sweepspear." Even today, portholes provide product identity to Buick.

Ned Nickles designed both the sweepspear and the portholes, which were dubbed Venti-Ports. Several variations of the story about how the portholes originated exist, and they are all interesting. The official story often told is that Ned Nickles customized his 1948 Roadmaster convertible by cutting holes into the sides of the hood, each with a light inside electrically attached to the distributor so that each would fire in sequence with the spark plugs. When Edward Ragsdale, Buick's assistant body engineer and soon-to-be manufacturing manager, saw the setup, he told Harlow Curtice that Nickles had

Harley Earl showed the low height of this experimental Buick four-door sedan, which was part of a 1947 GM Proving Grounds exhibit. The enclosed wheel openings were similar to an experimental Cadillac from about the same time. No other information was available from GM Media Archive on this unusual car. Note the sleek fastback at left in the background. (Photo Courtesy GM Media Archive)

The Roadmaster Riviera two-door hardtop arrived late in the 1949 model year. Early examples had the straight body-side molding as seen on this show car. The venue here, though, is the GM building in downtown Detroit. (Photo Courtesy GM Media Archive)

"ruined" his car. Curious, Curtice went to look at Nickles' car. He liked the idea so much he ordered the portholes, minus the lights, added to the 1949 models, which were already designed and seven months away from the start of production. However, according to retired GM engineer Ken Pickering, the story he heard was that Buick chief modeler, Joe Funk, purchased some drain escutcheons and "for a joke placed them on the front fender of a clay model. Thus were born the Venti-Ports." Pickering, however, did see Nickles' car in action and thought it "quite a sight."

However, portholes were not unique to Buick. For instance, the 1947 Pinin Farina Cisitalia 202 carried a pair of them on the front fenders. What influence, if any, this might have had on using the feature on the Buick is apparently not recorded.

Venti-Ports were used to signify status, four portholes were for the top-line Roadmaster series and three were reserved for the Super.

The sweepspear molding was initially used for the two-door hardtop Roadmaster Riviera, but it was added some time after the model's introduction in July. The molding was an option for the Riviera convertible. The hardtop body style is often attributed to the wife of Ed Ragsdale, who loved to drive a convertible but only with the top raised. She liked the look of the car, but did not want to ruin her hairdo, an inevitable result of top-down driving. Thus, the best of both worlds was achieved, the look of a convertible with the top up and closed car without the wind in the hair. Initially, the style was labeled as a hardtop convertible only to be shortened to simply, hardtop. Ned Nickles, though, claimed he began working on the concept in 1945. He built a 3/8-scale model of his hardtop design. Upon seeing it, Harlow Curtice wanted to know if it was practical to build, and Ragsdale said that it was. Body construction was similar to that of a convertible, particularly in the lower body area.

Standard issue with the Roadmaster Riviera included power windows, chrome bows across the headliner, and a combination leather and cloth interior.

Also released one month after the Riviera (on August 8) was the new Special series with 1950 styling; the rest of the Buick line continued with 1949 styling until late December. (There were some 1948-styled 1949 Specials sold, but the model was out of production from December 1948 until the release of the 1950 model. Some of the new 1949s were reportedly titled as 1950s.) Offered as a two-door sedan, four-door sedan, and as a three-passenger business coupe, the Special proved to be quite popular; 81,817 were sold before the start of the 1950 model year, on December 28.

The public loved the new 1949 models, portholes and all. Despite higher prices, production soared 49 percent over the number built the previous model year. A total of 327,321 were assembled, which includes 4,343 of the Riviera hardtops. The Series 50 Super accounted for approximately 70 percent of the total output.

Buick: 1950–1953

For 1950, Buick had new B- and C-bodies; the latter, shared with Cadillac, was used for the longer wheelbase Super and Roadmaster Riviera. The new bodies did away

This combination grille-bumper guard design for the 1950 Buicks lasted one model year. It was composed of nine individually shaped pieces, which created a bit of an inventory headache for dealers who had to stock the replacement parts. This photo was taken inside the GM Building. (Photo Courtesy GM Media Archive)

with the old bolt-on rear fenders and instead used rear panels, which fit flush with the doors.

Late in the 1950 model year, the Riviera sweepspear molding replaced the straight one used on the Roadmaster Series 72 sedans.

Somewhat controversial at the time was the new "buck-tooth" combination bumper guard and grille used only for this model year. The design was originally considered for the Le Sabre during the brief time it was to be a Buick. It consisted of nine vertical bars, each of slightly different sizes and shapes, which went across the bumper. Some thought that the design was ugly. Others worried about the cost of repairs after an accident, despite the fact that repair costs were reduced over that of unified grilles

Ned Nickles: The Versatile and Creative Designer

Ned Nickles was a Wisconsin native, but little seems to be known about his early life. Nickles taught himself the art of car design, frequently during his high school general science class. Officially, his teacher was not pleased with his inattention to the lesson, but actual punishment was not forthcoming. Instead, Nickles was told to stand in front of the class and show the students his sketches.

After graduating from Waukauna High School, Ned went to work for his father. About five years later, he read an article about Detroit's auto manufacturing industry in *Life* magazine, which inspired Nickles to send some sketches to General Motors. According to *The Buick: A Complete History* by Terry Dunham and Lawrence Gustin, the package he sent was accidentally addressed to "Earl Harley." Evidently, the typo did not leave a negative impression on Earl. Several weeks later, Nickles received a letter telling him to report to work the following Monday.

During the war years, Nickles performed camouflage work for GM tanks and trucks. In 1945, Nickles was appointed to Chief Designer of the Advanced Design Studio, and soon thereafter he succeeded Henry Lauve as the Chief Designer of the Buick Studio (although some sources state this happened in 1947, even specifying the month of May as well). In that studio is where the designs were created for which Nickles is largely known. Reportedly, one of his earliest assignments there was to redesign the Buick Y-Job's hood ornament for use on the 1946 Buick. The "gun sight" hood ornament was used through the 1958 models. Nickles is also credited with the design of Buick's daring grilles, portholes, and the hardtop body style. However, his career at General Motors continued through 1973.

Former GM Design engineer Ken Pickering remembers Nickles well: "Ned Nickles was just a wonderful person, talented and always on an even keel. All of the studio doors were locked, but when you had business in the Buick Studio, Nick welcomed

Designer Ned Nickles is most known for his work as head of the Buick Studio. He is credited with the design of Buick's daring grilles, portholes, and the hardtop body style. His career at General Motors continued through 1973. (Photo Courtesy GM Media Archive)

you. The Buick Division was at the forefront of Styling as former Buick executive, Harlow Curtice, was now president of General Motors. Nick was single and lived alone in the Lee Plaza Hotel on West Grand Boulevard. At noontime, Nick always ate at Topinka's Restaurant . . . and always picked up the check. Nick was a great designer and a great manager."

In 1958, Ned Nickles was appointed as Chief Designer of the Advanced 1 Studio, a post he held through the end of 1967. The following year he was transferred to the position of Chief Designer of Advanced Design, Canadian and Overseas Studio. From 1971 until Nickles' retirement two years later, he held the position of Chief Designer of the Experimental Design 1 Studio.

The popularity of fastbacks was fast fading in the early 1950s. This rendering shows a 1951 Buick Custom Special Jetback (Model 46D), a model in its final year of production. The body style was produced only as a Super this year and brought only 1,500 sales. (Photo Courtesy Bob Najjar Collection)

This Terrace Green and Beach White 1952 Buick Special Deluxe Tourback sedan was far and away the most popular in the Series 40 lineup consisting of a half-dozen offerings. The Deluxe had a one-piece windshield, rocker molding, and bright fender fins affixed to the rear fenders. A total of 63,346 were built. The car pictured here is original with only 19,300 actual miles.

This 1953 Buick Roadmaster Estate Wagon (Model 79R) was exceptionally rare when new; only 670 were constructed. The body (constructed for Buick by Ionia Manufacturing of Ionia, Michigan) continued to have a combination of wood and steel construction. Buick's first all-steel wagon arrived the following year. (Photo Courtesy Wayne Ellwood)

because individual grille pieces could be replaced. However, the cost of stocking so many individual pieces was bothersome for dealers. Thereafter, the design reverted back to a more conventional one.

The so-called bucktooth grille did not have a negative effect on sales. In fact, apparently, it was just the opposite. A new high was established for Buick with 670,256 being built for the model year; the Special accounted for nearly half of them.

Golden Anniversary

Buick turned 50 years old in 1953 and celebrated its birthday in style. It delayed the release of its new V-8 until this year, improved the Dynaflow (which some called dyna slush), updated its B- and C-body cars for the final time, and released the Skylark.

The new Fireball V-8 displaced 322 ci in its original form and, when installed in a Roadmaster or Skylark, it produced a maximum horsepower of 188 at 4,000 rpm. The engine for the Super series was equipped with the 2-barrel and 8.0:1 compression. Output was rated at 170 hp at 4,000 rpm. Performance of the Roadmaster-Skylark engine was better due to a 4-barrel carburetor and a higher compression ratio. The old 263-ci straight-8 still powered the Special, but at least had an improved combustion chamber, resulting in slightly higher horsepower.

A Twin-Turbine Dynaflow helped deliver 10 percent more torque to the rear wheels. It felt less "slushy" and was also quieter than the original design.

Styling refinements included a raised front fender and hood line and a taller deck. Oval headlight bezels much like those of the 1951 XP-300 concept car were also included.

The release of the 1953 Skylark about mid-model year made the rest of the Buick line seem outdated.

The 1953 Buick Special convertible accounted for just 4,282 of Buick's 488,805 sales for the model year. Even though Buick released a new V-8 for 1953, the Special continued to be powered by the old straight-8, perhaps to amortize the costs of its tooling.

However, the Skylark forecasted the general look of the 1954 models.

Sales for the 1953 Buicks were exceptionally strong. A total of 488,805 were sold, the second best in Buick's history and over 50 percent more than the number produced for 1952.

Buick: 1954

Among the highlights of the 1954 model year was the return of the Century to the Buick lineup after an absence of a dozen years. As before, it combined the Roadmaster's upgraded 200-hp engine with the Special's body. Performance was on the minds of buyers, so the time was right to bring back the Series 60 Century. The Century was only about 70 pounds heavier than the Special, so performance was impressive for the day. With the Dynaflow attached, a Century could reach 60 mph from a standing start in 10.6 seconds, as shown by writer Griff Borgeson, who tested the model for *Car Life*.

Additional new features included the speedometer and the dash. Dubbed the Redliner, a red and black drum turned up a red line as speed increased. As innovative as it was, the Redliner met with mixed reviews. The speedometer, as well as the new double-roll dash, was similar to what was forecasted by the 1953 Buick Wildcat dream car. The Redliner speedometer appeared only on the Super and Roadmaster series. Other Buicks (including the Skylark) in the lineup used a pair of round gauges, one of which was the speedometer.

The Century came in almost all body styles: four-door sedan, two-door hardtop, convertible, and a station wagon. The new body design for this year's Buick featured smoother lines (more slab-sided), shorter and lower hoods, longer and higher deck lids, a wraparound windshield, and full wheel cutouts on two-door models (except on the Special two-door sedan). Windshield posts were upright on the Roadmaster series (C-body), but were slightly reverse-canted on the Super and Special series (B-body). Buick's new styling was promoted as "The Beautiful Buy." Evidently, the claim was considered true as shown by the 444,609 Buicks sold for the model year. The two-door hardtop, or Riviera, was offered in all series; the Super and Special versions were the most popular with a combined 210,831 built, thus accounting for nearly half of all Buicks built for 1954. This number even far exceeded the number of the lower priced Chevrolet Bel Air two-door hardtops built that year, a peculiar fact since sales of four-door sedans typically sold in higher numbers.

Buick: 1955

Greater expectations for Buick came from GM president Harlow Curtice. He expected Buick to maintain its third place position in the marketplace in a

The first all-steel bodied station wagons arrived at Buick for the 1954 model year. This Series 60 Century version, shown with optional Kelsey-Hayes 40-spoke wire wheels, was not a major seller with only 1,563 purchased. The output of the other station wagon offered by Buick, the Series 40 Special, found about as many buyers, at 1,650.

Among the features of the restyled 1955 Buicks were a multitude of two-tone and even three-tone paint patterns. This Cherokee Red and Dover White Roadmaster is equipped with the optional Kelsey-Hayes 40-spoke wire wheels. Hardtop models had the radiused rear wheel openings rather than the low-cut type of four-door sedans. (Photo Courtesy Gary Klecka)

The Series 60 Century convertible was one of five body styles offered to the general public in that line for 1955. A sixth (a two-door sedan) was available exclusively to the California Highway Patrol, which ordered 268 of them. As for the convertible, 5,588 were built.

year of new designs from competitors, as well as from General Motors.

Hardtops were very popular, so a four-door hardtop was added to the Special and Century this year. As a result, the Riviera name was dropped from the four-door sedan in the Super and Roadmaster series. Strangely, the Riviera name, which had originally signified "hardtop," was watered down starting with the 1950 models. These hardtops had the rounded wheelhouses given to all two-door models. Although the four-door hardtops used the B-body, their rear windows and roof pillars were much like those of the C-body two-door hardtops.

Due to a variety of monotone, two-tone, and even tri-tone paint patterns, 200 color schemes were offered to buyers this year.

The V-8 benefited from changes that pushed output to as high as 236 hp. Furthermore, the Dynaflow received improvements; the Variable Pitch feature of the transmission, as the name implies, varied the pitch of 20 stator blades according to acceleration. The improvement provided better acceleration and fuel mileage.

Sales, indeed, met with the expectations of Curtice as a new record was set with the production of 738,814 cars, which was more than enough to keep Buick in third place. Even Canadian production set a record high. Again two-door hardtops were the most popular and accounted for nearly two-thirds of overall production. However, this success came at a price: build quality began to suffer; it was only worse the following year.

Buick: 1956, the Start of a Downfall

A revised grille and bumper, new sheet metal in front with a V-profile hood, oval-shaped portholes, and a modified taillight design helped distinguish the 1956 Buicks from those of the prior model year. It would be the last use of the 1954 body.

Buick's general manager, Ivan Wiles, set a goal of building 900,000 Buicks in plants not nearly designed for that level. First quarter sales declined, and the expected spring surge did not materialize. Production was cut.

During 1955, according to, *The Buick: A Complete History*, "One Buick official of the time recalled, 'We were building engines so fast we were building some of them off the assembly line. We were running the foundry three shifts, running overtime beyond capacity. There was a problem with the rear axle. A number of them failed after

Buick's trademark Venti-Ports had different shapes since their inception in 1949. Three signified a lower series car, such as the Special seen here, and four denoted a car in the upper price bracket, such as the 1957 Buick Convertible (either a Century or a Roadmaster), also shown in this photo next to the Special. (Photo Courtesy Brian Lawrence)

20,000 miles.'" An executive was also quoted as saying, "There was a big feud between engineering and manufacturing; engineering wanted to design a new axle; manufacturing wouldn't do it." A variety of problems went unresolved for 1956.

This year all Buicks shared the 322, and all but the Special now had the Dynaflow as standard equipment. Production dropped by 22.5 percent from 1955's output. Recovery was years away.

Buick: 1957

Buicks for 1957 were longer and lower. Lower series cars were nearly 3½ inches longer and higher series were 1.7 inches longer. Their "Low Sweep Silhouette" partly came as a result of a new chassis with center "X" bracing.

In their original form, the Roadmaster Rivieras from this year had twin bright moldings on the deck and roof, which were connected by bars across the rear windshield, resulting in a three-piece design, a styling feature intended to give the roofline a longer appearance. However, it met with complaints about visibility and simply on looks, so an alternative was offered. A single-pane rear window was offered in the model 73A, the Roadmaster four-door, and the model 76A, the two-door version. An undivided rear window was also used on the interim Roadmaster Series 75 Riviera, which featured an extremely plush interior. The Century and Special series Riviera four-door hardtops had C-pillar posts much like those of the 1955–1956 Riviera four-door body style, while the Super two- and four-door hardtops had reverse-slant pillars similar to the 1956 Buick Centurion shown at the GM Motorama. Furthermore, a four-door hardtop dubbed the Caballero was added to the station wagon lineup. It was equipped with a distinctive upholstery pattern.

The styling of the new Buicks was not well accepted by the public, and sales were down; they would have been down even without the recession that began that year. However, Harlow Curtice, GM president and former general manager of Buick, thought they were beautiful cars! The public's opinion counted more: Buick lost its third place spot, slipping behind Plymouth.

Buick: 1958 Limited

An exclusive model, the Series 700, was introduced for 1958. It was labeled "Limited," a name that had last been used by Buick in 1942. Of it, the sales literature said, "There's no other car on the road quite like it, from the Dynastar grille right back to the twin tower taillights." All 1958 Buicks shared that Dynastar grille, composed of four rows of bright, faceted squares creating a jeweled look; the Limited differed visually from the rest with exclusive quarter panel trim layout (three sets of five simulated louvers) and taillights, as well as being longer than any other model offered, overall length measured 227.1 inches or nearly 19 feet! The Limited was a full 8 inches longer than the Roadmaster and Super with the additional length being added to the deck.

According to Buick Studio chief Ned Nickles, the design of the 1958 Buick Limited came about from a strange set of events. The stylists had two proposals to show to Harley Earl, and each of them was illustrated with two cardboard mockups with clay extrusions on them. To help make moving the exhibit to its viewing area for Earl to inspect easier, the designers pinned both proposals to the side of the model. Once they were moved, the stylists planned to show Earl the proposals one at a time. After moving the model, the men went back to the studio briefly, then started back to the viewing area but were met by Harley Earl's administrative assistant, Jules Andrade, who told them, "Mr. Earl just looked at it, and he says you should release it exactly as it is shown." The group was stunned, but of course did as they were instructed.

According to retired GM engineer Ken Pickering, however, this story was "folklore" around General Motors, and furthermore was associated with Oldsmobile. Even so, Pickering believes that if Nickles said the story applied to the Buick Limited, then it must be accurate.

The Century Estate Wagon remained in the lineup for 1957, but it was not a big seller. Only 10,186 were produced. Like other Century styles, trim was similar to the Special but with four portholes instead of three, and the series designation was placed in the rear quarters or doors within the dip in the sweepspear molding.

The 1958 Buick Limited was the top-of-the-line model and was actually intended to be a competitor to Cadillac. It was offered in two-door hardtop form as seen here, as well as a four-door sedan, and a convertible. The Limited could be distinguished from the lower series cars by its exclusive side trim, consisting of three sets of five simulated vents and special taillight treatment. Only 1,026 of the two-doors were sold. Total production amounted to just 7,436 units. (Photo Courtesy Jim Jordan)

Tales of the Wells Fargo was a popular western broadcast on NBC with Buick as a sponsor. The shows' star, Dale Robertson, received this modified 1958 Limited convertible after it was used briefly as a show car. The car's exterior differed from production models in having a longhorn steer's head overlaying the stock V-8 hood emblem, wheel covers modified with a three-bar "flipper," and simulated woodgrain inserts overlaid with "Wells Fargo" in chrome-plated block letters within the looped quarter panel moldings.

Continued for one more model year was the Caballero Estate Wagon, a four-door hardtop model. Only 4,456 were produced for 1958. Introduced for 1957, it was Buick's entry into the short-lived four-door hardtop station wagon market. Note the longitudinal moldings on the roof, a modification of the concept of the indentations used on the 1955–1957 Nomad. (Photo Courtesy GM Media Archive)

Any "hot rod" image Buick had disappeared with the 1958 models. Buick was about luxury this time and as with the prewar Limited, it was meant to take on Cadillac in that regard. Curtice had tried it with the original Limited and was doing so again. It proved to be the wrong car at the wrong time. Of course, the timing could not be foreseen when the 1958s were being designed, as the economy showed no signs of slowing then.

Cadillac: Still the Luxury Leader

Cadillac had overtaken Packard for supremacy in the luxury car market, but past success did not guarantee future success. The perpetually creative Harley Earl did not stop looking ahead even during the war years. Inspiration for the design of the first truly new Cadillac to emerge after World War II took shape with a fortuitous visit to view an advanced fighter plane with engines built by GM's Allison Division.

During the immediate post-war years, there was a design proposal for the first truly new Cadillac that was ultimately judged as too radical for the times. A functional prototype dubbed "C.O." was constructed. It featured enclosed wheels at all four points, recessed headlights, rounded lines, and a very aerodynamic-looking shape. Notably absent were tail fins.

Chapter Seven: Tail Fins, Chrome, Gadgets and More!

The 1947 Cadillac Series 75 Limousine continued to use the front fender shape from 1941. Its body was not shared with other Cadillac models. Five versions were offered ranging from five- to nine-passenger capacity. (Photo Courtesy Cadillac & LaSalle Club)

The Cadillac Series 61 was the low-priced model in the lineup. A flared-out lower body distinguishes the Series 61 from the higher-level models. This 1947 version, sometimes called a Sedanette but officially labeled as a Club Coupe, accounted for 3,395 sales that model year. The Club Coupe style was also offered in the Series 62 line. (Photo Courtesy Cadillac & LaSalle Club)

This functional experimental Cadillac dubbed the "C.O." from 1946 had highly advanced styling for the time: enclosed wheels, recessed headlights, wraparound windshield (two-piece construction), flush-fitting rear fenders, etc. Ultimately it was apparently judged as a bit too advanced for the public's tastes. Incidentally, GM's British division, Vauxhall, also had a very similar prototype but with stubby tail fins similar to those of a 1948 Cadillac. (Photo Courtesy GM Media Archive)

The Cadillac C.O. evidently led to this clay mockup labeled XP-5. Note the stubby tail fins, the forward leaning windshield posts, and the hood recessed below the cowl to create an air intake. The date of the photo is December 8, 1948. (Photo Courtesy GM Media Archive)

1948: The Arrival of Tail Fins

In the late 1930s, the legendary Kelly Johnson led Lockheed Aircraft. One of his most famous designs was the twin-boom P-38 Lightning, powered by two Allison-built V-1710 engines. Allison was a division of General Motors. Sometime during 1939, Harley Earl was offered a chance to view an early version of the P-38; that invitation changed automotive history.

The Cadillac P-38 C-body design was developed under Frank Hershey with, of course, direction coming from Harley Earl. Other than the fins, the Lightning also inspired the pontoon-like fenders and propeller spinner–shaped bumper guards. The bumper guards were eventually dubbed "bumper bombs," but were more famously known as, "Dagmars," after the shapely actress who went by the singular name, Dagmar. Those stubby fins, which launched a styling fad lasting into the early 1960s, were not at first well received when the clay mockup of the proposed 1948 model was shown to executives. Reportedly, Harley Earl then ordered the fins to be removed, but Hershey only covered them with a cloth, a bold move, to say the least, because Earl could easily fire anyone not following orders. Later, management had second thoughts and wanted to view the clay model again. Earl was pleased that Hershey had left the fins in place because the idea met with full approval the second time.

Apparently, those fins took a little time to accept. When dealers had their first look at the all-new Cadillacs, they were also dubious of the feature. Public reaction to the design changed their minds, though. Sales for the finned cars reached 52,706 units.

The Sedanette body style was offered through 1950. With the advent of the hardtop body style, fastback styling faded away for quite some time. Shown is a 1949 Series 62. (Photo Courtesy Steve Plunkett and Paul Sontrop)

All of Cadillac's body styles from 1948 were carried forward for 1949, but the new Coupe de Ville, a two-door hardtop model, joined them. Late in the model year, one of the Coupe de Villes became Cadillac's 1-millionth car. (Photo Courtesy GM Media Archive)

Incidentally, the 1948 Cadillac was not the first Cadillac with tail fins. Harley Earl built a custom 1931 Cadillac for actor Buck Jones. Among its custom features was a set of three fins across the rear of the car. This car still exists and at last report was under restoration.

1949: A New Model and a Modern V-8

Few things changed for Cadillac in 1949. The revised grille was the only minor styling update applied to the new models. Introduced at about the middle of the model year was the Coupe de Ville, a two-door hardtop. Bringing great excitement for the second year in a row was a replacement for the old L-head with an overhead-valve (ohv) V-8. The new powerplant displaced 331 ci and provided significantly greater performance and fuel economy. Compression ratios were on the rise due to the availability of higher octane gasoline (up to a rating of 88 by 1948). Still higher ratings were being planned for the future, thus the new engine was designed for a compression ratio of up to 12:1. The engineers apparently did their work well because the engine continued in its basic form through 1963. Because of the lively performance of the new Cadillac V-8, a number of racers (including Briggs Cunningham and Allard) used it to power their race cars. The only other street car that could measure up to Cadillac in terms of performance was Oldsmobile's V-8.

Cadillac: 1950–1953

A new body arrived for 1950. The bolt-on rear fender was gone and body sides were smoother. A chrome-plated, simulated vent was attached to the forward end of the quarter panel as well. From 1951 to 1953,

Cadillacs underwent minor styling tweaks. Examples of these include back-up lights below the taillights for 1951, a higher, squarer profile for the deck lids of the 1952 and 1953 models compared to the 1951s, and a dual-exhaust bumper, which helped differentiate the 1952s from the previous year. For 1953, Cadillacs received a one-piece rear windshield, thus replacing the three-piece arrangement, as well as rear bumper guards, or "bombs," much like the front ones.

In 1952, Cadillac celebrated its golden anniversary. In recognition of that, Cadillac created a "gold package" composed of an anodized gold "V" and Cadillac crest, a feature that continued to be used through the 1958 models. The division also fielded a couple of show cars dubbed El Dorado and Townsman.

Perhaps the best view of a 1954 Cadillac Coupe de Ville is in motion. The CDV model was distinguishable from a Series 62 by its wider rocker panel moldings and special script on the upper quarter panel next to the rear pillar. A gullwing-like front bumper design was revived for 1954 after a one-year absence. (Photo Courtesy I. W. Harper Photography)

"El Dorado" was a label applied to the fabled city of gold and other riches supposedly somewhere in South America. This fact, combined with the golden anniversary, made the moniker El Dorado entirely appropriate. The public's reaction to the El Dorado, later simply Eldorado, resulted in a limited-production, almost identical version becoming available for 1953.

The Townsman was a modified Sixty Special painted in Nubian Black with a golden linen-grained coated fabric roof covering padded with felt. Its interior was upholstered in gold and black cloth with Cadillac-crested emblems of gold metallic thread.

Another mild facelift defined the 1953 Cadillacs.

Cadillac: 1954–1956

Model year 1953 was enormously successful for Cadillac, but the 1950–1953 body was retired and replaced with an all-new one for 1954. It had been in the works for more than two years under the direction of Ed Glowacke. Frontal styling, consisting of a finely textured cellular grille integrated with a gullwing bumper, visored headlights, round parking lights, and "bomb" type bumper guards, was essentially the same as that of the 1953 LeMans dream car shown at that year's GM Motorama. Also, included was a wraparound windshield for all models. Windshield posts were vertical, unlike those of the B-body Olds and smaller Buicks. A 2-inch visor over the windshield helped reduce glare from the sun. The tail fins with integrated taillights were similar in style to those of the past but were somewhat larger. Exhausts exited through the far ends of the rear bumper; while the design looked good, it eventually resulted in corrosion unless the owner kept it clean and waxed on a regular basis.

In keeping with Harley Earl's lower, longer, wider motif, the cars were lengthened, with wheelbases for all models receiving a 3-inch stretch, thus spanning 129 inches for the Series 62 line, 133 for Sixty Special, and 149.25 inches for the Series 75. Overall length of the cars, of course, was similarly increased with the exception of the Series 62 sedan, which was, strangely enough, 7 inches shorter than the two-door hardtop. The end result was a car about 2 feet longer than the contemporary Chevrolet.

Eight models were offered in the three series. In the Series 62 were the two-door hardtop, Coupe de Ville, six-window sedan, convertible, and Eldorado convertible. The latter no longer had the extensive body modifications required to create the original 1953 version. However, it was less distinctive, leading to some complaints in that regard. That issue was resolved the following year. Because the model was built directly from a Series 62 convertible body shell, the price could be drastically reduced from the 1953 price of $7,750 to $5,738, thus accounting for the larger production run of 2,150 units.

The Fleetwood Sixty Special was 11 inches longer

This 1955 Cadillac Series 62 two-door hardtop owned by Angelo Van Bogart, editor of the publication, Old Cars Weekly, is one of 27,879 built during Cadillac's record-breaking model year in which production reached 140,777. Production was even higher the following year. (Photo Courtesy Angelo Van Bogart)

The air-conditioning system on this 1955 Cadillac Series 62 sedan required a lot of space; the bulky evaporator was placed in the trunk compartment. Note the air intakes on top of the quarter panels and the plastic tubes emerging from the rear shelf. The paint color was labeled Deep Cherry.

than the Series 62 and distinguished with a set of eight small chrome-plated louvers on the rear doors. Inside was a more upscale interior with 12 trim options offered to the buyer. Standard equipment included a two-way power seat, power windows, and the Autronic Eye automatic headlight dimmer.

Series 75 offerings numbered just two: sedan and a limousine. Either could seat up to eight comfortably, thanks to an overall length of just a fraction more than 237 inches, or about 3½ feet more than a Chevrolet.

All series of Cadillacs were powered by a 331 V-8 rated at 230 hp at 4,400 rpm, 20 hp more than the previous year. At least that was what was advertised. In reality, the 1953s were deliberately underrated. With no changes to the 1953 engine, there was no real increase in the output of the 1954 engine.

A shorter model year accounted for fewer sales compared to 1953's output of 103,538 cars; a total of 98,680 were produced for 1954, which far surpassed the combined output of competitors Lincoln (nearly 37,000) and Packard (nearly 31,300). Evidently, the majority of luxury car buyers believed that Cadillac was indeed the "standard of the world."

As good as the 1954 model year had been for Cadillac, it paled in comparison to the number of cars sold for 1955. The total of 140,777 cars sold represented a new high point for the division. There were no drastic changes to the 1954 body, but rather minor refinements, which included a coarser grille, parking lights relocated and reshaped to rectangular units, and an L-shaped body-side molding (except on the Series 75). However, the Eldorado was again a much more distinctive model thanks to exclusive rear styling with tail fins and taillights virtually the same as those of the 1954 Cadillac La Espada and El Camino dream

This 1955 Eldorado has some unusual features. For one, Cadillac did not offer a hardtop version until 1956. This is a "shop order" car (SO 2542) built especially for Cadillac's chief engineer at the time, C. F. Arnold. It was also outfitted with 1956-style upholstery. (Photos Courtesy Clint Ruby)

Chapter Seven *Tail Fins, Chrome, Gadgets and More!*

This Alpine White 1955 Cadillac Series 62 convertible is one of 8,150 built for the model year. Note the use of anodized gold hood ornamentation. (Photo Courtesy I. W. Harper Photography)

The Florentine curve of the rear roof is quite distinct in this near profile view of a 1956 Cadillac Series 62 two-door hardtop. This feature was adopted six years earlier. Upper roof color on two-toned cars extended down to the beltline, as seen on this Sonic Blue and Alpine White car. (Photo Courtesy Jim Jordan)

cars. Also included and copied from the two dream cars were Sabre Spoke wheels. The standard fender skirts of the other models were deleted from the Eldorado as well.

This time horsepower actually increased for Cadillac's 331 V-8 due to a three-quarter-point compression increase to 9:1, redesigned combustion chambers, and a higher lift cam. These changes raised the output to 250 hp at 4,400 rpm. However, the standard engine for the Eldorado had twin 4-barrel Rochester carburetors; it was rated at 270 hp at 4,800 rpm. The Eldorado engine was a $161 option in other models.

The 1954 body received one more restyle before being replaced with another all-new one. Changes for 1956 were again mild and were composed of finer mesh grille, squared tail fins, new wheel covers, and "slip-stream" rear fender styling. The latter was a tubular contour that tapered from near the forward edge of the rear fender and extended back to join the exhaust outlet extensions. Chromed vertical ribs were attached on Series 62 models, while the Sixty Special had the entire fairing covered with a ribbed chrome-plated molding.

Added to the lineup was a two-door hardtop version of the Eldorado. To distinguish the two styles, the hardtop was labeled as the Eldorado Seville and the convertible became the Eldorado Biarritz. Also new was the Sedan de Ville,

The elegant setting of the Webb Institute in Glen Cove, New York, was appropriate for this equally elegant 1956 Cadillac Eldorado Seville equipped with the optional anodized gold alloy Sabre-spoke wheels. Twin windsplits mounted at the front center of the hood replaced the goddess hood ornament, standard on lower-priced Cadillacs. (Photo Courtesy Lou Commisso)

This 1956 Cadillac Eldorado Seville, like the one before it, was made much more distinctive with exclusive rear styling. Note the exhausts that exit through the bumper end caps. A hardtop version, labeled Eldorado Biarritz, was added to the line this model year. (Photo Courtesy Lou Commisso)

This Mountain Laurel 1957 Cadillac Eldorado Seville is fitted with the optional anodized gold Sabre-spoke wheels. Exclusive rear styling set apart the Eldorado from other Cadillac models. (Photo Courtesy Cadillac & LaSalle Club)

a four-door hardtop equipped with leather and cloth upholstery, chromed headliner bows, power windows, and power seat. It was the most popular model with more than 41,700 being sold.

Engine output was improved due to a bore increase, the first since the type was released in 1949, and a compression boost to 9.75:1. The 365-ci V-8 was rated at 285 hp at 4,600 rpm, except for the twin-carb Eldorado engine, which produced 305 hp at 4,700 rpm. The Hydra-Matic received improvements to create smoother shifts as well.

Sales of Cadillacs shot up again for 1956, thus setting yet another record; in all, 154,577 were produced and sold, thus pushing Cadillac up one notch to ninth place in overall automobile sales. This record would stand until 1962.

Cadillac: 1957–1958

The new 1957 Cadillac models borrowed many styling cues from dream cars of the 1954 and 1955 GM Motorama: the La Espada, El Camino, Park Avenue, and Eldorado Brougham. Headlight treatment (quad type for 1958), bumper-grille combo, front and rear windshield slant, roof architecture, tapered tubular shape on the quarter panels, tail fins, and taillights of the 1957 and 1958 Cadillacs strongly resembled those of the listed dream cars.

The Eldorado Seville and Biarritz remained especially distinctive again with exclusive rear styling consisting of tapering quarter panels topped off with shark-like fins with taillights beneath them. Also part of the Eldorado styling was special moldings for the rear wheel opening and aft to the rear bumper, a low deck lid, and a unique rear bumper.

Also distinctive was the Sixty Special. Even though this four-door hardtop lacked exclusive bodywork, it was instantly recognizable due to unique ribbed moldings along its lower quarter panels. These Sixty Special–only moldings were redesigned for 1958.

Ed Glowacke, along with assistants David Holls, Ron Hill, and Bob Scheelk, developed the styling of the 1957 and 1958 models. As explained in the August 1997 issue of *Collectible Automobile* magazine, "Thanks largely to Glowacke . . . the marque moved serenely from model year to model year in a steadily recognizable progression. Cadillac styling marched along at an evolutionary pace (as it had since 1941) always leading the industry

A vinyl-covered top was standard issue on the Eldorado Biarritz. Shown is a 1957 model painted Glade Green. Those fender-top twin windsplits were used only for the Eldorado. (Photo Courtesy Cadillac & LaSalle Club)

Cadillac added the Sedan de Ville four-door hardtop to the Series 62 lineup in 1956. The Sedan de Ville differed from the Series 62 four-door hardtop in having its interior fitted with leather and cloth instead of all cloth or combination cloth and vinyl. Additionally, chromed headliner bows were included, as were power windows and seat. Shown is the 1957 model, of which 23,808 were produced.

and always instantly recognizable. Not only did the tail fins say Cadillac, but also from 1954 through 1957, Earl insisted on the traditional gullwing front bumper with Dagmars (a touch appropriated from the Le Sabre show car) and an egg-crate grille texture. These all stood out as Caddy hallmarks."

Despite the "evolutionary" design and "recognizable" traits, the appearance of the 1957 Cadillacs received some criticism from dealers and the public. Their complaint, oddly enough, was that the cars looked short! The illusion of shortness was caused by the front end, which leaned back and the fins, which were canted forward. To remedy the problem, the Cadillac Studio revised these features for the 1958 model year.

On the plus side was a new interior with a more user-friendly instrument panel layout. At the center of the dash was a large glove box with the release button offset to the left to provide easy access to it for the driver. Radio pushbuttons were also placed left of center for the same purpose, and switches for the lights and windshield wipers were on the left corner of the instrument panel wraparound. All controls had lighted bezels for easy viewing at night.

Quad headlights and a new bumper-grille were new features of the 1958 Cadillacs. However, the quad lights first appeared on the flagship model dubbed Eldorado Brougham, released in 1957, but with the 1958s, all models had the feature. The gullwing bumper was replaced with one designed by Pete Wozena, who ran a special studio at Design. His replacement for it was a broad, full-width jeweled grille with pointed, rubber-tipped bumperettes at each end. Underneath each bumperette was a U-shaped, combination parking/fog light. Incidentally, Chevrolet's bumper-grille resembled that of the Cadillac's.

Yet another compression ratio boost (this time to 10:1), along with a new low-profile 4-barrel carburetor with larger secondaries helped push horsepower to

New frontal appearance of the 1958 Cadillac lineup included quad headlights as well as a completely new massive bumper and grille arrangement. This Dakota Red Eldorado Seville is one of only 815 built. (Photo Courtesy Cadillac & LaSalle Club)

Reportedly, a total of five Raindrop Cadillacs were built for the 1958 auto show circuit. Each was fitted with a system similar to that installed on Harley Earl's Le Sabre. The convertible top folded down to fit under a flush-fitting cover in lieu of a conventional convertible top boot. If the top was down and the car parked at the time rain began to fall, a rain sensor would activate the mechanism to raise the top and windows. This particular photo was taken of one of the surviving cars at the 2013 Amelia Island Concours d'Elegance.

Carl Renner: Making Styling Concepts a Reality

Carl H. Renner was born in Nuremberg, Germany, on February 12, 1923, and immigrated with his family to the United States about four years later, settling in Detroit, Michigan.

As a teenager, Renner's passion was to work for Walt Disney, and at the age of 20 moved to California to work at the Disney Studios as a cartoon animator. However, he found the work was simply production-oriented and did little toward his interest in using his imagination. He returned to Detroit one year later.

In April 1945, however, Renner had his chance to use his creativeness when, after interviewing at General Motors, he was hired to work in Styling as a junior designer in the Orientation Studio. He was promoted to senior designer by the fall of the following year and was transferred to the Chevrolet Studio, where

Carl Renner (left) joined General Motors in 1945 after working for one year for Walt Disney Studios. He is best known for his work on the 1954 Nomad dream car and the 1955 Chevrolets, but his long career also included work on many other projects, such as the Corvair and Cadillac Cyclone. (Photo Courtesy GM Media Archive)

Carl Renner penned these designs, which include a proposal for the XP-100, the dream car that ultimately became the 1956 Corvette Impala. Note the Pontiac with a "flying wing" deck. (Photo Courtesy GM Media Archive)

Carl Renner: Making Styling Concepts a Reality CONTINUED

he was later deeply involved in the design of the original Corvette. Among the work there for which he is most known was designing the 1954 Nomad dream car and adapting its roof for use on the Bel Air body to create the production version of the Nomad. His other contributions while in the Chevrolet Studio include the notch belt fender line, 1955–1956 hood ornaments, and the deluxe steering wheel.

In late 1953, Carl Renner was promoted to Assistant Chief Designer in the Body Development Studio, where he assisted the head of the studio, Chuck Stebbins. This studio played an important role in developing the A-B-C body interchangeability system created by Harley Earl. In an interview of Renner published in the May 1997 issue of *Collectible Automobile*, he noted that his time in the Chevy studio was "an exciting era . . . first under Ed Anderson, then Ed Glowacke, and finally Clare MacKichan. It was the time of the postwar boom; the era of Harley J. Earl and Ed Cole; the origin of the Corvette, Nomad Motorama car, and the 1955-1957 Chevys."

Renner also served as Assistant Chief Designer in the Oldsmobile (working under Art Ross), Pontiac (under Paul Gillan), and in the Advanced I Design studios (under Ned Nickles). He was also involved in the design of the LaSalle II roadster. He even penned a Corvette styling proposal based upon this concept car. During a tour for the people of GM's German Opel Division led by Tom Christiansen, Administrative Director for GM Styling, one of the Opel tourists noticed a drawing of the LaSalle II roadster on Renner's desk. Renner had signed it in the corner. The German tourist thought that name to be the name of the car and noted how appropriate it was for the design. Christiansen asked what *Renner* meant and was told that, in German, it meant *racer*.

As Assistant Chief Designer working with Ned Nickles in the Advanced I Studio, Carl assisted in the design of the 1960 Corvair. He went on to serve as Chief Designer in the Advanced II and Advanced IV studios. Under him, while of course working with Harley Earl, the Cadillac Cyclone was crafted.

Carl Renner retired from General Motors in November 1980.

---

300 at 4,800 rpm. An optional version was even more powerful, 325 hp at 4,800 rpm; the extra dose of power came as a result of a dual 4-barrel carb setup. For 1958, the dual-fours were replaced with a trio of 2-barrel carburetors. Compression was bumped up to 10.25:1, thus adding another 10 hp to both the single carb and 3 x 2-barrel engines.

Despite some pushback from dealers and the public regarding the short look of the 1957 models, Cadillac sales were strong, but not quite as strong as the previous model year. In all, 146,441 were built. The revised 1958s generated 121,474 sales.

Specialty Models: Fiesta, Skylark and Eldorado

During the 1953 model year, General Motors released for sale three semi-custom models: the Oldsmobile Fiesta, Buick Skylark, and the Cadillac Eldorado. All were partially hand-built cars with prices high enough to keep their production limited. These three models were introduced to the public at that year's GM Motorama, along with several dream cars featuring the new wraparound windshield. The Fiesta and the Eldorado had the feature, so both had some dream car styling.

Fiesta

The Fiesta was a part of the 98 series even though the Fiesta shared little with the 98, just the grille, bumpers, taillights, and a few trim pieces. It featured a low, wraparound windshield, frameless "wind wings" rather than conventional vent windows, a notched beltline (known as the "Darrin dip," named for the stylist Howard "Dutch" Darrin), and a so-called hockey stick molding on the quarters, which would show up on Oldsmobiles the following model year. Standard equipment included a tuned version of the 303 producing 170 hp (5 more than that of a 98), a Hydra-Matic transmission, power steering, power brakes, left and right outside rearview mirrors, heater/defroster, super deluxe radio, leather upholstery, Autronic-Eye (automatic headlight dimmer), back-up lights, spinner wheel covers (like those installed on the 1953 Oldsmobile Starfire dream car), and wide whites.

Exterior color schemes at first numbered just four with two of them being two-tone: Polar White, Black, Noel Green with Nile Green, and Surf Blue with Teal Blue. Interior offerings were limited to light green, light blue, or black buffed leather trimmed with ivory leather. Color selections were later expanded to include such two-tones as Polar White with Raven Red and Polar White with Regal Turquoise, and additional upholstery colors were of course added to match. The convertible top (of either canvas or Orlon) was offered in black, white, dark blue, and dark green.

As the wraparound windshield and notched beltline indicated, there were structural changes made to the Oldsmobile convertible to transform it into a Fiesta. The trailing edge of the hood, front fenders, instrument panel, and cowl had to be reworked to accommodate the shape of the windshield. Doors were, of course, modified for the Darrin dip. This, in turn, forced the quarter panels to be altered, too. Even the deck lid differed from a standard Olds. The low height of the windshield meant the convertible top had to be lowered in overall height by 2.5 inches, which made necessary changes in the standard convertible top frame. The top-operating hydraulic cylinders needed additional clearance, so the rear wheel housings were indented to accommodate it. Despite all the changes, the Fiesta was not as difficult to engineer as the Eldorado.

Despite the reduced difficulty of engineering the Fiesta, it still carried a high price tag. As a result, of the 334,462 Oldsmobiles built for 1953, only 458 of them were Fiestas. The following year the model was replaced by the Starfire, a convertible, which shared many of its components with the lower series cars, thus reducing its production cost and selling price.

Skylark

A customized 1951 convertible designed by stylist Ned Nickles inspired the Skylark. Buick's general manager, Ivan Wiles, liked it so much he thought a special show car, which was dubbed "Skylark," should be built for the 1952 auto show circuit. The Skylark prototype with Carlo Borrani wire wheels was claimed to be the "answer to the European sports car," although how such a big car could be labeled a sports car is beyond explanation. It was at least sporty. A Buick press release said the car would be put into production if enough interest were shown in the Skylark. In reality, it was already scheduled for production.

The body of the Skylark, or Model 76X, received a "chopped" windshield rather than the wraparound type as found on the Fiesta and Eldorado, a lowered beltline, radiused wheel openings, and a deck lid with a faster slope. A "bombsight" hood ornament was recessed into the hood and by then traditional Buick Venti-Ports were deleted from the front fenders. The top of the front seat was lowered to align exactly with the beltline, resulting in a car that appeared dramatically lower as compared to other 1953 Buick models. Indeed, it was about 3 inches lower. This lower look gave Skylark a sporty look, which was apparently enough to advertise it as having "sports

For 1953, General Motors offered specialty model convertibles in its top three divisions. Shown here is the Oldsmobile 98 Fiesta. It was a virtually hand-built, factory-customized 98 convertible with a wraparound windshield and other body modifications. Most Fiestas were two-toned like the pictured car. Only 458 were built due to its high price of $5,715. (Photo Courtesy GM Media Archive)

The 1953 Buick Skylark was inspired by a customized 1951 Buick convertible designed by stylist Ned Nickles. Built from a Series 70 Roadmaster convertible, the Skylark's windshield, convertible top, and doors were all cut down. However, unlike the specialty cars from Oldsmobile (the Fiesta) and Cadillac (the Eldorado), it did not have a wraparound windshield, which would have required further body modifications. The pictured car, one of 1,690 built, was restored over a period of 20 years.

car" qualities. Just as the dream cars were predictive of future styling characteristics, the Skylark was, too, since Buick's 1954 models would receive radiused wheel openings and the sweepspear trim. The 1953 Skylark's special body sat on a Roadmaster chassis with a wheelbase of 127 inches.

Enhancing the sporty look of the Skylark was a set of 40-spoke, chrome-plated Kelsey-Hayes wire wheels. Its radiused wheel openings not only helped show off the glittering wheels, but also the wheelwells, which were painted a contrasting color. Sweeping over the wheel openings was a "rapier-styled sweepspear" molding unique to this model. The sweepspear would soon become a tradition appearing in one form or another on Buick's cars into the 1960s. Its shape helped to highlight the fender line that flowed into the door and the hopped-up quarters.

Standard equipment for the Skylark, other than the wire wheels, included tinted glass, whitewall tires, leather upholstery with narrow pleats, special carpeting, foot-controlled signal-seeking Selectronic radio, tinted glass, heater, power brakes, steering, seat, windows, antenna, and top (which was of synthetic Orlon), plus the 188-hp 322 4-barrel V-8 and the Twin-Turbine Dynaflow transmission. Furthermore, the owner's signature was sealed into the Lucite steering wheel hub. With a price tag of $5,000, the special model was priced nearly $1,500 more than a Roadmaster convertible and about $700 more than a Cadillac Series Sixty Special.

Buick Engineering in Flint built one or perhaps two prototype 1953 Skylark hardtops. However, the roofline combined with the dipped beltline appeared awkward. No production versions were forthcoming.

The 1954 Skylark was based upon the revived Century, which had been last produced in the war-shortened 1942 model year. Buick's Century combined the relatively light weight of the Buick Special with the highest output engine available (200 hp), which was standard equipment for the Roadmaster. The lightweight body combined with a high-performance engine was a concept that would emerge in the 1960s as the muscle car.

The heavily restyled and distinctive Skylark was given body panels unique to the model. These included deeply scooped wheel openings, which in some cases had their inner surfaces painted a contrasting color, unique quarter panels with chrome-plated, bolt-on fins doubling as taillight housings, and a sloping deck decorated with a set of twin ridges running lengthwise. The special rear end styling was very similar to that of the 1954 Buick Wildcat II dream car on display at that year's GM Motorama. Unlike the prior model year, the new Skylark had a wraparound windshield, too, which was standard issue on the 1954 Buick line.

Other than the Roadmaster engine, the Skylark came with leather upholstery with a unique embossed square pattern and power accessories, as well as the 40-spoke wire wheels used for 1953. All Buick models this year received an updated instrument panel patterned after that of the 1953 Buick Wildcat I. It was revised to include the "Redliner" speedometer, although only on the Super and Roadmaster series.

Despite a nearly $650 price cut, only 836 of the 1954 Skylarks were built, about half as many as the 1953 version. Its $4,355 list price was almost as costly as a Cadillac Series 62 convertible. The special model was discontinued afterward, even though a 1955 version had been on

Also part of the Skylark's appeal was a special interior with a unique appliqué across the instrument panel that wrapped along the door panels. Full leather upholstery was included in the $5,000 price.

The Skylark continued to be offered for 1954. It was distinguished by elongated wheel openings with inner fenders sometimes painted a contrasting color as well as styling in back patterned after that of the 1954 Buick Wildcat dream car.

the drawing board. However, the Skylark was probably doomed anyway as General Motors learned price mattered to Buick buyers, but not so much to Cadillac buyers.

Eldorado

From the day the Eldorado became available for sale, it was one of the grandest possessions of status-seeking individuals. Its name was synonymous with wealth due to the centuries-old tale of the lost city of gold. It represented America's most expensive production car at the time and was the flagship of Cadillac's luxurious fleet. Of course most people could not afford this model, but it drew attention to Cadillac dealerships filled with very prestigious Coupe de Villes and Series 62 sedans, which sold very well. Cadillac's cars ruled the luxury car market, and the Eldorado represented automotive elegance taken to a higher level.

The first Cadillac Eldorado was a prototype built for display on the 1952 show circuit (and was actually the El Dorado, two words). Cadillac presented the production version of the Eldorado at the 1953 General Motors Motorama. The first production Eldorado, painted Artisan Ochre, premiered at the GM Motorama's opening show at the Waldorf-Astoria in January, while another painted Azure Blue was displayed on a five-car platform in the Waldorf-Astoria's grand ballroom.

The virtually hand-built Eldorado featured a wraparound windshield, Darrin dip beltline, chrome-plated wire wheels, padded dash, special leather upholstery, and a white or black Orlon (a shiny synthetic fiber) convertible top that, when down, was completely concealed underneath a nearly flush-fitting cover. Only the drivetrain, front fenders, quarter panels, deck lid, and floor pan were shared with the other Cadillacs in the lineup. Like its Oldsmobile counterpart, the Fiesta, even the dashboard was different so as to fit the dogleg created as a result of the wraparound windshield. By the way, the Eldorado's windshield did not interchange with that of the Fiesta, thus making it a unique component of the Eldorado. The special-bodied cars were lower than the regular Series 62 convertible; road clearance and overall height was 1 inch and 3 inches less, respectively. Extensive use of lead was required in building these cars and no two were exactly alike, a consequence of handmade modifications.

Standard equipment for the limited-production Eldorado also included Hydra-Matic transmission, power windows and seat, power steering, heater, wide whitewall tires, fog lights, signal-seeking pre-selector radio, windshield washer, oil filter, license plate frame, and outside rearview mirror. Incidentally, a fire at GM's Hydra-Matic transmission plant in August 1953 resulted in the top-of-the-line Eldorado and Series 75 limousine receiving priority for the Hydra-Matic, while other automatic transmission-equipped Cadillacs received Buick's Twin-Turbine Dynaflow.

Very few options and accessories were needed for the well-equipped 1953 Eldorado. "E-Z-Eye" tinted glass and the "Autronic-Eye" automatic headlight dimmer were the only factory-installed options. An Eldorado-specific spotlight kit and door-edge guards were accessories offered

This fully restored Azure Blue 1953 Cadillac Eldorado is one of only 532 built for the model year. Its ultra-high price (reportedly $7,750 but most were likely sold for less) was the result of hand-built modifications to the Series 62 convertible from which they were built. Revisions included a reshaped cowl and dash to accept the wraparound windshield. Azure Blue was one of only four colors initially offered for the Eldorado.

Another of the many modifications that comprised an Eldorado was the installation of a flush-fitting lid to hide the power-operated Orlon convertible top. Top colors were either white or black.

Cadillac's Eldorado for 1953 had many elegant refinements, such as a ripple-pattern door-sill plates, black-lined headliner for the convertible top, and special door panels.

by the dealer. Today, some 1953 Eldorados are equipped with a Continental kit, but this was not offered as a factory option or dealer accessory. Air-conditioning was not available on Eldorado convertibles until 1956, though a few 1953 Eldorados have been retrofitted with A/C.

Not available at the time was power brakes. However, a power brake installation kit (part number 146 2266) for retrofit became available for the 1953 Eldorado and other Cadillacs (1950–1953) the following model year.

List price for the 1953 Eldorado is often quoted as having been $7,750, although there seems to be no surviving dealer-to-customer invoice to support the claimed figure. For 1953, only 532 Eldorados were built, so one could argue these were prototypes of the 1954 Eldorado. The latter shared all of its body components with other Cadillacs, making it much less costly to build, thus substantially lowering its retail price. Today, the exclusivity of the 1953 Eldorado makes it one of the most desired and valuable cars of the 1950s. Examples rated in condition number one or two sell well into the six-figure dollar range. After 1953, the Eldorado shared its body components with the lower series Cadillacs all the way through 1966, after which it acquired its own body design, as well as front-wheel drive.

The Eldorado Brougham: Supreme Standard

Competition is said to bring out the best in rivals. The adage must be true because from the moment Henry Leland incorporated Cadillac over a century ago, the company has always sought to produce cars that were ahead of its contemporaries. Many consider Cadillac's smooth running and powerful V-16 engines, produced throughout the 1930s, as the best prewar automobile engines in the world. In 1947, Cadillac outsold Packard, a leader in the luxury car field, for the first time since 1934 and continued to do so until Packard's demise. Then, of course, there was the tail fin age begun by the 1948 Cadillac, followed the next year by the advanced overhead-valve V-8, which provided significantly greater performance and fuel economy than the engine it replaced.

Great styling and an advanced V-8 helped Cadillac maintain a sizable lead over its rivals, which included Lincoln and Imperial. Its success allowed for the opportunity to offer the expensive image-building car, the Eldorado, for 1953. The elegance bar was set even higher four years later with the limited-production Eldorado Brougham.

Like the name "Eldorado," the label "Brougham" has its origins in the past. The term came from the days of the horse-drawn carriage with the driver seated outside in front. It is a name that is also associated with 18th and 19th Century England; Henry Brougham, a political figure in that country in the 1800s, is credited with the design of the aforementioned carriage.

A brushed stainless steel top was exclusive to the 1957 and 1958 (shown) Eldorado Brougham. (Photo Courtesy Angelo Van Bogart)

1952 Cadillac El Dorado Prototype

During the 1952 auto show circuit, General Motors displayed a prototype of the limited-production 1953 Eldorado. The press release about the car issued on Jan. 22, 1952, said, "The motorist who shares the craftsman's pleasure in exquisite handicraft will instantly find kinship with Cadillac's fabulous ELDORADO. This exotic convertible dramatically blends two great fields of human endeavor. In an expression of the ageless arts, ELDORADO reveals a treatment of gold on a gleaming, ivory-like surface. A sports car in character, the long, low body of the ELDORADO is finished in a dazzling, white lacquer. Bright, East Indian, Pepper Red leather heightens the enchanting effect of the artistic interior. The seatbacks are piped in modern horseshoe pattern with door inserts of the same theme. Crash pad and instrument board top are of an expanded Royalite skin, perfectly matching the leather. The steering wheel carries . . . its covering of hand sewn, East Indian, Pepper Red leather, which is baseball stitched on the back. The ELDORADO's instrument board inserts, door moldings and kick strips are of gold plated, ripple patterned material."

The claim of the Eldorado being a "sports car

For 1952, Cadillac celebrated its golden anniversary with the construction of a couple of show cars, one of which was the El Dorado. The El Dorado went into production on a limited basis the following year, although as the "Eldorado." This photo shows the prototype 1952 version; the date and location are unknown. (Photo Courtesy Jim Jordan)

in character" was certainly a stretch, even when one considers that at the time GM officials did not fully grasp what a true sports car was, as was soon revealed by the Corvette, which went into production the same model year as the Eldorado.

In the immediate years prior to the commencement of production of the Eldorado Brougham, the head of GM Styling, Harley Earl, was discovering through the traveling auto show, the GM Motorama (see Chapter Eight), what Cadillac buyers expected to receive when they purchased a Cadillac. Visitors to the Motorama clearly showed a preference for the four-door sedans, Orleans (1953) and Park Avenue (1954), which revealed to Harley Earl that Cadillac was headed in the right direction for a flagship model. These cars led to the concept and proposal of the Eldorado Brougham in mid-1954. Earl was quoted as saying the Brougham concept "was created with the intent of capturing the appeal of those who wanted the finest product, whether it be their home, clothing, jewelry, or their car."

The next prototype in the series leading to the production of the Brougham was another four-door pillarless sedan, the 1955 Eldorado Brougham, with design influences from the 1954 Park Avenue, including an egg-crate grille and a brushed aluminum roof. It was also low in height, standing only 54 inches high. In front were quad headlights, which were at the time not a legal setup in many states. The laws in those states were in the process of being changed by the time production of the Brougham became available.

Reportedly, initial discussions between Earl and Cadillac's general manager, Don Ahrens, resulted in a rejection of the Eldorado Brougham for production due to cost considerations, at least for a while. However, when word spread of Ford Motor Company's plans to create the Continental division to produce its version of the ultimate luxury car, the Mark II, the issue of cost was no longer paramount. During this time, those in charge at Ford Motor Company were seriously attempting to close the sales gap between Lincoln and Cadillac. One facet of its plan to establish Ford as a leader in the luxury car market was the creation of the Continental division. General Motors could not allow Cadillac's status as the "Standard of the World" to be challenged. The prototype 1957 Eldorado Brougham was completed in mid-1955 and then displayed at the Paris Salon and throughout the 1956 GM Motorama tour. Additional tweaks to the car resulted in a grand luxury automobile to offer to Cadillac buyers who desired and could afford the best car money could buy in 1957.

On March 18, 1957, General Motors began releasing Broughams to the dealers. The announced list price was a stratospheric $13,074, which was far more than the original target of $8,500. For the list price of the Eldorado Brougham, one could have bought a new two-door hardtop from nearly all of GM's auto divisions; that amount of money would have bought a Cadillac Series 62 ($4,609), Buick Series 40 Riviera ($2,204), Oldsmobile Rocket 88 Holiday ($2,854), as well as a Pontiac Chieftain Catalina ($2,529) and such a buyer would have still had about $800 to make a down payment on a new Chevrolet. Also notable is that the Brougham's price was nearly $400 more than a 1957 Rolls Royce Silver Cloud.

What made the Brougham so expensive? One reason was that its body panels did not interchange with anything else in the Cadillac lineup. Moreover, the standard equipment list included nearly everything available: 325-hp, 365 V-8 with dual 4-barrel carburetors, Hydra-Matic transmission, air-conditioning, individual front and rear heating systems with under seat blowers, six-way power seat with memory settings, power windows, power ventipanes, automatic power door locks, power deck lid, air suspension, automatic headlight dimmer, drum-dial clock, polarized sun visors, all-transistor AM radio with front and rear speakers and automatic antenna, quadruple horns, wide oval narrow band whitewall tires, forged aluminum wheels, fully carpeted trunk, a brushed stainless-steel roof, and automatic engine restart should the engine quit running due to a minor problem.

Cadillac's flagship Eldorado Brougham continued into 1958 virtually unchanged. This one was originally owned by actor-comedian Bob Hope and is now part of the collection of Steve Plunkett. Just 304 Eldorado Broughams were built for this model year. Its special body panels, which did not interchange with Cadillac's other models, and extensive standard equipment resulted in its stratospheric price of more than $13,000, thus explaining the low production figure. (Photo Courtesy Wayne Ellwood)

Buyers were offered in excess of 45 interior combinations with lambskin or Karakul carpeting and 15 exterior colors. Additionally, inside the glove box were two compartments containing several items included as standard equipment: a fold-out shelf to support six magnetic tumblers (which when not in use were stored within a two-piece screw-together plastic case and secured with a leather strap), a plastic case for one pack of cigarettes, a tissue dispenser, and a cosmetic case with two compartments, with the front of the case covered in color-coordinated leather.

The front compartment contained a mirror, lipstick holder, and a powder puff, as well as a place to hold one nickel for the parking meter; the back compartment was for loose cigarettes. The rear fold-down armrest was divided into sections to hold several other useful items: a beveled mirror, perfume atomizer with a one-ounce volume of Arpége Extract de Lanvin, Cross pencil, and a color-coordinated leather-covered notepad. An early GM press release stated men's cologne would also be included, but evidently that feature was deleted at the last minute.

One other feature offered to the Brougham buyer was mentioned in the factory service manual: on the back of the first page of this manual is the advisement to Cadillac's service personnel that, "Brougham service should receive priority over all other service assignments."

Originally, power disc brakes, Hydra-Matic transaxle, and fuel injection were to be included as standard equipment for the Brougham, but with the costs escalating far beyond expectations, these features were wisely eliminated. One more item that should have been dropped from the list of gadgets was the air suspension, which proved troublesome because of so many potential leak points. Still it was the first of its kind to go into production (although Citroën had a hydro-pneumatic suspension in production a bit earlier). According to a report in the September 1957 issue of *Modern Motor* the leveling controls were so sensitive that they went into action the moment a door was opened. The setup was intended to provide a constant ride height even when fully loaded and to give the smoothest possible ride; obviously highly desirable qualities for the finest car money could buy. Unfortunately, the sophisticated system did not significantly improve the ride qualities beyond those of a steel coil spring to justify its expense and lack of reliability.

Production for the ultra-sophisticated Cadillac totaled just 400 units in 1957 and another 304 were constructed for 1958. Differences between the 1957 and 1958 models were minor and, in fact, the serial numbers continued consecutively throughout the two-year run of this design, thus they were numbered from 1 to 704. However, General Motors retained Brougham number two for engineering tests of a fuel-injection setup. When General Motors completed its testing, the car's repainted body was mounted on a 1958 chassis and received the new designation of car number 475.

The market for such an expensive car was a small one as Cadillac and Continental managers soon learned. Of course the market size was never the point anyway. Image was the reason for building the Eldorado Brougham. The Lincoln division of Ford absorbed the Continental division, and the costly Mark II was dropped. Cadillac continued with the Eldorado Brougham model for two more years but quit building the bodies in Detroit; instead, it contracted with Pinin Farina to construct the special body. Only a total of 200 Pinin Farina Broughams were built for the 1959 to 1960 model years, after which the Eldorado Brougham faded into the past. Today, they are among the most prized models by collectors of Cadillacs of this era.

Chevrolet and GMC Pickups: Passenger Car Styling

Technically, the first passenger car–styled trucks were the sedan delivery type, which shared a passenger car chassis and front sheet metal. Although car-based, these vehicles were classified as trucks.

In terms of Chevrolet and GMC *pickup* trucks, passenger car influence did not come along until the redesigned 1954s. The following year an even more stylish set of pickups went into production: one for Chevrolet named Cameo (or sometimes referenced as Cameo Carrier), and the other, the GMC Suburban Carrier. Each had its bed and tailgate constructed of fiberglass, along with a chrome molding to hide as much as possible the gap between the bed and cab. The sides of the bed fit flush with the cab. As originally envisioned by designer Chuck Jordan, the cab and bed would have been constructed as one piece. However, body flex issues prevented that arrangement. Another feature, a first for pickup trucks, was the wraparound windshield.

Fins never made it to GM's pickups, but they were considered as shown by this mid-1956 photo of a clay mockup named "Daytona."

Although the vehicles were very similar to each other, there were notable differences. The GMC version was about 4½ inches longer, had a different grille with large GMC lettering, and used either the GMC 248-ci 6-cylinder or the Pontiac V-8 for power rather than Chevrolet's straight-6 or V-8. Additionally, there was extra bright work on the instrument panel for the GMC version.

In 1955, Chevrolet's Task Force Trucks had a new model added to the lineup, the Cameo. It was a stylish pickup with a wraparound windshield and a fiberglass bed that fit flush with the cab. GMC also offered a similar pickup, dubbed as the Suburban Carrier. Shown is a restored 1956 GMC Suburban Carrier with the extra-cost exterior sun visor.

Chapter Seven Tail Fins, Chrome, Gadgets and More!

Stylist Charles "Chuck" Jordan began working for General Motors in 1949. His career was briefly interrupted by military service. During that time he continued to create renderings such as this one illustrating a one-piece cab and bed. Upon his return to General Motors he worked in the truck studio where he created the Cameo and Suburban Carrier pickups before moving on to passenger car design and ultimately GM's fourth head of Design.

The 1955 Cameo pickups were finished in Bombay Ivory with red accents; the GMC was offered in other colors. Upholstery was upgraded over that of standard pickups, more like that of the 1954 Bel Air. More befitting the sportier look of the Cameo and Suburban Carrier were bright two-tone paint schemes in 1956. Eight combinations were available, with the more spectacular being Cardinal Red over Sand Beige, Golden Yellow over Jet Black, Bombay Ivory over Cardinal Red, or as in the case of the featured vehicles, Bombay Ivory over Indian Turquoise.

Besides optional V-8 power and two-tone paint, there were other amenities. Available at extra cost were power steering, power brakes, and Hydra-Matic automatic transmission.

As stylish as the Cameo and Suburban Carrier trucks were, they did not sell in high numbers. The Cameo was intended as a low-volume seller, but the Suburban Carrier was considered as a promotional vehicle to help build traffic to showrooms. With a price about 30 percent higher than a regular Chevrolet pickup, low sales were guaranteed. The Cameo and Suburban Carrier were discontinued after 1958. Chevy and GMC Fleetside pickups offered a flush-fitting steel bed, which took away some "thunder" from these special models.

The Chevrolet Cameo light-duty pickup returned for 1957. Cardinal Red and Bombay Ivory was one of several paint color schemes offered for the stylish pickup.

THE GM MOTORAMA

CHAPTER 8

"These men are the stylists of the vast General Motors Corporation. With Mr. Earl, the corporation's key 'man of the future,' they are the most restless of executives. Discontent with virtually everything that smatters of the 'present' has turned them into what the world is pleased to call 'dreamers.'"

– Christian Science Monitor, *April 18, 1956*

During the mid-20th Century, General Motors staged an elaborate automobile show largely remembered today for its spectacular dream cars. The first two were dubbed Transportation Unlimited (1949) and Mid-Century Motorama (1950); subsequent shows were titled The GM Motorama. The moniker, "Motorama," probably did not originate with General Motors and was likely a name derived from the British "Motor Show" in which various "motor cars" were displayed. Furthermore, the letters spelling "ama" translates into "spectacle."

The GM shows held consecutively from 1953 to 1956 are the most remembered because of the numerous "dream cars" (concept cars in today's vernacular) shown at these shows. The GM Motorama was an outgrowth of the prewar "Industrialist Luncheons" held at the Waldorf-Astoria and of other auto shows sponsored by General Motors.

Harley Earl developed the concept of the GM Motorama, which some insiders called, "Harley Earl's circus." Earl had been pushing General Motors for years to display more than just GM's production cars at the auto shows in which the company participated, and he finally convinced management to go along with an idea. The all-GM show was created to promote the products of

A car from each of GM's passenger car divisions occupied a five-car platform at the 1955 GM Motorama. At bottom center is the Cadillac Celebrity show car, which was painted bright red and had a matching vinyl top. (Photo Courtesy GM Media Archive)

The 1953 Cadillac LeMans was quite a departure from what Cadillac owners expected. This sporty, three-passenger convertible possibly tested the market for a Cadillac with sports car attributes. It definitely forecasted the frontal design of the 1954 Cadillacs. Inspiration for the LeMans may have originated with a one-off, 1952 Cadillac Custom Convertible that Harley Earl had built for friend and co-worker Harold R. Boyer. Boyer was the plant manager of Cadillac Motor Car Division's Cleveland tank plant. (Photo Courtesy GM Media Archive)

the corporation, which included not only automobiles from Cadillac, Buick, Oldsmobile, Pontiac, Chevrolet, and GMC, but also its auto parts and non-automotive divisions. More notably, it featured the dream cars to test public reaction to new ideas. These cars also exposed the public to advanced concepts, a relatively simple but effective way to introduce features that would definitely or potentially be found on automobiles in the near and distant future. Earl knew the public did not respond well to too much change too soon, but he knew people could, and would, regard changes as desirable by the time they appeared on production cars. In that way, GM's Motorama prepared the public for what was to come. GM's traveling extravaganza also spotlighted the company's varied products through interactive exhibits, orchestras, and troupes of dancers who performed at half-hour intervals, amid lavish décor. It was an elaborate spectacle absolutely worthy of an "ama" title.

General Motors spent a small fortune to bring its show to high-population cities across the United States. In the beginning, the GM Motorama was an approximately $5 million production. The costs included the dream cars such as the Buick Wildcat and Cadillac LeMans, which cost six figures to design and build. In addition, the show required transportation of all the displays to five or six major cities, buying local advertising, adding special décor stage shows, and so on. No admission was charged, which would have helped cover or at least reduce the cost of the exhibition. Of course, back then General Motors could afford such expenditures. By 1955, the company operated 119 plants in 65 communities in 19 states, 6 plants in Canada, manufacturing facilities in 18 foreign countries, and had a net income of more than $1 billion, thus becoming the first company in the auto industry to top that figure. The company also had a 50 percent market share. General Motors had clearly become a giant since it was organized in 1908.

The GM Motorama was said to be "GM's top salesman, its best prognosticator and barometer of business." Sales soared for 1953 and continued to climb during most of the Motorama years. An example of its impact is illustrated by a sale to an Iowa resident, who, while visiting relatives in Miami, attended the GM Motorama, then immediately purchased a new GM car when he returned home. Enormous orders for new cars at each venue more than offset the cost, at least for a while. However, the expenses increased yearly and by 1956 were twice the initial figure.

In Miami, the large Dinner Key Auditorium provided three times the space of the Waldorf-Astoria. General Motors took advantage of the additional space by displaying many more cars and other exhibits. The larger show required 300 carpenters, 200 exhibit demonstrators, 100 ushers, 35 guards, and 30 members of GM's public relations department. Another 60 dancers, singers, musicians, and models were part of the cast of the stage shows. GM of Canada even staged a limited Motorama display at the Canadian National Exhibition in the early 1950s and later an exhibition mirroring that of the type held in the United States.

More than 2.3 million people attended the 1956 GM Motorama in the five cities it visited, making it the most successful of all. As reported in the May 1956 issue of *Auto Age*, General Motors received $1.3 million in orders for its cars at the New York City showing alone. Despite this, the 1956 tour was the last of its kind; the Firebird III was the only dream car exhibited for the 1959 and 1961 shows in the United States.

Eventually, the increasingly high cost of the Motorama and the popularity of television helped put an end to the grand spectacle. Management found that, with more and more people owning a TV set, advertising through television was more cost effective. Additionally, GM's ideas were essentially being given away to its competitors for free. Anyone, including stylists from Ford Motor Company and Chrysler Corporation, could and did attend the GM Motorama.

The late Chuck Jordan, who began his career at General Motors in 1949 and headed the design of two GM Motorama vehicles, explained the sudden departure of the GM Motorama: "After the 1956 Motorama, things changed. Because of continually increasing costs and new corporate marketing opportunities, the 1957 Motorama was canceled. GM Styling's annual crop of dream cars also came to an end because, as the style leader, General Motors was giving away too many valuable design ideas to our competitors. GM Styling's program of concept cars continued, but now in secret behind locked doors. One fact was certain: Our Motorama experience had taught us the importance of creativity and the value of advance design as we charged ahead.

"The Motorama produced many benefits for General Motors, not the least of which was increased sales and a brighter image. To GM Styling it was a priceless experience. In my 43 years at GM Design, I have never known a time that was more exciting, more creative, and more productive than the Motorama years. I believe the design of our Motorama cars had a profound influence on America's golden era of automobile design of the 1950s and 1960s."

Another contributing factor to the demise of GM's auto show was that design work for multiple concept cars did take away from efforts toward production cars. There was only so much manpower available to go around. Company president Harlow Curtice undoubtedly noticed the matter and probably considered it in making the decision to cancel the 1957 show tour. (An in-depth account of the cars of the GM Motorama can be found in my book, *Motorama: GM's Legendary Show and Concept Cars*, published by CarTech Books.)

General Motors' Traveling Auto Show

GM's Transportation Unlimited of 1949 and Mid-Century Motorama of 1950 featured a number of production cars wearing non-production paint and upholstery; the former was used to exhibit prototype two-door hardtop models for Cadillac, Buick, Oldsmobile, Pontiac, and Chevrolet. Cadillac's Coupe de Ville, Buick's Roadmaster Riviera, and Oldsmobile's Holiday Ninety-Eight two-door hardtops went into production later that year, while the remainder, Pontiac's Catalina and Chevrolet's Bel Air, debuted the following model year. Three modified Cadillacs also shown were a Western-themed Series 62

Among the many displays at General Motors' 1949 Transportation Unlimited auto show was this 1949 Chevrolet Bel Air two-door hardtop prototype. The Bel Air became available the following model year, as did a two-door hardtop for Pontiac dubbed Catalina. (Photo Courtesy GM Media Archive)

convertible named El Rancho and two altered Fleetwood Sixty Specials dubbed Caribbean and Embassy, both fitted with antiqued silver hardware and special upholstery. As reported in the February 1949 issue of *General Motors World*, Cadillac described its special Cadillac show cars as "sleek sybaritic specimens of automotive splendor."

The prototype two-toned Coupe de Ville differed from what actually went into production later. It was built on the Fleetwood's 133-inch wheelbase chassis and had hydraulically operated windows, a simulated rear fender air scoop, a 1950-style Series 75 backlight, a one-piece curved windshield, short-wave telephone, and a pullout desk. Of the four show cars, only the Coupe de Ville prototype is known to still exist.

The New York show was a major success. According to an article published in the January 21, 1949, edition of the *New York Times*, "New York's unabated craving for new cars and insatiable curiosity as to what makes the automotive wheels go around were emphasized yesterday by the 65,000 visitors attending the opening session of the General Motors exposition 'Transportation Unlimited' at the Waldorf-Astoria Hotel.

"Show officials estimated that one out of every three who inspected the automobiles on display wished to purchase at once and take delivery at the same time. On receiving the sad tidings that they could place orders with dealers and hope for the best, at least 80 percent of those who applied turned away with long faces." Such results were typical of the GM's special auto show over the years. After the show at the Waldorf, Transportation Unlimited went on to Detroit.

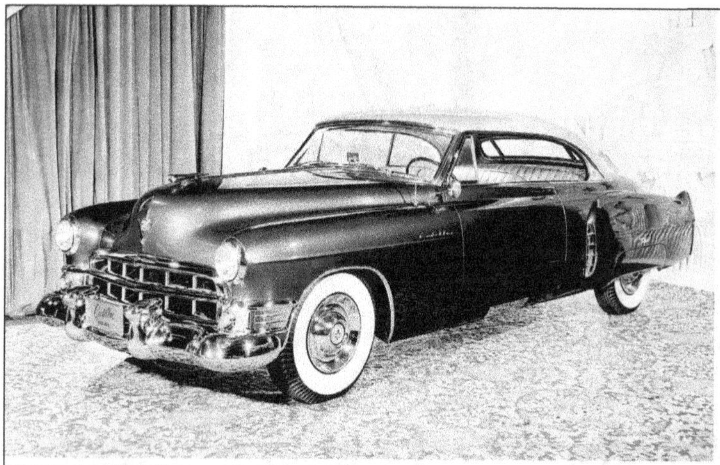

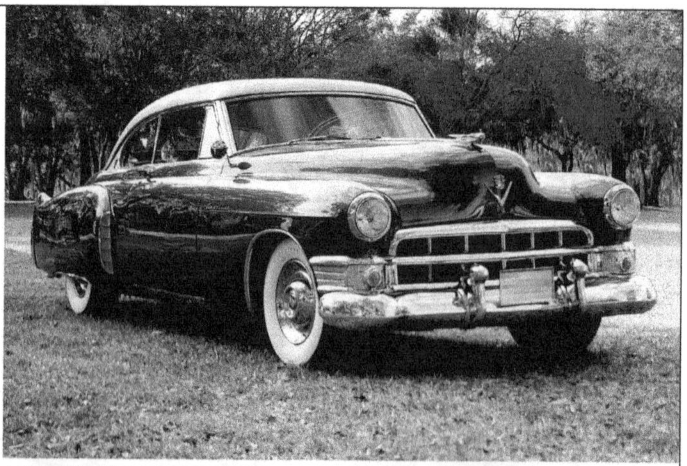

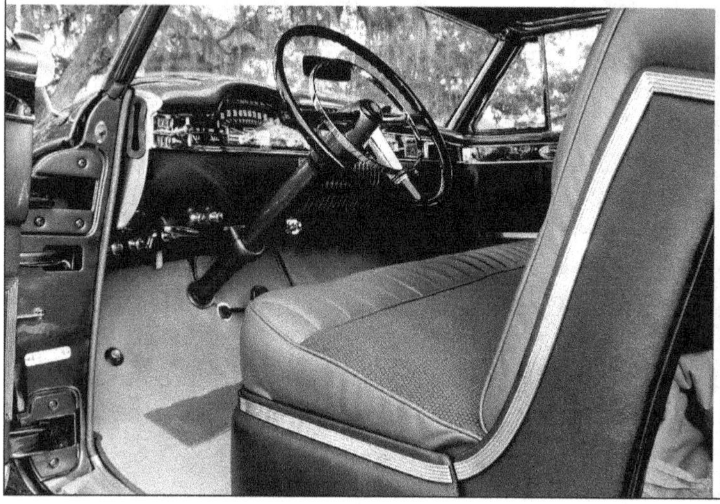

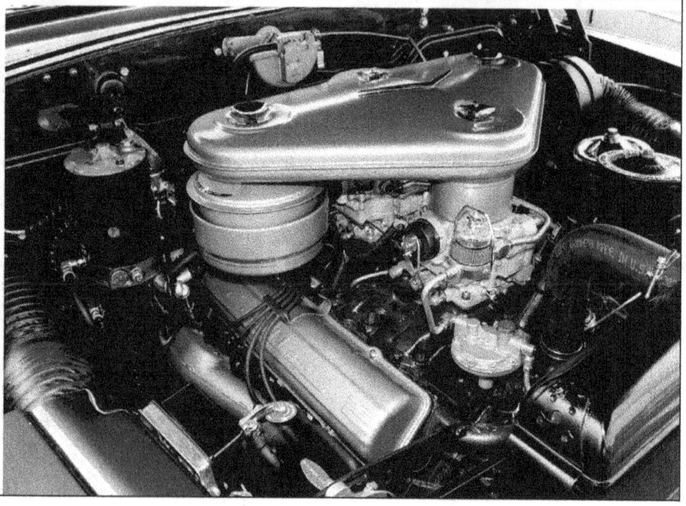

Page Six THE OLDSMOBILE NEWS February 1950

320,000 See Oldsmobile at GM New York Show

Catharine Ames (upper left) watches the inner workings of a "Rocket" engine. Mary Ashworth (upper right) admires the eye-catching "Palm Beach" Holiday "98". Gen. Lucius Clay (center, left) chats with General Manager S. E. Skinner. Irene Rich (center) tries out the Palm Beach. Bette Adams (center, right) reclines on the rich upholstery, Irish linen nylon with alligator.

Interested spectators (above) hear a talk on the operation of the "Rocket" engine. A curved dash Oldsmobile (right) replaces the horse in stage presentation.

Phyllis Nelson (above) opens the door of the "Palm Beach" to show the green alligator leather and cane mesh trim in the door panel. Floor mat is woven flax.

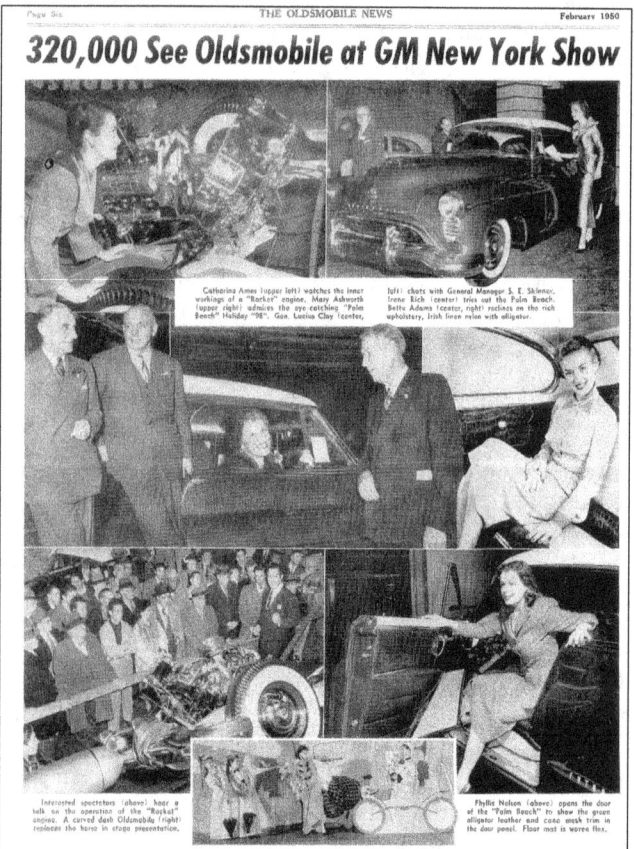

The 1949 Cadillac Coupe de Ville prototype was shown at that year's Transportation Unlimited auto show produced by General Motors. It differed from the production version released some months later in having the longer wheelbase of the Fleetwood Sixty Special. Well-known Cadillac collector Steve Plunkett restored this car a few years ago. (Photos By David Temple, Courtesy GM Media Archive)

For the 1950 Mid-Century Motorama held only at the Waldorf-Astoria, an Oldsmobile Holiday Ninety-Eight, rechristened as the Palm Beach, was painted Cabana Sand over Surf Green and upholstered in green alligator leather with a contrasting fine cane mesh fabric. There were other non-standard cars shown, too. Most remembered of them, though, is the Cadillac Debutante featuring Tawny Buff Yellow paint, 24-carat gold interior trim, and leopard skin upholstery.

With the outbreak of the Korean War, the Motorama was put on hold; there was no justification for trying to push

***GM Styling upgraded a 1950 Oldsmobile Holiday 98 with alligator hide and special nylon fabric. It drew the attention of numerous VIPs at the preview night for GM's Mid-Century Motorama, as reported by the February 1950 issue of the internal publication,* The Oldsmobile News.**

The Cars of Harley Earl

The 1950 Cadillac Debutante Series 62 convertible was among the major attractions of GM's Mid-Century Motorama. It was painted Tawny Yellow Buff with a pearl luster effect achieved by using miniature moon-shaped fish scales that were sprayed over the base paint. The fine scales were obtained through a special process of dissolving large fish scales, leaving only the tiny pearl essence. (Photo Courtesy GM Media Archive)

sales beyond what wartime materials (steel, nickel, copper, etc.) restrictions could allow. However, as the 1953 model year approached, General Motors was ready and able to go on the road again with a much larger show.

Motorama: 1953

When the 1953 model year arrived, sales of GM's automobiles had been on a two-year decline. The GM Motorama with its half-dozen dream cars, along with a glittering array of production models, was expected to be one way to boost sales.

On January 17, 1953, General Motors unveiled to the general public at the Waldorf-Astoria six new dream cars, one of which (the Corvette) entered production sooner than planned. (The Corvette is detailed in Chapter Five.) Also displayed were two older dream cars, the 1951 Buick XP-300 and the 1953 GM Le Sabre (both detailed in Chapter Four). The Le Sabre had a fresh look after some

Building the Dream Cars: An Eyewitness Account

Former GM engineer Ken Pickering was involved in developing convertible top mechanisms for some of GM's dream cars for the Motorama shows. About the cars he said, "The Motorama cars were absolutely beautiful automobiles and most were running models, and many others could be made roadworthy with a little work. All of this was possible because during the design phase, a small group of dedicated engineers and shop personnel worked with the studio to bring these models to reality.

"The Body Development Studio (BDS) did the basic packaging and established the 'hard points' [fixed criteria that regulates the rest of the design process] for the studio. Earl was a strong participant in this phase as the work in the BDS was a high priority for him.

"But in addition to locating the driver with these 'hard points,' BDS and Advance Engineering also provided the studio with the entire packaging for the vehicle, including the total engine configuration and drivetrain. They also developed the front hinge pillar limit lines (a little-understood constraint when doing different production model door skins), rocker panel sections, windshield and center pillar sections as well as door glass drops. In other words, they make the building of the car possible.

"Prior to moving to the Tech Center, the Wood and Metal Shops were housed on the eighth floor of the Argonaut Building on West Milwaukee Street. Plaster, Plastic, Paint, and Trim were in the old Fisher Plant 8 about one mile away. All were later consolidated when we moved into the GM Design Building at the Tech Center.

"The men who worked in these shops were gifted world-class craftsmen and could build anything in a very short time. It was absolutely amazing that these Motorama cars were fabricated in such detail in a matter of a few months or sometimes just weeks. For designers, there is always a better solution tomorrow, and it was extremely difficult to get HJE [Harley J. Earl] and his designers to 'freeze' the clay.

"As the Motorama days approached, usually about six weeks before the Waldorf opening, the shops [consisting of Wood, Metal, Plaster, Plastic, Paint, Trim, and the Sculpture Studio] went on extended-hour shifts beyond their 'normal' nine hours. This was when Earl brought in Al Greene, the noted Detroit restaurateur, to cater every meal for the shops and everyone else who was working overtime. Al Greene served outstanding fare.

"When the Waldorf show preview was scheduled, Earl arranged for some of us and our wives to travel to New York City on the train to attend, all expenses paid for the four-day trip. The ladies loved it, and it was Earl's way of 'payback' for all the long hours we had worked on the cars there."

Cadillac was well represented at the 1953 GM Motorama. This scene from the show in Kansas City includes the new Eldorado (on turntable), the fiberglass-bodied LeMans dream car (background on turntable), and a couple of regular production Cadillacs each fitted with a vinyl top.

The 1951 Buick XP-300 was included in the 1953 GM Motorama six-city tour. This scene is from Fair Park in Dallas, Texas, the fifth venue of the traveling exhibition.

mild upgrades. The remaining cars were the Pontiac Parisienne (sometimes called La Parisienne), Oldsmobile Starfire, Buick Wildcat, Cadillac Orleans, and Cadillac LeMans. Such names alone must have been enough to stir interest in attending the special auto show. All but two of these cars were built of fiberglass; the two exceptions were built from production vehicles, which of course were fabricated in steel.

Other than the Corvette, none of these were intended for production, a fact emphasized in GM press releases, although officials noted that if there was sufficient interest in any of these dream cars, they could enter production. The one-week shows went on to Miami (February), Los Angeles (April), San Francisco (early May), Dallas (mid-May), and Kansas City (June). (Dallas and Kansas City were dropped from future tours after 1953. Chicago was a venue for 1954, and Boston was added for the 1955, 1956, and 1959 tours.) The display of new GM automobiles, mildly modified production vehicles, and dream cars, along with Broadway-style stage shows, attracted 1.5 million visitors to the tour in 1953.

American Sports Car Prototype

The Polo White sports car revolving slowly on its turntable fascinated a lot of attendees of the GM Motorama, so much so it was hurriedly rushed into production by the end of June. The show prototype gave an accurate preview of the production version. Even though it had the right looks for a sports car, it did not have the power to match.

Parisienne: Retro Design

The Parisienne, a design exercise meant to impress potential Pontiac buyers, although not considered for production, brought an opulent aura to an otherwise relatively pedestrian car. A 1953 Chieftain

The 1953 Corvette prototype show car impressed many attendees at the GM Motorama. Reaction was so strong that production was pushed ahead many months from the planned 1954 model year.

A production Chieftain was used to create the 1953 Pontiac Parisienne. Overall height of the car was 56 inches, which represented a decrease of a full 7 inches from a stock Pontiac. To achieve the lower height, the car did not simply receive a decreased roof height, but also extensive body reconstruction consisting of a sectioned hood, a lowered cowl shaped to accommodate a wraparound windshield, and cut-down front fenders, doors, rear deck and quarters. A fixed landau-styled top made of fiberglass covered the passenger compartment and, of course, there was the open chauffeur's compartment.

was reconstructed into the form of a chauffeured town car. The town car design was similar in concept to the landaulet design, which originated from the days of the horse-drawn carriage, but the town car differed in having a fixed rear roof section as opposed to a folding one. Wealthy owners typically purchased town cars with the open chauffeur's compartment, which could be covered in inclement weather, but the type had given way to fully enclosed limousines. So, the Parisienne offered a nostalgic look back at such an automobile rather than a serious look at the future for General Motors.

The Regal Starfire

The Regal Turquoise six-passenger Oldsmobile Starfire convertible was named after the US Air Force's F-94A Starfire interceptor powered by the J-33 turbojet manufactured by GM's Allison Division. Arthur "Art" Ross, chief of the Oldsmobile Studio, headed the styling effort of this dream car. Its two-tone turquoise and white interior was one of its most important features as it gave a preview of what was to come in the near future. Other styling ideas placed into production (some as early as 1954) included the Starfire's wide-oval-shaped bumper-grille combination, side trim, and beltline dip.

Revolutionary Wildcat

The three-passenger Buick Wildcat I offered a look at stylish and functional concepts. One such idea was "Roto-Static" hubs on the front wheels, wherein the outer wheel revolved around air scoops used to cool the brake drums. However, this concept did not make it into production. Nevertheless, the Wildcat was one of the more predictive concept cars in terms of ideas that actually were to be put into use. Its combination bumper/grille and buffer bombs were similar to what appeared on the 1954 through 1957 Buicks (although without the concave grille). The sweepspear showed up on many Buicks, beginning with those in the mid-1950s. Furthermore, its modest fin design was used on production Buicks in 1954, as was the double-roll dashboard.

Cadillac: Competing Ideas

The two special Cadillacs on display (the Orleans and the LeMans) were quite opposite in concept. The Orleans was essentially the first prototype of what would ultimately become the Eldorado Brougham, an ultra-luxurious and ultra-expensive automobile. It was

The Starfire was painted a stock color from the 1953 Olds color palette, Regal Turquoise. Its "Panoramic" windshield was said to provide "unusual forward visibility . . . permitting the driver to see the top of the right front fender." Other features of the Starfire included power steering, power brakes, and power twin aerials. (Photo Courtesy GM Media Archive)

The 1953 Wildcat I was designed under the supervision of Buick's chief stylist, Ned Nickles, who some years earlier oversaw the design of Buick's first hardtop, the 1949 Riviera. Under the direction of Nickles, the fiberglass three-passenger Wildcat described by General Motors as a "revolutionary sports convertible," showcased many fresh styling and mechanical elements, one of which never entered production: its "Roto-Static" front brake hubs with air scoop. The air scoop drew in air to cool the brakes to reduce fade encountered from repeated stops. It was fixed while the wheel revolved around it. Eventually, more effective means to reduce brake fade were found. (Photo Courtesy GM Media Archive)

a pillarless four-door hardtop with reverse opening rear doors (or expressed using the more common slang term, "suicide doors"). The car was probably built as much for Charles E. Wilson as it was for show purposes. Wilson served as president of General Motors from 1941 until his departure from the company in 1953, after being appointed as Secretary of Defense by the newly elected president of the United States, Dwight Eisenhower. The Orleans drew the interest of those who bought Cadillacs and preferred the hardtop body style but wanted four doors for convenience.

The silver-blue LeMans was named for the 24-hour race held near Paris, France. It showcased something unusual for a car wearing the Cadillac name: sports car attributes. Its fiberglass body was low with an overall height of 51 inches and its wheelbase relatively short at 115 inches.

The LeMans may have tested the market for such a car, for which some projected a demand for up to 5,000 per year. It was not designed as a true sports car but instead some elements of a sports car with the luxury for which Cadillac was known. Indeed, one of GM's press releases about the car stated, "The LeMans represents an ideal of motor car enthusiasts, combining elegance with power." In the end, it did not make production, but its styling forecasted that of the 1954 Cadillac line.

Three limited-production cars made their public debut, too, at this year's GM Motorama: Cadillac Eldorado, Buick Skylark, and Oldsmobile Fiesta (all covered in Chapter Seven).

Motorama 1954: A Large Array of Dream Cars

The 1954 GM Motorama toured five cities this year: New York City, Miami, Los Angeles, San Francisco, and Chicago. It showcased 13 dream cars, which was the largest group ever to be displayed during the Motorama years. These included a turbine-powered car resembling a jet fighter plane, a set of Corvette-based concepts, and some sporty Oldsmobiles.

Corvette Concepts

Two Corvette-based concepts, the Nomad station wagon and a Corvair fastback, offered stunning attractions when they debuted at the Waldorf-Astoria in January 1954. The following month a modified Corvette with a prototype detachable hardtop, roll-up windows, and

The Damascus Steel Gray Cadillac four-door hardtop, which sat 2 inches lower than a standard Coupe de Ville, had its roof covered with champagne-colored Naugahyde. Extensive modifications were required to convert a leftover 1952 Coupe de Ville body shell into the Orleans, including the reshaping of its cowl for the installation of a "Panoramic" windshield. Shortening the coupe's doors was also required, as was the installation of rear doors. The arrangement did away with the standard center pillar post to which front doors were normally latched and to which rear doors were normally hinged. The result was a pillarless four-door hardtop, a concept inspired by a Lancia show car seen by Harley Earl at a European auto show. (Photo Courtesy GM Media Archive)

unique upholstery, along with the Nomad and Corvair, was on exhibit at the Dinner Key Auditorium in Miami.

The Corvette-based Nomad did not go into production, but its roofline was adapted to the Bel Air, resulting in a sporty, two-door station wagon for 1955 through 1957.

The 1954 Corvair offered a look at a closed version of the sports car. Its swept-back roofline ended in a "jet-like exhaust opening," as it was described in a GM press release. The fastback body style had fallen out of favor with car buyers a few years earlier, but for a sports car it was definitely viable. Other than its fastback roofline, the Corvair's other features included engine compartment heat vents integrated into twin bulges on the hood, as well as a ventilation system composed of a stack of three small, rectangular intake vents on the fenders and exhaust vents located on the C-pillars, which could be opened and closed with a manual control. The so-called jet exhaust opening was fitted with the license plate mounting, a license plate light, a pair of back-up lights, and was filled with a bright metal plate with well over 200 Chevrolet bowtie emblems cut into it. Incidentally, the Corvair's rear styling was considered a styling update for the 1955 Corvette, but no money was released to fund the necessary tooling changes because of the poor sales of the sports car.

The other special Corvette displayed during this year's GM Motorama tour showcased a prototype of a detachable fiberglass top, roll-up windows, and an interior much like that of the 1956–1957 Corvettes. The hardtop became optional equipment starting with the 1956 models.

Pontiac Changes Direction

Like the other GM divisions, Pontiac was represented by more than one dream car for the 1954 GM Motorama. One was a sports car dubbed the Bonneville Special and the other a sporty and luxurious sedan named Strato Streak.

The Bonneville Special was named after Utah's expansive Bonneville Salt Flats, where many automotive speed records were set. Eddie Miller was one of the record setters there, and his Pontiac-powered racer was the inspiration for the Bonneville Special's design.

The car signaled a new direction for Pontiac, one that was away from the dull but reliable family-toting car to one emphasizing performance. Its fiberglass body with long hood-short deck proportioning was low in height at only 48½ inches. It was painted a brilliant metallic

The Corvette and Corvette-based show cars were posed together in Miami prior to the opening of the GM Motorama there in February 1954. The Corvette with the prototype detachable hardtop and roll-up windows forecasted features that would be included on the 1956 and later Corvettes, while the Nomad provided the roof design for a Bel Air version of the station wagon. Low sales of the Corvette kept the fastback body style out of production.

The Bonneville Special was named for Utah's Bonneville Salt Flats where numerous land speed records were regularly set. Among the features of the two-passenger dream car was a plexiglass roof with only a minimal amount of framing and flip-up panels to ease entry and exit. According to a news release from Pontiac regarding this feature, "Hinged at the center, the canopy raises at each side on counterbalanced springs at the touch of a release catch. The doors are then opened from the inside. There are no outside door handles."

red-copper and sported many features not found on cars of the day such as a wide frontal opening but without a grille and a bubble-top canopy with flip-up panels to ease entry and exit. Scoops located on the cowl at the end of the silver streaks running along the hood funneled air into the interior for ventilation. The car's short deck ended with a built-in, functional "Continental kit."

Sporty Strato Streak

The low-slung Strato Streak, described in GM press releases as a "spectacular sports car," was a pillarless four-door four-passenger car. It was described as a sports car, but it was too big to truly be one. In fact, it was a luxury car with sports car attributes. Its windsplits, which ran along the deck and roof, were integrated into the rear windshield, resulting in a three-piece window. General Motors adopted the concept for production of the 1957 Buicks and Oldsmobiles, but it was not a popular feature. The interior of the Strato Streak featured leather upholstery with fabric inserts, swivel front seats, and a full-length console housing the radio and controls for the air vents and heater.

Oldsmobile Sports Cars

A pair of two-passenger sports cars (the Cutlass and the F-88) represented Oldsmobile at the 1954 GM Motorama. The iridescent copper 1954 Cutlass was the more unusual of the two. Inspiration for some aspects of the styling of the Cutlass was actually sourced from its namesake, the US Navy's unconventional F7-U fighter jet.

The term "unconventional" well describes the aircraft canopy-like roof and louvered backlight of the Olds Cutlass, a feature not adopted for production. However, its combination bumper-grille design was used for the 1956 Oldsmobiles. Other features of the Cutlass included teardrop-shaped wheel openings with polished stainless-steel inner fenders, engine compartment heat vents, 13-inch wheels, and a spare tire stowed in a compartment behind the fold-down center section of the rear bumper. Since the Cutlass had no deck lid, access to the luggage compartment was through a panel in the body-colored filler assembly behind the seats.

The instrumentation layout was identical to that of the F-88; a set of competition-style instruments were arranged across the driver's position then extended vertically to the transmission tunnel. Copper-and-white leather upholstered seats swiveled to facilitate entry and exit. A console between the bucket seats carried a radio/telephone, a feature many years away at that point. The F-88 was essentially that division's version of Chevrolet's Corvette. This model is detailed in Chapter Eleven.

Buick Landau

Like Pontiac, Buick was represented with two completely different designs at the 1954 GM Motorama. One of them, the four-door Landau built from a Series 70 Roadmaster, was an elegant retro offering with a fold-down rear roof section and a padded detachable trunk complete with functional leather hold-down belts. Both were features reminiscent of the landaulets of the early classic era. The spare tire was stored in a compartment accessed via a fold-down, center section of the rear bumper.

The Landau's passenger compartment was upholstered in tan leather with matching cloth inserts, and the front

The three-piece backlight of the sporty and luxurious 1954 Strato Streak was adopted for the 1957 Oldsmobile and Buick. Also adopted was its pillarless hardtop concept for the 1957–1958 Eldorado Brougham. Cadillac used the pillarless-hardtop concept for the limited production Eldorado Brougham, which debuted for 1957.

The F-88's body sat on a Corvette frame modified to accept the Rocket V-8. This car's wheelbase remained the same as the Vette's at 102 inches. Overall length of the car stretched to 167.25 inches and its overall height at the peak of the windshield frame was a low 45 inches. Wheel size was the same as that of the Cutlass at 13 inches. (Photo Courtesy GM Media Archive)

In 1954, the GM Motorama went to Chicago for the only time. This overview contains about half of the dream cars General Motors displayed. Starting at left center and moving left to right are the pearlescent silver Cadillac El Camino, copper-red Pontiac Bonneville Special, turbine-powered GM Firebird I, metallic blue Chevrolet Nomad, Electric Blue Buick Wildcat II, and the iridescent copper Oldsmobile Cutlass. (Photo Courtesy GM Media Archive)

was upholstered in dark blue leather. Front and rear compartments were divided by a retractable glass partition.

Buick Wildcat Redo

The Wildcat II departed completely away from traditional Buicks in being a two-passenger sports car. Buick's chief designer, Ned Nickles, was placed in charge of the Wildcat II project. In the end he and his team created a dream car with highly distinctive features such as biplane bumpers similar to those of the 1934 Cadillac and LaSalle, free-standing parking lights, and "flying wing" fenders with polished inner liners and engine compartment heat vents, as well as hidden fuel fillers beneath the taillight assemblies. Tubular-shaped rear bumpers (also known as nerfing bars, a hot rodder's term) were used in lieu of a conventional rear bumper. The Wildcat II was quite low in height with an overall height (top up) of just over 48 inches.

The Wildcat II's stunning white leather interior contrasted sharply with its Electric Blue exterior. Brushed aluminum inserts and chrome trim decorated the door panels, and a twin-pod gauge cluster sat on a pedestal atop the Wildcat II's transmission tunnel.

The Wildcat II was titled to Harlow Curtice for a while. During that time it was repainted a metallic tan or rose-beige color. The car was still this color when it was donated to the Alfred P. Sloan Museum in Flint, Michigan, in 1976. Many years later it was restored to its original color scheme.

The Buick Landau, built from a Series 70 Roadmaster, was an elegant retro design with a fold-down rear roof section. The Landau was equipped with power windows, power brakes, power steering, radio, and a Dynaflow automatic transmission. Also, a fold-down armrest in the center of the rear seat contained a cocktail shaker and goblets. After it was no longer needed as a show car, the Landau was used as an executive courtesy car in New York City. General Motors sold it in 1959, and since then the one-of-a-kind show car has passed through a number of owners including Joe Bortz, Bill Warner, and Bob Coker. It is now in the Cars of Yesteryear, a private museum in New Orleans, Louisiana.

The Electric Blue 1954 Buick Wildcat II was powered by a 220 hp, 322 V-8 coupled to a Dynaflow transmission. Its engine was modified with four side-draft 2-barrel carburetors with flame arresters. The Wildcat II's chrome-plated suspension consisted of four coil springs, direct-acting shocks, and an 11/16-inch-diameter front stabilizer bar.

Cadillac Park Avenue: Prototype for the Future

The four-door pillarless sedan Park Avenue was very similar in concept to the 1953 Cadillac Orleans and was the next link in the chain after the 1953 Orleans, leading to the 1957–1958 Eldorado Brougham. The car's lower body was painted dark Antoinette Blue and the roof was hand-brushed aluminum. Its tail fin shape was virtually the same as that of Harley Earl's Le Sabre and was a feature adopted for the Series 62 and Sixty-Special Cadillacs of 1957–1958. However, its tiered drive, stop, and park lights were not put into production. Below the rear deck lid of the Park Avenue was a compartment housing the spare tire, which could be removed by lowering a bright chrome-trimmed door, which also served as a bumperette and license-plate mounting.

Sporty Cadillacs: La Espada and El Camino

Two nearly identical two-passenger dream cars, the La Espada and El Camino, a convertible and a closed coupe, respectively, combined sportiness with luxury. Cadillac's press release regarding the La Espada (Spanish for "the sword") stated the car was "a compact, well integrated, personalized type of car containing the traditional luxury, conveniences, quality of finish and fineness of materials traditionally identified with Cadillacs." The same could have been said about the El Camino (Spanish for "the Royal highway"). Both the La Espada and the El Camino drew a lot of attention, but just as was the case with the preceding LeMans, people who were serious about buying a Cadillac were more interested in owning a car more like the Park Avenue. The concept of such a personal car bearing the Cadillac crest was dismissed by GM afterward and did not reappear until the Allante three decades later. Ford, on the other hand, released its version of a personal car, the Thunderbird, the following year.

Like the Park Avenue, these two dream cars had aluminum alloy turbine-blade wheels designed to aid in brake cooling, air-conditioning, and a spare tire compartment concealed by a chrome-trimmed door underneath the lower lip of their deck lids.

The El Camino's lower body was painted pearlescent silver-gray and its roof was brushed aluminum. Its interior was upholstered in gray leather (seats, door panels, and upper instrument panel), and its headliner was of perforated gray Naugahyde with sound deadening qualities. Gray nylon chord covered the El Camino's steering wheel.

Turbine Research

The 1954 XP-21 GM Firebird I resembled a jet-powered fighter plane, and indeed, its styling was heavily

Both the La Espada and the similar El Camino had wheel bases spanning 115 inches and an overall length of 200.6 inches. Two La Espadas were built: The first was painted Apollo Gold (a stock Cadillac color) with a black and yellow interior, and the other was painted Sword Silver and upholstered with a black and silver interior. The latter car appeared at the GM Motorama in Chicago, the last stop of that year's tour. Both cars were shown (separately) during the 1954 and 1955 Parade of Progress.

The fuel, temperature, and oil gauges, ammeter, and the clock of the 1954 Cadillac La Espada were, according to Cadillac press releases, "scientifically engineered for perfect visual control." Brushed-aluminum trim was in abundance. An aircraft-style joystick mounted on a machine-ground, stainless-steel trimmed tunnel between the seats served as the gear selector lever. Harley Earl posed alongside the La Espada; sitting in the car was Don Ahrens, Cadillac's sales manager.

The Cars of Harley Earl

The Firebird I was posed with an F-84F fighter plane for this publicity photo. It served to emphasize the jet engine technology demonstrated by the Firebird, the first in a series of turbine-powered research cars tested by General Motors.

influenced by the shape of the US Navy's delta-winged F4D Skyray interceptor. It was the perfect showcase for its GT-302 Whirlfire Turbo-Power engine. GM's styling boss, Harley Earl, explained the origin of the Firebird's design in an article he authored for the Saturday Evening Post titled, "I Dream Automobiles." He wrote, "The Firebird tickles me because of its origin. In our 1953 Motorama the spotlight model of the dream cars was the Le Sabre, and just after it had been first shown to company officials, I was on an airplane trip. I picked up a magazine and noticed a picture of a new jet plane, the Douglas Skyray. It was a striking ship, and I liked it so well that I tore out the picture and put it into my inside coat pocket.

"Subsequently, a traveling companion who was also a GM officer, stopped at my seat to congratulate me on Le Sabre. 'But,' he added, 'now what will you do for next year?' At that moment, I had absolutely nothing in mind. But I patted the pocket where the picture of the Skyray was tucked away. 'I have it right here,' I said. I was joking. I was merely answering his banter in kind. Then, bingo, I decided I had kidded myself into something. The result, as you may have seen, is that the Firebird is an earth-bound replica of the Skyray airplane."

The British tested the world's first turbine engine for an automobile in 1950. Interest in the possible application for turbine led to research on the topic in the United States not long after the end of World War II. GM's Research Laboratories Division began work on the GT-300 and then wanted to proceed with testing the turbine in trucks and buses. However, Harley Earl's interest in the subject led to the Firebird. Reportedly, Earl had to provide some incentive for GM's lab to test the engine in a car by threatening to have Boeing build the engine for the Firebird!

Indy champion Mauri Rose, who had been hired by General Motors, did some of the test driving of the Firebird. In a report written by Rose for the April 1954 *Motor Life*, he stated, "The steering was absolutely true. The car wanted to behave. It wanted to keep going straight ahead. It was perfectly stable." He also said with a note of strong conviction that, "With absolute sincerity I can say that the car itself is an outstanding job from both styling and engineering standpoints." However, all was not perfect with the Firebird; it was somewhat noisy, very fuel thirsty, and the exhaust temperature was approximately 1,000 degrees Fahrenheit. The upcoming Firebird II benefited from the lessons learned with the first Firebird.

Motorama 1955

The 1955 GM Motorama toured five cities this year: New York City, Miami, Los Angeles, San Francisco, and Boston.

At center in this photo taken in the Grand Ballroom of the Waldorf-Astoria is the 1955 GM LaSalle II Sedan, a car showcasing a mockup of an experimental V-6 engine. From left, going clockwise are the Buick Wildcat III, Chevrolet Biscayne, Oldsmobile 88 Delta, Cadillac Eldorado Brougham, and the Pontiac Strato-Star.

A full array of the virtually all-new 1955 Chevrolets were available for close-up inspection by visitors to that year's GM Motorama. Among the cars seen in this photo are a Bel Air two-door hardtop, Bel Air convertible, and a Townsman station wagon.

Cutaway cars were displayed at the GM Motorama shows to give visitors a unique look at the inner workings of GM cars. This one is a 1955 Pontiac four-door sedan.

Another scene from one of the five venues of the 1955 GM Motorama gives us a look at the 1955 Eldorado Brougham (just left of center), which was painted a highly iridescent color called Chameleon Green developed solely for the prototype. At bottom center is the Pontiac Strato-Star (renamed Strato-Chief when shown in Canada the following year) featuring a cantilever roof and a gullwing front bumper. Behind the Strato-Star is the two-tone blue Olds 88 Delta featuring a brushed aluminum roof and blue-tinted glass.

Chevrolet's Biscayne: Exploration in Elegance

The Biscayne, a four-passenger, pillarless four-door hardtop, was described by General Motors as "an exploration in elegance . . . a superlatively luxurious experimental car that illustrates an entirely new way of thinking about automotive design."

The frontal design of the Biscayne was unusual and was most likely inspired by the Kurtis sports car. Long fairings for the headlights, which stretched across the hood, ended just ahead of the inlets for interior ventilation. Vertical chrome bars sat over the fine mesh-filled frontal opening. Parking lights and an anodized gold "V" were fitted into the end of the projectile-style front fenders. The latter noted the presence of Chevrolet's new small-block 265 V-8, said to produce 215 hp. In reality, the Biscayne was non-functional. A so-called Stratospheric wraparound windshield curved upward into the roof panel, a feature that was adapted for production for 1959. In fact, the fiberglass-bodied Biscayne previewed numerous styling cues, which were applied sooner or later to various GM cars. One of the immediate applications was its side coves, or indented side panels as General Motors described them, for the Corvette beginning the next model year. The side coves of the Biscayne, though, were reversed as compared to the Corvette and wrapped around the back of the body.

Interior features of the Biscayne included thin-shell, swiveling front bucket seats to aid ingress/egress for the driver and front passenger. The bucket-type rear seats were separated with a small console serving as a storage area and an armrest. Chrome-plated brass trim framed the green-and-white leather-covered seats.

Pontiac Strato-Star: Daring Design

General Motors claimed the Dark Silver Metallic 1955 Strato-Star to be, "The most daring new design ever displayed." The Strato-Star's most significant feature was an unusual roof design utilizing two slim-section cantilever pillars growing upward from the flat rear deck and extending forward as windsplits through the roof section

Chevrolet was represented at the 1955 GM Motorama by the Biscayne dream car. The four-door pillarless hardtop was said to be an "exploration in elegance." A number of its features appeared over the next five years on GM's production cars. (Photo Courtesy Bortz Auto Collection)

The 1955 Oldsmobile 88 Delta was a two-toned blue, four-passenger, two-door hardtop standing only 53.1 inches high. Wide-set vertical ovals housed the headlights, parking lights, and scoops used to cool the front brake drums. Between the wide ovals was a bumper/grille combination with a set of thin horizontal bars divided centrally with a chrome vertical bar. Standing with the car was pop music star, Patti Page, who served as a spokesperson for Oldsmobile at the time. (Photo Courtesy Jim Jordan)

and gradually tapering to join the windshield bar. These same rear pillars also flowed back across the deck to form fins. Panoramic quarter glass in the rear, along with the panoramic windshield, provided excellent visibility for the driver in all directions. Because of the car's low overall height of a fraction over 53 inches, flip-up panels in the roof opened and closed automatically via an electric circuit when the doors were opened to assist with entry and exit of the driver and passengers.

Deeply extended wheelwells in the front were painted a contrasting vermillion and were perhaps inspired by a Bertone-bodied Abarth designed by Franco Scaglione four years earlier. Other unusual styling features of this dream car included its protruding headlight fairings, which extended all the way back to the cowl, and divided gull-wing bumper with pod-mounted parking lights hanging underneath. The wheels for the Strato-Star were experimental units formed as a deep-draw section of chrome with a brake cooling air intake styled like a turbine impeller.

The six-passenger Strato-Stars featured a bench seat interior upholstered in vermillion red leather and a gull-wing shaped dash. The door and rear side panels were sculpted with a concave projectile form upon which were mounted projectile-shaped armrests.

Oldsmobile 88 Delta: Supersonic Shape

The Oldsmobile 88 Delta dream car was a two-toned blue, four-passenger, two-door hardtop. Its frontal styling was spectacularly different with its wide-set vertical ovals housing the headlights, parking lights, and air scoops for cooling the front brake drums. Between the wide ovals was a combination bumper-grille; the grille was split with a vertical divider. The hood spanned the entire width from fender crown line to fender crown line, and the hood cut-lines were neatly concealed with chromed trim. All of the glass was tinted light blue to blend with the blue-tinted brushed aluminum roof, even though the backlight was given a darker tint to give the impression that it was a continuation of the roof panel. Vent windows, standard equipment on cars of the day, were deleted on the 88 Delta. Slim vertical A-pillars were blended into the frame of the wraparound windshield.

Other noteworthy features of the 88 Delta included 15-gallon fuel tanks in the quarter panels, polished stainless-steel inner fenders, six-lug wheels with exposed brake drums, and swiveling front seats. Sweeping side trim with a frontal loop trim on this dream car provided a dividing line for the two-tone paint scheme. Colorful two-toning became an important styling trend, and Oldsmobile offered 89 two-tone combinations for 1955.

The Buick Wildcat III: More Conservative

The red fiberglass, four-passenger Wildcat III was a much more conservative design and more reflective of Buick design than the Wildcat II. Among its many features was its hood, which sloped in front to improve visibility immediately ahead of the car and was also recessed beneath the cowl, where an upright air intake for passenger compartment ventilation was located. Furthermore, the dream car's compound curved panoramic windshield provided improved protection from wind blast when the top was down. A cooling slot in the quarter panels for the

The 1955 Wildcat III was painted Kimberly Red, a name chosen to honor racecar driver and SCCA member Jim Kimberly, who was well known for his wins at Sebring, Road America, Watkins Glen, etc. This dream car's hood sloped in front to improve visibility immediately ahead of the car and was also recessed beneath the cowl where an upright air intake for passenger compartment ventilation was located.

rear brakes sat at an angle immediately above the dip in the sweepspear molding.

The Wildcat III's profile view was similar to that of production Buicks largely due to its sweepspear molding and circular wheel openings. However, it was clearly lower in height and shorter in length than any production model built by the division. When down, the convertible top was concealed under the deck lid, which incorporated the upper portion of the quarter panels. The latter feature improved access to the trunk compartment. Despite the sophisticated top stowage arrangement, the Wildcat III never actually had a convertible top installed.

The red interior had swiveling bucket seats in front and a bucket-styled bench type seat in back, all covered in leather and trimmed in gleaming chrome. Bucket seats, along with the bucket-styled rear bench seat, would become a 1960s trend.

The Eldorado Brougham: Completely Functional Prototype

Unlike most dream cars of General Motors, the *steel-bodied* Eldorado Brougham represented a serious design proposal because it was yet another refinement of the production Eldorado Brougham, which emerged for 1957. A number of features of the preceding Cadillac show cars, the Orleans and Park Avenue, were carried forward in the design of this car, including a brushed aluminum roof, reverse-opening rear doors, no center pillars, and no vent windows. Another idea carried forward from other Cadillac showpieces, the La Espada and the El Camino, was the quad headlight design. Quad headlights were illegal in some states at the time, but legislation was later passed to legalize them in all states.

Inside the prototype were specially designed lounge seats for four passengers, vanity case, and unique padded instrument panel. Other equipment included an Autronic Eye automatic headlight dimmer mounted at the top of the windshield, leather and silk interior, pivoting front seats, map light, and storage compartments in the dash and between the front seats.

GMC's L'Universelle: Stylish and Practical Cargo Vehicle

There was a time when trucks were thought of as more utilitarian than stylish. However, that attitude changed in the 1950s. At the 1954 GM Motorama, GMC exhibited its all-new pickup featuring passenger car–styling attributes. Then in 1955, GMC had its only dream vehicle for the GM Motorama, the L'Universelle, which was a prototype for a cargo van designed for comfort and ease of loading. This advanced panel delivery prototype was equipped with front-wheel drive, two-way radio/telephone, torsion-bar front suspension, fold-up cargo doors, and a mid-mounted Pontiac V-8 rated at 180 hp.

The design provided a 13-inch floor height (compared to 28 inches for conventional half-ton panel trucks), a 1,000-pound load capacity, and 173 cubic feet of cargo space. This prototype was nearly 1 foot lower than conventional panel trucks but could carry more cargo and do so with the comfort of a standard passenger car.

Styling for the L'Universelle was as important as ease of loading and cargo capacity. To avoid the boxy look, a sharp crease wrapped around the front to the sides and curved downward to the rear wheels, resulting in a forward-leaning edge. The prow of the L'Universelle was slanted just enough to avoid appearing bus-like. Forward-leaning roof pillars similar to those of the new Nomad also enhanced the styling. The L'Universelle

GMC's only dream vehicle for the GM Motorama, one that served as a prototype for a vehicle designed for comfort and ease of loading, was dubbed the L'Universelle, a kind of all-purpose vehicle. This advanced panel delivery prototype was equipped with front-wheel drive, two-way radio/telephone, torsion-bar front suspension, fold-up cargo doors, and a mid-mounted Pontiac V-8 rated at 180 hp. It almost went into production.

ultimately influenced the design of the first compact passenger vans from Chevrolet in the 1960s.

GM's LaSalle II Roadster and Sedan: V-6 Showcases

The GM LaSalle IIs featured an advanced V-6, an engine out of step with the V-8 fad. Furthermore, both dream cars were quite small for the day, which also went against the trend of lower, longer, and wider. The two dream cars were named after the first car Harley Earl designed for GM (the 1927 LaSalle), Cadillac's companion model last produced in 1940.

The rather compact six-passenger, four-door pillarless hardtop LaSalle II Sedan had a wheelbase of 108 inches (just 6 inches longer than that of the Corvette) and an overall length of 180.2 inches, which was about the same length as some alternative sports cars of the day. As for the Roadster, it was even more compact with a wheelbase of 99.9 inches and an overall length of 151.7 inches. Both cars were quite low in height: the hardtop stood 49.8 inches high and the Roadster, just a mere 42.8 inches high. Each used a drop-floor construction made possible by offsetting the transmission downward with a consequent lowering of the driveshaft and driveshaft tunnel.

Frontal styling for both LaSalle IIs featured vertical grille openings very similar to those of the canceled 1941 LaSalle. The side coves of the pearlescent white cars were painted Bahama Blue on the Roadster and Le Sabre Blue on the Sedan. This feature gave a preview of the styling for the upcoming 1956 Corvette.

The 60-degree V-6 engines for both LaSalles were non-functional castings without provisions for internal components but represented all-aluminum, fuel-injected, double-overhead cam (DOHC) powerplants expected to produce a maximum horsepower of 150 in finished form. Even though these particular V-6 prototypes were simulated, General Motors had a serious V-6 research program over the preceding seven years. The V-6 was actually ready for production as a Chevrolet engine, but GM managers suddenly reversed their decision to release it due to a variety of factors such as production cost, as well as the fact the division had just released its new V-8 and a virtually all-new Chevrolet.

A full set of gauges, along with a 140-mph speedometer and 5,500-rpm tachometer, were included in a compact instrument cluster for the LaSalle II Roadster. A switch for adjustment of the driver's seat was placed on the console and power window switches are on the door panels. All of this was simulated since this dream car was not originally built as a functional vehicle.

Motorama 1956

The 1956 GM Motorama toured the same five cities as the prior year. At the time no one realized there would be no 1957 GM Motorama (although GM of Canada continued its Motorama through 1961).

Among the seven dream cars shown were another turbine-powered research vehicle, the GM Firebird II, and the final prototype of the Eldorado Brougham, which went into production the following model year.

Corvette Impala

The Corvette Impala was an automobile styled to give a little Corvette "flavor" to a five-passenger luxury car. Its toothy grille and rounded quarters revealed its

The 1955 GM LaSalle II Roadster was a very compact design for the era with a wheelbase of 99.9 inches, an overall length of 151.7 inches, and an overall height of just 42.8 inches. Like its companion, the LaSalle II Sedan, it featured a mockup of an experimental V-6. I took this photo of the restored car at the 2013 Amelia Island Concours d'Elegance. It languished in a junkyard for nearly 30 years before being purchased by dream car collector Joe Bortz, who had the unique car restored over a period of 20 years.

The Corvette-like grille of the 1956 Chevrolet Corvette Impala was proposed for use on the big Chevrolets for 1958 but was rejected due to cost considerations. Its lance-shaped windsplit along the body sides was inspired by the 1954 Fiat V-8 coupe. The show car appears to have been painted in a color somewhat similar to Aegean Turquoise, a color offered for the 1958 model year. Note the brushed aluminum roof. (Photo Courtesy GM Media Archive)

styling was influenced by the newly restyled first-gen Corvette. A special brochure about the Corvette Impala stated the car "incorporates wholly new considerations in fine passenger car design from the standpoint of sleekness, safety, and luxury."

Styling of the Corvette Impala foretold much of the styling of the 1958 Impala (detailed in Chapter Seven) such as the integral bumper and grille, wraparound rear windshield, and the beltline dip near the reverse slant C-pillars.

Designing safety into the interior of cars was still in its infancy in the 1950s, but the Corvette Impala was certainly advanced in that regard for the era. A unique, air-foil shaped, padded strut emerged from the steering column and angled upward before transitioning into a horizontal component extending across the entire width of the interior. Flush-fitting controls for the heater/defroster, headlights, and windshield wipers were located on the surface of the strut.

Also included in the interest of safety were seatbelts stored in the recesses between the backrests and seat cushion, a steering wheel with a padded single spoke, and a sloped, recessed package shelf, along with a padded rear window header.

Pontiac Club de Mer

The 1956 Pontiac Club de Mer was distinctive and exotic, to say the least, so its French moniker, which translated into "Beach Exclusive," a name inspired by Miami's fashionable Surf Club, was certainly fitting. This dream car suggested Pontiac was very serious about changing its image from a dull, yet dependable car to that of a performance car, an image much more appealing to the emerging youth market of the era. This two-seater was compact and very low in height, standing only a little more than 38 inches tall, and was barely more than 180 inches long.

The dream car's outer body panels were made of clear anodized brushed aluminum painted translucent Cerulean blue. Its body panels rolled under to seal the entire undercarriage for cleaner airflow underneath. Removable panels bolted over openings throughout the underside

With the model standing alongside the Club de Mer, its low height is very apparent. The Club de Mer stood only a fraction of an inch over 38 inches high. Its body panels rolled under to form a belly pan for improved airflow past the undercarriage. Regardless of its clean lines and racy looks, the Club de Mer was only for show; it did not run. (Photo Courtesy GM Media Archive)

allowed access to mechanical systems. The belly pan was an attribute of European race cars and sports cars such as the Mercedes-Benz 300SL, which had a bolt-on belly pan.

Other styling characteristics of the Club de Mer included twin-bubble windscreens and a shark-like dorsal fin.

A rich vermillion red interior contrasted spectacularly well with the exterior finish and featured chrome-trimmed bucket seats upholstered in soft grain crush leather separated by a chrome-plated console housing the controls for gear selection, remote deck release, ignition, and the radio. The console served as the tube through which the driveshaft ran to connect the engine to the rear trans-axle.

A custom-fabricated steel tube chassis with a modified stock front suspension supported the body. A 300-hp Strato-Streak 317 V-8 fitted with dual 4-barrel carburetors was said to supply the power.

Oldsmobile Golden Rocket

The 1956 Golden Rocket's profile view resembled a metallic gold rocket laid on its side as a result of its twin-torpedo, pontoon-shaped fenders and tapering quarter panels with stubby tail fins, so its name was quite fitting. Its styling was surely inspired by that of the 1953–1955 B.A.T. (Berlina Aero-Technica) series featuring a split backlight. However, as for the split backlight, the feature dates back at least as far as the Bugatti Type 57SC Atlantic of the 1930s. Harley Earl was no doubt familiar with all of these European cars.

The split backlight of the Golden Rocket ultimately was adopted for the second generation, or C2, Corvette, but for only the first model year of the type, 1963. This was not happenstance. The split window was a favorite theme of Bill Mitchell, who would succeed Harley Earl just about three years after the Golden Rocket made its national tour. Interestingly, an earlier C2 Corvette design rendered in clay in 1955 (and intended for production as a 1958 model) was styled very much like the Golden Rocket, including its split rear window.

Flip-up roof panels were provided to ease entry into and exit from the Golden Rocket, which had an overall height of only 49.5 inches. Opening and closing the doors automatically activated these panels. Seats swiveled and the lower steering wheel folded under race car-style to ease entry and exit.

The projectile-shaped nose, pontoon-like fenders, and tapering quarter panels with stubby tail fins gave the 1956 Oldsmobile Golden Rocket a rocket-like profile, something very befitting for a show car representing Oldsmobile, which used "rocket" as a marketing theme. Its roof design was intended for the canceled second-generation Corvette to have been released as a 1958 model. (Photo Courtesy GM Media Archive)

Buick Centurion

The red and white Centurion was designed as a four-passenger model. A Roadmaster-style sweepspear molding divided the contrasting colors.

Other than the sweepspear and open wheelwells, no other outward features associated it with Buicks of the day. The sloping nose featured a deeply recessed, horizontally divided grille and a turbine-like bezel surrounded each recessed headlight. Fresh-air scoops shaped like those of the restyled Corvette served as functional inlets for the air-conditioner system; they were located on the cowl near the front fenders. Air scoops were also incorporated into the wheel discs to help dissipate heat from the finned brake drums. A transparent roof panel, combined with the car's wraparound windshield and backlight, covered the Centurion's passenger compartment. Only the required framing around the glass interrupted the outward view. Rear end styling was dramatic with a flared rear deck area, which foretold the look of the 1959 Chevrolets and Buicks. Lights were integrated into individual units with the stop and backup lights being grouped behind a chrome-plated "Dagmar" at the end of the tail cone, while the parking and directional lights were paired on the far ends and positioned just above the exhaust outlets.

Just above the tail cone sat a patented rear-facing, wide-angle television camera connected electrically to a 4- x 6-inch screen located in the center of the instrument panel. The functional camera took the place of a conventional rearview mirror. Even at night the system provided a suitable view.

Inside the Centurion were four bright red leather-covered bucket seats, each with seatbelts and adjustable headrests. In place of a conventional steering column was an aircraft type cantilever arm attached at the centerline of the car.

The Centurion is now a part of the collection of the Alfred P. Sloan Museum's Buick Gallery in Flint, Michigan.

Cadillac Eldorado Brougham Prototype and Eldorado Brougham Town Car

The fiberglass Eldorado Brougham on exhibit at the 1956 GM Motorama was a near final-form prototype of the production version of the Eldorado Brougham, which emerged the following year.

Another fiberglass Cadillac shown was the Eldorado Brougham Town Car, a chauffer-driven car as the name suggests with an open chauffeur's compartment separated from the passenger compartment via a divider window.

The chauffeur's compartment contained two bucket-type seats covered in black Morocco leather. A dual pane, horizontally sliding glass divider separated the passenger section from the front compartment, and

The chauffer-driven 1956 Cadillac Eldorado Brougham Town Car was simply a styling exercise rather than a serious proposal for production. It was based upon the then upcoming, limited-production 1957 Eldorado Brougham.

a partition bulkhead included several comfort and convenience items, such as a radio/telephone unit to communicate with the chauffeur, air-conditioning, a vanity compartment, a cigar humidor, and a thermos bottle with accompanying gold-plated tumblers.

According to a GM-issued press release, "The inner doors are cloaked in black leather while beige broadcloth in a 'biscuit & button' design covers the rear seat. It blends tastefully with the deep-pile beige [Mouton] carpeting and beige broadcloth headlining." The radio/telephone unit was not actually functional, but it looked convincing; the chauffeur's unit was trimmed in chrome while the passenger's was gold-plated.

GM Firebird II

General Motors built upon the lessons learned with the Firebird I when it designed its next turbine-powered research car, the 1956 Firebird II. Two were built: one of fiberglass and the other of titanium. The former was "the first American gas turbine passenger car *specifically* designed for family use on the highway," according to a GM-issued press release. The Titanium car was non-functional and was the display car at the GM Motorama.

Two Firebird IIs were built, but only one was operational. The second in a series of turbine-powered research cars was exhibited at the Road America race held at Elkhart Lake, Wisconsin. (Photo Courtesy GM Media Archive)

This photo offers a rare look at the construction of one of the 1956 GM Firebird IIs. (Photo Courtesy John Richmond)

The fiberglass Firebird II was more than a turbine engine research project. It was used to test experimental suspension and braking systems, as well as the concept of an electronic highway in which cars of the future might be controlled electronically for speed, direction, and spacing interval in order to eliminate driver error in the operation of an automobile. The other version tested advanced construction techniques with an alternative metal.

The Firebird II's GT-304 had a more efficient regenerator, which recycled 80 percent of the exhaust heat wasted in the GT-302. As a result, fuel economy improved to almost that of the average piston engine of the day. Exhaust gases, which traveled through a set of stainless-steel pipes running through the rocker panels and onward to ports on top of the rear fenders, exited at about the same temperature as that from a conventional automobile. Noise was also reduced to nearly that of a conventional car through the use of a silencer built into the nose of the Firebird II.

Motorama 1959–1961

For 1959, the GM Motorama was revived at the request of northeastern GM dealers, who were feeling the slump in sales. It traveled only to New York City and Boston. When it opened at the Waldorf-Astoria, Harley Earl was just a few weeks from retirement. This time the GM Motorama focused almost exclusively on the products, which could be purchased by consumers; the only dream car present was the 1958 GM Firebird III, a further refinement of the turbine-powered car. General Motors of Canada kept its traveling exhibition going continuously from 1955 to 1961. For the 1960 and 1961 show circuit, it displayed the 1959 Cadillac Cyclone, a dream car not shown at the American version of the GM Motorama.

GM Firebird III

Turbine engine research moved ahead with the 1958 Firebird III. It proved to be the last of its kind, though, for in 1964 General Motors trotted out the Firebird IV, which was said to be turbine-powered. In fact, it was a non-functional show car without an engine.

According to GM's booklet, *Flight of the Firebirds*, Harley Earl "envisioned an entirely different type of car, 'which a person may drive to the launching site of a rocket to the moon,'" when he considered the styling for the next turbine car. For the times, the styling, which included a twin-bubble canopy and multiple tail fins, certainly fit Earl's vision.

Contained within the car's fiberglass body were a regenerative gas turbine GT-305 and a separate two-cylinder, 10-hp aluminum engine to run the electrical and hydraulic accessories consisting of steering, braking pumps, brake flaps, air suspension, and air-conditioning systems. The engine represented a significant advance over the GT-304; it was 25 percent lighter, more compact, developed 225 horsepower at 33,000-rpm gasifier speed, and provided a 25 percent increase in fuel economy.

Turbine research for passenger cars at General Motors ended with the Firebird III, but turbine research continued in the form of large trucks in the 1960s.

Cadillac Cyclone

The Cyclone incorporated numerous advanced systems, all functional rather than simulated. When an object or automobile was approaching, proximity-warning radar alerted drivers via a warning light and an audible signal. Initially when something came into the path of the Cyclone, the warning light flashed and a digital readout appeared on the proximity and stopping distance display window. As the distance decreased between the Cyclone and the approaching object, the audible alarm activated, and the pitch of the signal increased as the driver moved closer to the object. Before an impact could occur, the system automatically applied the brakes if no action was taken. That was the theory at least. Reportedly, no one actually tested the last part of the setup. Common braking action was accomplished via a power-boosted system using a pressure servo, drawing pressure from the air-ride reserve tank. Up front, the wheels and brake drums were designed as an integral unit; rear brakes were made of conventional cast-iron and mounted inboard.

An autopilot system controlling both speed and steering through a sensor bar underneath allowed the car to follow a guide wire buried in the road surface. This idea appeared earlier on the 1956 GM Firebird II as part of the "Highway of Tomorrow" concept.

The doors were another unconventional feature of the Cyclone. Instead of swinging open, they popped out 3 inches with the activation of an electric switch, and then were manually slid back over the quarter panels; ball bearings provided smooth operation. When either door was opened, the electrically operated plastic canopy automatically rose if it was in place. When not in use, the one-piece canopy was stowed in the rear storage compartment. A cable release hidden behind the driver's side gas filler (one was placed on each side) unlocked the entire rear section (deck and quarter panels), which swung back as a unit. Communicating with the outside world with the canopy in place could be accomplished with a two-way intercom. A small panel on each door acted as a pass-through for exchanging small objects such as coins.

According to GM's booklet, Flight of the Firebirds, with the 1958 GM Firebird III, Harley Earl "envisioned an entirely different type of car, 'which a person may drive to the launching site of a rocket to the moon,'" when he considered the styling for the next turbine car. A GT-304 turbine engine, considerably more advanced than those of the previous Firebirds, powered it.

One of Harley Earl's final projects was the construction of the 1959 Cadillac Cyclone. The fully functional dream car had many styling and mechanical innovations, including a proximity warning radar to alert drivers via a warning light and an audible signal when an object or automobile was approaching, an autopilot system that could control both speed and steering through a sensor bar underneath the car, which followed a guide wire buried in the road surface, and many others. (Photo Courtesy GM Media Archive)

CHAPTER 9
PARADE OF PROGRESS

"The GM Parade of Progress is undertaking to bring industry to people... to increase confidence in the future of America."
— Alfred P. Sloan describing the Parade of Progress

GM's Parade of Progress, which was briefly labeled Caravan of Progress, is often associated with the GM Motorama. Indeed, they were *two* separate traveling exhibitions. The Parade of Progress, or PoP, held in the 1950s, did include some of the dream cars first seen on a turntable at the GM Motorama on its tour. Sometimes second or third copies of such cars were on display. However, the PoP began well before the GM Motorama came along, even before the Buick Y-Job was built. A total of eight Streamliner buses were constructed. These unconventional-looking buses were outfitted with displays to illustrate GM's scientific and technical advances.

The origin for the idea of the General Motors Parade of Progress is credited to Charles "Boss Ket" Kettering, who was in charge of the GM Research Laboratories from 1920 to 1947. Five years after earning his BS in electrical engineering and working at various jobs, Kettering, along with a partner, founded Delco–Dayton Engineering Laboratory in 1909. He and his colleagues developed electric ignition, lighting, and starting systems for automobiles. The electric starter became standard equipment for the 1912 Cadillac and subsequently, General Motors bought Delco and left Kettering in charge. During his career he obtained more than 140 US and international patents.

General Motors' Parade of Progress (briefly labeled Caravan of Progress) began in 1936 using a set of nine Streamliner buses like this one. (Photo Courtesy GM Media Archive)

The Cars of Harley Earl 153

The driver's compartment of the 1936 Streamliner does not appear to have been especially comfortable. A sharply angled steering column and wheel was typical of buses of the era. (Photo Courtesy GM Media Archive)

His idea to have a traveling exhibition largely emerged from GM's exhibits at the 1933 "Century of Progress" World's Fair held in Chicago. After viewing the myriad displays of the "Wonders of Science—Wonders of Art" and "An Eye to the Future—an Ear to the Ground," people would go back home to tell family and friends of all the amazing sights they had seen. Among the sights there were the prototype Cadillac Aerodynamic Coupe, an actual Chevrolet assembly line from which visitors could actually purchase a car they had just watched being built, music on a beam of light showing how music played on a phonograph record could be turned into a beam of light, which when projected onto a photoelectric cell receiver connected to a loud speaker would be turned into music again, and other fascinating exhibitions.

During the fair's two-year run, 48 million people had attended. Kettering realized General Motors had an opportunity to reach many more people by creating a nationwide road show to showcase the company's scientific and technological advancements, as well as tell of even greater future advancements. He went to Detroit to suggest the idea to company president Alfred P. Sloan Jr. With Sloan's support, along with that of public relations director, Paul Garret, the board of directors approved the plan.

Sloan described the purpose of the traveling show thusly: "The GM Parade of Progress is undertaking to bring industry to people, and by showing the individual citizen in his home community what the contributions of industry mean to him and his family, to establish a basis of mutual understanding and friendliness and at the same time to increase confidence in the future progress of America."

Two years were needed to put together a staff, concepts, and equipment for the Parade of Progress. The eight chromium-trimmed Streamliners were designed by Harley Earl's Art and Colour Section and then assembled by GM's Fisher Body Fleetwood plant. A GMC 6-cylinder gasoline engine powered the buses.

Finally, after a special ceremony outside the GM Building, the first PoP began a 1,500-mile trek 15 days in advance of the February 11, 1936, opening of its inaugural show in Lakeland, Florida. The eight red-and-white Streamliners, emblazoned with "General Motors Parade of Progress," rolling into town would certainly have been an impressive sight to onlookers. Upon arrival, the parade staff, called "Caravaneers," immediately went to work preparing the grounds, setting up tents and displays, and getting everything ready. Among the many displays were various models of GM's 1936 cars.

The Parade stayed at each destination for about five days. During that time visitors were able to view walk-through exhibits such as a 19th Century home compared with a modern one, a blacksmith's shop compared with a modern service station, and so on. Inside a large silver tent a film was shown, "Progress on Parade," and in between showings up to 500 people could watch scientific demonstrations such as music on a light beam, how a voice appears in sound waves, and other such marvels. Other displays included a running 4-cylinder engine with a quartz glass window to allow spectators to

The Parade stayed at each destination about five days. During that time visitors viewed walk-through exhibits and saw cars from GM's five passenger-car divisions. Charles "Boss Ket" Kettering, the head of the GM Research Laboratories from 1920 to 1947, developed the concept for the Parade of Progress.

The Parade of Progress was interrupted by World War II but resumed in 1953 with the replacements for the Streamliners, a total of 12 Futurliners. Each of the 12 carried a unique display related to GM research. (Photo Courtesy GM Media Archive)

watch the entire process of combustion, studying sound with an oscillograph, photoelectric cells, and automotive safety through engineering. Six of the Streamliners in sets of three formed a walk-through exhibit when parked side-by-side and covered with a canvas canopy. One opened up to be used as a stage, and the other was used to move equipment.

Also during this time, a single custom-built streamlined bus made tours. It was billed as "Previews of Progress." The 28-foot long vehicle, which was built on a GMC chassis, had enclosed front and rear wheels and a rounded front. Presentations consisting of scientific demonstrations lasted about 45 minutes and were held at schools, colleges, and auditoriums such as Carnegie Hall.

With styles changing, Harley Earl saw a need to replace the Streamliners with something more up-to-date. Styling's Industrial Design and Exhibit department was put to work designing the next set of buses for the Parade of Progress. In 1939, construction began on the 12 buses, named Futurliners. They were hand-built and were significantly larger than the old Streamliners, with dimensions of 33 feet long (considerably longer than the nearly 18.6-foot long Streamliners), 8 feet wide, and 11 feet 4 inches tall and had a weight of 12.5 tons. A set of 16-foot long panels could be opened on one side of the Futurliners to reveal differing exhibits. The red and silver vehicles reportedly cost $100,000 each. A bubble canopy was fitted over the driver's compartment, and each was shaped over a wooden form in a vacuum chamber. Over the years, the buses underwent various cosmetic upgrades, including a new grille design and an increase in the number of aluminum moldings on the exterior.

The new Futurliners were ready to be put into service in 1941, but with the United States having to commit itself to fighting in World War II, the Parade of Progress

In mid-October 1953, the Parade of Progress went to the central business district of Pittsburgh, Pennsylvania, known as the Golden Triangle. (Photo Courtesy GM Media Archive)

The Cars of Harley Earl 155

In late August 1953, the Parade of Progress traveled to Pontiac, Michigan. The caravan of tractor-trailers and Futurliners entering town attracted much attention at every venue. Washington Junior High School was the location for this showing. (Photo Courtesy GM Media Archive)

was brought to a halt; the buses were put into storage in early 1942. By the end of the 1941 tour, approximately 12.5 million people spread out over 251 cities (including Mexico City in 1938 and Havana, Cuba, in 1939) had attended the Parade of Progress since its inception.

In 1946, some of the buses were freshened up to be driven in a parade celebrating the Golden Jubilee of the Auto Industry in Detroit but were evidently rarely, if ever, used afterward, at least not until sometime around late 1952 or early 1953, when the decision was made to resume the Parade of Progress. Its success at reaching the public had not been forgotten.

Before the tour resumed, the Futurliners were improved. Among the changes performed were the installation of air-conditioning and the replacement of the original acrylic plastic dome over the driver's compartment with a curved, tinted "E-Z Eye" glass windshield with a panel overhead because of uncomfortable heat buildup for the driver and crew. Furthermore, engines were switched from the 4-71 two-cycle diesel engine and standard-shift transmission to a GMC 302 6-cylinder gasoline engine connected to a Hydra-Matic.

The Parade was finally resumed again in April 1953 with the first stop at the University of Kentucky at Lexington. There were 27 additional venues for the PoP that year, ending in Atlanta, Georgia, in December. For 1954, 47 cities were on the schedule. During 1955, 10 Canadian cities were among the 49 visited by the Parade.

As before, the PoP was used to display products related to GM's modern engineering, science, ongoing research, the newest line of cars, and on occasion a smattering of dream cars such as the 1954 Buick Wildcat and Cadillac La Espada. Upon the resumption of the Parade of Progress, Harlow Curtice announced, "The new and exciting 1953 version of the Parade is an ultra-modern presentation, highlighting the enormous progress the country has made in recent years. Visitors, for example, will hear the scratchy reception of the radio of 1925 as compared to modern high-fidelity microwave transmission, will watch a tiny jet plane swoosh across the stage and take a fanciful flight into outer space."

Other exhibits and demonstrations included such things as a two-cycle diesel engine, how high-compression engines boost fuel economy and power, animations of how a car was built, a cutaway jet engine, plus science lectures. The most popular was "America at the Crossroads" carried by Futurliner number two. This 16-foot-long diorama showed the transformation of a rural crossroads community of a half-century earlier into a thriving, modern community and how the automobile played a part in it.

With the final venue, the 26th of the year, held at Spokane, Washington, in early July 1956, the Parade of Progress came to an end. By the time it had ended, the PoP had crisscrossed the United States from coast to coast, with visits to 35 of the 48 states comprising the United States at that time. Increasing costs helped put an end to the impressive spectacle, just as happened with the GM Motorama.

Among the exhibits at this Parade of Progress stop in Georgia were some of GM's finest cars of 1954, an Eldorado, Corvette, and a Skylark. (Photo Courtesy GM Media Archive)

CHAPTER 10
HARLEY EARL'S DAMSELS OF DESIGN

"I don't know why the ladies shouldn't be represented in the designing of cars, refrigerators, and other appliances."
— *Harley Earl*, Christian Science Monitor, *1958*

In the mid-1950s, Harley Earl hired several women to work at GM Styling that the press dubbed the "Damsels of Design." The group included Dagmar Arnold, Jane van Alstyne, Ruth Glennie, Gere Kavanaugh, Jeanette "Jan" Krebs, Sandra Longyear, Marjorie Ford Pohlman, Helene Pollins, Peggy Sauer, and Suzanne Vanderbilt. However, they were not the first women hired by Earl; he had hired the first one, Helene Rother, in 1943.

What is special about this group is that they were hired as a group for the purpose of obtaining the woman's point of view on how cars and appliances should be designed. The woman's viewpoint had become especially significant because by 1955, women much more often than not had the final say on what car the family purchased. Despite that fact, Earl took a lot of criticism for hiring the women, from the upper management at General Motors to the men asked to work with them in Design. Regardless, he firmly believed his decision was the right one.

These women were by no means hired "off the street." Harley Earl selected these women because their background gave them experience related to designing automobiles. They all had college degrees and knowledge of industrial design. Seven of the nine graduated from the art school Pratt Institute, and the other two had master's degrees in fine art. Harley Earl tasked them essentially the same way he had with his male staff; use your imagination, or in other words, "think outside the box."

Suzanne Vanderbilt said of the experience, "It was an exciting notion to start at the bottom and create a new car from scratch. But the truth is I didn't know one car from another then." However, there was at least one exception regarding the latter statement among the women; Jan Krebs was a car enthusiast who could perform minor repairs on her own car. In fact, to her, the performance capabilities of a car were an important consideration.

Their original assignments involved interior design considerations such as color, texture, and trim for interior fabrics and shaping seats, door handles, and armrests,

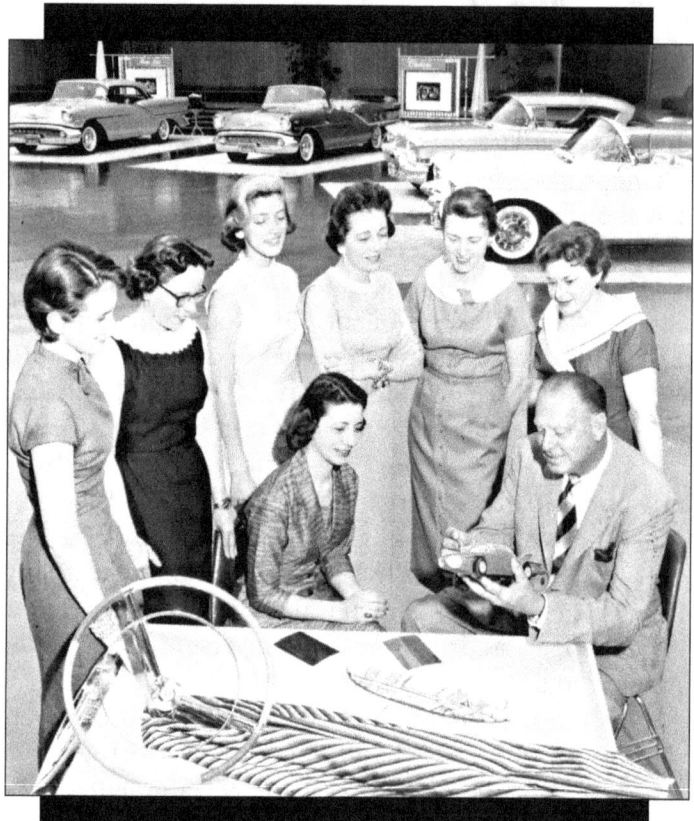

The Damsels of Design assigned to styling automobiles posed with their boss, Harley Earl, for this publicity photograph taken in 1957. Standing, from left to right are Dagmar Arnold, Jane Van Alstyne, Jan Krebs, Gere Kavanaugh, Peggy Sauer, and Helene Pollins. Sandra Longyear is seated next to Earl, who is holding a model of the Firebird II. (Photo Courtesy GM Media Archive)

before moving on to much more substantial projects. Some of those projects came to fruition in 1957 and again in 1958 with cars from each of the five divisions of General Motors to be evaluated in private showings (virtually the equivalent of fashion shows) at Design. At least some of the cars were later displayed at auto shows. The Damsels, incidentally, were also responsible for the GM

The Cars of Harley Earl 157

Jan Krebs (sitting in chair) was responsible for the ideas exhibited on two "feminized" 1957 Pontiacs, including this Star Chief convertible painted Chiffon Pink. (Photo Courtesy GM Media Archive)

Frigidaire "Kitchen of Tomorrow" exhibits at the 1956 and 1959 GM Motorama.

The Damsels' Designs for 1957

For 1957, two cars from each of GM's passenger car line received makeovers by the Damsels. Not satisfied with their ideas for imaginative exterior colors, fabrics, and accessories, special names were given to most, if not all, of the cars as well. They were shown inside the GM Design dome in May 1957.

Few details are known about the 1957 Trieste, a modified 1957 Bel Air. Its monotone color scheme may have been inspired by the color of the sand on the beaches of the Italian city located on the Adriatic coast for which it was named. Without documentation or a color photo, one can only guess at its actual color. (Photo Courtesy GM Media Archive)

Chevrolet Mademoiselle and Trieste

Both the Chevys were Bel Air models; the Mademoiselle was a convertible and the other (dubbed Trieste) a two-door hardtop. The Mademoiselle featured paint accents to the wheel covers and the quarter panel trim insert, which were color-keyed to the exterior paint color. (The color scheme, though, was not uncovered during research for this book.) Interior upgrades included multicolored fabric inserts similar to what was used for the 1958 Impala and special door and rear side panels.

As for the Trieste (pronounced tree-est), its namesake was the Italian city. It also featured special upholstery, along with unique door and rear side panels. Brushed aluminum was applied to the lower portion of the door panels. Its leather and contrasting fabric upholstery was sewn to form "V" patterns on both the seat uprights and seat cushions. The exterior color may have been light tan. Whatever its exterior color, much of the interior was the same shade, including the dash and steering wheel.

Pontiac Catalina and Star Chief

Jan Krebs was responsible for the ideas exhibited on the two feminine Pontiacs. These two cars likely had special names given to them, but they could not be determined during the research of this book. Even a Pontiac press release about them in the files of the GM Heritage Center does not reveal such names. The press release noted Krebs' "combination of styling skill and feminine point of view has resulted in the superb styling of two

The 1957 Oldsmobile Chanteuse was a modified 98 Starfire convertible painted high-luster violet with an interior in medium and dark violet. The glove compartment was stocked with a leather-bound vanity case. (Photo Courtesy GM Media Archive)

A 1957 Oldsmobile 98 Holiday Coupe was transformed into the pearlescent tangerine Mona Lisa by Peggy Sauer. Among the alterations were an interior finished in tangerine leather and tangerine fabric in a striped design with a Caribbean motif tastefully combined in the upholstery and accented with cream insert stripes and a vanity case stored in the glove compartment. (Photo Courtesy GM Media Archive)

Pontiac cars: Star Chief convertible and Star Chief Catalina, both currently winning the admiration of men as well as women."

The Star Chief convertible's exterior was painted in acrylic Chiffon Pink and the car-length accent panel received Magenta Red paint. Matching metallic Chiffon Pink leather and multicolored Aztec nylon fabric covered the seats. The nylon was used only on the upper left front seat and the upper right rear seat. Thick pink carpeting covered the floor, and the glove box compartment door contained a lift-out vanity in matching leather, along with a notepad and tissue dispenser.

Kreb's Catalina was finished primarily in Onyx Black inside and out. Its seats were covered in calf grain and patent leather. Black mouton carpeting covered the floor. According to the aforementioned press release issued by Pontiac, "The car is receiving favorable attention from male car buyers due to its handsome Ivy League looks.

Oldsmobile Chanteuse and Mona Lisa

The Olds Starfire 98 Chanteuse convertible was the work of Peggy Sauer. It was painted a high-luster violet with a matching violet interior. The convertible top boot and seat panels had contrasting light-green stripes. Seats were upholstered in medium and dark-violet leather. Also in harmonizing violet were the steering wheel, instrument panel, and door panels. Carpeting was boucle (wool) looped pile in light violet, and the glove compartment was lined in light green leather with a matching leather-bound vanity case. Also included was a chrome-plated tube attached to the lower right door panel housing a violet-colored umbrella.

A Ninety-Eight Holiday Coupe dubbed the Mona Lisa was also the work of Miss Sauer. The car was painted a brilliant pearlescent tangerine while the interior was finished in tangerine leather and tangerine fabric in a striped design with a Caribbean motif tastefully combined in

A Series 70 Roadmaster two-door hardtop was converted into the Alouette, equipped with a distinctive interior. (Photo Courtesy GM Media Archive)

the upholstery and accented with cream insert stripes. The steering wheel, too, was covered in cream leather, as was a vanity case inside the cream leather-lined glove compartment. Like the Chanteuse, the Mona Lisa also had its floor covered in boucle looped pile carpeting. The Mona Lisa was included with five other production-type Oldsmobiles displayed at the 1957 Michigan State Fair in Detroit.

Buick Alouette, Bolero

Few details are available from the GM Heritage Center on the two "Damsel" Buick Roadmasters, the Alouette and Bolero. Photographs do clearly reveal the former was a two-tone, Series 70 Roadmaster two-door hardtop, and the latter was a monotone Series 60 Century convertible.

The interior of the Alouette was a combination of leather and cloth. Cloth inserts for the seats and door panels were sewn in a wide, pleated pattern. Placed within the recessed portion of the back sides of the front seat was a pull rod to move the seat back into the upright position after a passenger had entered the rear compartment. The lower portion of the door panels were covered in cut-pile carpeting just like that used for the floors. A leather-bound vanity case and notepad were placed within recesses located in the backside of the glove compartment door.

Mildly contrasting leather was used on the interior of the Bolero convertible. Seat inserts were darker and the

The interior of the 1957 Buick Alouette was of a combination of leather and cloth. Cloth inserts for the seats and door panels were sewn in a wide, pleated pattern. (Photo Courtesy GM Media Archive)

The work of the Damsels of Design was exhibited at the Spring Fashion Festival of Women-Designed Cars held inside the dome building at the GM Design Center. (Photo Courtesy GM Media Archive)

same color was applied to the instrument panel, steering wheel, and steering column. The recessed back of the front seat had a pull cord to aid in returning the seat back to the upright position after entering the rear passenger compartment. Carpeting was the same as that used for the Alouette.

Cadillac Allegro and Elegante

Like the Alouette and Bolero, details are sparse for the Cadillac Series 62 Allegro convertible and the Coupe de Ville Elegante. The Allegro featured leather and tufted fabric seats.

As for the Elegante, it had a monotone color scheme inside and out. Pleated leather covered the seats. Like the Allegro, a leather-covered vanity kit was fitted into recesses on the back of the glove box door.

The Damsels' Designs for 1958

About one year after evaluating his Damsels' creations, the outgoing head of GM Design, Harley Earl, reviewed another set of his all-female designers' cars at the Spring Fashion Festival of Women-Designed Cars held again inside the GM Design dome. As before, two cars from each passenger car division received a feminine makeover. He found the group had not expended their imagination with their earlier works.

Chevrolet Fancy Free and Martinique

A Corvette received the "Damsel" treatment. Ruth Glennie feminized the sports car with special slip-on seat covers. The stitch lines of the seat covers were vertical with molded outer edges and sides of white leather. Two-inch

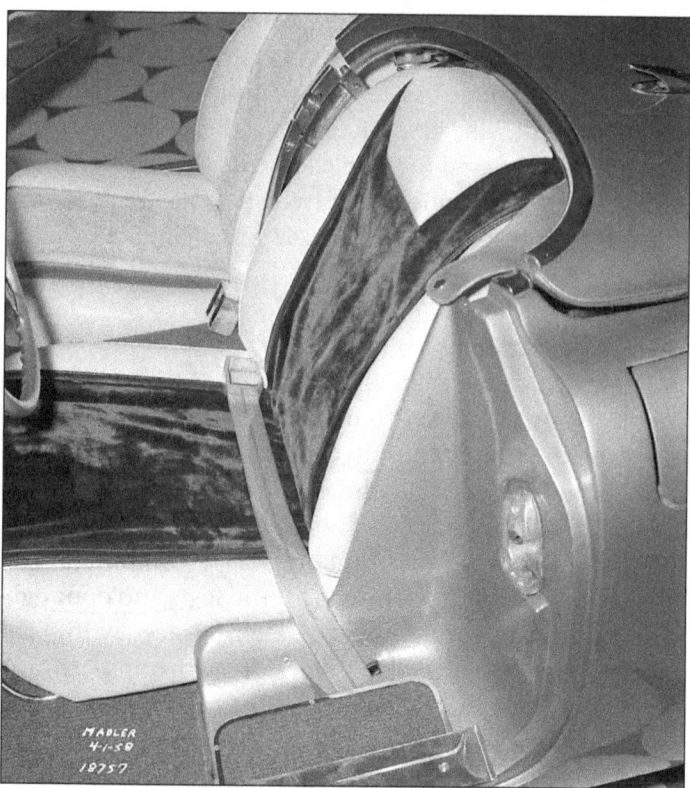

Ruth Glennie added a number of practical and novel features in creating the Corvette-based Fancy Free. These included self-adjusting retractable seat belts, seat covers for each season of the year, color-coordinated instrument faces, white phosphorescent gauge numerals and needles, etc. Shown in place is the imitation black fur seat cover for winter. (Photo Courtesy GM Media Archive)

The only "Damsel" car known to still exist is the 1958 Corvette Fancy Free, created by Ruth Glennie. She chose silver-olive paint for the exterior. The car was photographed at the Gilmore Museum in Hickory Corners, Michigan.

The 1958 Chevrolet Martinique convertible is one of the more well-known cars designed by "Damsel of Design" stylist, Jeanette Linder. Its trunk had fitted, three-piece fiberglass luggage matching the pastel striped interior, a trunk compartment light, spare tire cover, and a lined inner trunk lid. (Photo Courtesy GM Media Archive)

stripes of silver-olive leather were inboard. The insert was silver-olive. In the summer, a bright yellow fabric could be installed in the center of the seat; for autumn, red-orange tweed was provided; in the winter, an imitation black fur could be used. Self-adjusting, retractable seatbelts were also included. The Fancy Free was painted silver-olive and had white leather trim inside. Among the other features included by Glennie were sun visors, color-coordinated instrument faces, white phosphorescent gauge numerals and needles, brushed aluminum appliqués for the instrument panel, leather-wrapped tray for purse storage, glove box storage bin, floor-mounted waste receptacle, contoured seats, leather door and kick panel trim, and a silver-olive paint accent on the wheel covers.

The pearlescent yellow Impala Martinique convertible was the work of Jeanette Linder. Its most significant features were fitted, three-piece fiberglass luggage matching the pastel striped interior, lighted trunk compartment, spare tire cover, and a lined inner trunk lid. The liner had two large pockets for additional storage.

Pontiac Bordeaux and Polaris

The green Pontiac Star Chief Catalina four-door hardtop Bordeaux was equipped with color-coordinated blankets to keep backseat occupants warm, as well as pockets in the trunk to secure luggage.

Sandra Longyear transformed a fuel-injected Starfire Blue Bonneville convertible into the Polaris. It featured a spectacular two-tone leather upholstery pattern with bucket-style seats front and rear. Between the front seats was a console with a sliding access door and grooved aluminum trim that continued rearward across the driveshaft tunnel. The console provided space to store picnic supplies, a thermos matching the interior, and a portable radio.

Oldsmobile Carousel and Rendezvous

The metallic blue Oldsmobile Super 88 Fiesta Carousel, the work of Peggy Sauer, had an interior designed

The child-friendly Olds Carousel station wagon had a magnetized back to the front seat. When used along with built-in flexible straps, this feature was meant to help hold toys in place. (Photo Courtesy GM Media Archive)

Sandra Longyear transformed a fuel-injected Starfire Blue 1958 Bonneville convertible into the Polaris. It featured a stunning two-tone leather upholstery pattern with bucket-style seats front and rear. (Photo Courtesy GM Media Archive)

The dark red 1958 Olds Ninety-Eight Rendezvous convertible had a leather and striped-cloth interior. (Photo Courtesy GM Media Archive)

Marjorie Ford Pohlman created the Royal Purple Shalimar from a 1958 Buick Limited. Among the amenities she included was a dictation machine, which slid out from the glove compartment. (Photo Courtesy GM Media Archive)

with children in mind. It featured a magnetized back to the front seat. When used along with built-in flexible straps, this feature was meant to help hold toys in place. The hardware used to open the rear windows and doors was removed and placed on the driver's instrument panel as a safety measure to prevent children from accidentally opening them. Door warning chimes were also included.

The dark red Ninety-Eight Rendezvous convertible had a leather and striped cloth interior. The backs of the front seat were equipped with large storage pockets; the one behind the driver's position had snaps while the other side opened and closed with a zipper.

Buick Shalimar and Tampico

Marjorie Ford Pohlman created the Royal Purple Shalimar from a Buick Limited. It was fitted with a removable cosmetic case and umbrella inside its fold-down armrest, as well as a dictation machine, which slid out from the glove compartment. Striped purple cloth covered the seats. A storage compartment was also included in the backside of the front seat. In back was a fur blanket.

Pohlman also styled a Buick Roadmaster convertible to become the Tampico. Its namesake was the port city in Mexico. Bright flaming-orange paint accents on the side moldings of the alabaster Tampico matched the largely flaming-orange leather interior designed to seat four. Alabaster leather accents shaped like a "T" were sewn into the seat backs. Paired cloth inserts were also sewn into the seat cushions and seat backs. A small console was placed between the front bucket seats. It housed a camera and binoculars.

Cadillac Baroness and Saxony

The black Cadillac Eldorado Seville Baroness was the work of Sue Vanderbilt. Inside was black mouton carpeting, a telephone, a pillow, and a lap robe made of black seal fur for the rear passengers. An umbrella was hidden in the passenger side armrest.

Marjorie Ford Pohlman transformed a 1958 Buick Roadmaster convertible into the Tampico. Bright flaming-orange paint accents on the side moldings of the alabaster Tampico matched the leather interior. (Photo Courtesy GM Media Archive)

Miss Vanderbilt was also responsible for the Saxony, a modified Series 62 convertible outfitted with a Dictaphone in the center armrest and a partitioned glove box.

The Damsels of Design Disbanded

"No women are going to stand next to any senior designers of mine," declared Bill Mitchell. He disbanded the group as soon as he became VP of GM Design. However, while the group was no more, not all of the women left General Motors, but rather took on new assignments. Suzanne Vanderbilt went on to eventually become chief designer for Chevrolet, followed by being appointed design assistant in charge of interior soft trim for all GM lines. She retired from General Motors in 1977.

Today, the men at GM Global Design far outnumber the female designers, which number in the hundreds versus thousands of male counterparts. While the Damsels of Design may today be thought of as pioneers in the field, they evidently did not think of themselves that way. As explained in a June 2010 article about the group published in the *New York Times*, "They shrugged off hurdles or obstacles by simply focusing on 'being really good' at what they did."

The black 1958 Cadillac Eldorado Seville Baroness was the work of Sue Vanderbilt. Its luxurious features included black mouton carpeting, a telephone, and a pillow and lap robe made of black seal fur for the rear passengers. (Photo Courtesy GM Media Archive)

The Damsels of Design had a part in designing the Firebird III. Bill Mitchell, who would later disband the Damsels, stands on the right. (Photo Courtesy GM Media Archive)

CHAPTER 11

HARLEY EARL'S PERSONAL F-88s

"On Saturday, February 25, 1955, Mr. Earl returned the subject car to the Styling Section and pointed out that the car was unsatisfactory for driving."
– March 4, 1955, memo to Bill Mitchell regarding F-88 number 2

For the 1954 GM Motorama, one of the dream cars gracing a turntable was a gold fiberglass two-seater convertible wearing an Oldsmobile logo. Other than that around-the-world emblem and its spinner wheel covers, there was not much else in a visual sense, which fit the public's perception of an Oldsmobile. However, this division of GM was known for its Rocket V-8, which powered NASCAR drivers to victory. Perhaps an Oldsmobile F-88 was not really so out of step after all. In essence, it was that division's version of Chevrolet's Corvette, but with V-8 power instead of a hopped-up Stovebolt Six.

Ironically, Oldsmobile was better suited to offering the sports car at the time, but an internal competitor to Chevy's Corvette had no chance of reaching production no matter how much anyone argued for it. Corvette would later catch up to what it was supposed to be, though, and there would be no more Oldsmobile two-passenger sports cars like the F-88, except for use by a few higher-ups at General Motors. Harley Earl was one of them. He really liked the F-88; he must have, because he had more than one!

XP-20, Also Known as F-88

The design of the F-88, referenced as the XP-20 during its design phase, was the responsibility of Art Ross, head of the Oldsmobile Studio. The fiberglass body of the F-88 show car was painted metallic gold with

The 1954 Olds F-88 used for the GM Motorama show circuit was painted metallic gold and had an interior color scheme of buckskin and green. Note the paint on the driver's door does not match the rest of the body, a situation that went without remedy probably due to lack of time. (Photo Courtesy GM Media Archive)

contrasting dark green wheelwells. Application of chrome trim was very restrained by 1950s standards. Up front was an oval-shaped honeycomb grille filling the opening of the combination bumper-grille surround. Large, chrome-plated "88" numerals were mounted over the engine heat vents on the front fenders. The only other brightwork applied to the body side was a bright molding that ran along the crown of the quarter panel to the dip in the beltline near the door opening, turned downward then turned rearward and finally terminated at the rear wheel opening.

Vertical, oval openings at the rear of the quarters outlined with a chrome-plated surround provided stylish exits for the dual-exhaust system. Also present were seven chromed bumper guards across the body-colored bumper. A set of conical taillights very similar to those used on the 1959 Cadillacs five years later completed the sleek car's profile in back. Wheel covers for the 13-inch wheels resembled a turbine with a three-blade spinner or "flipper" and, except for their diameter, were virtually identical to those of the 1954 Olds Starfire, a new model released that year. Just as on the Corvette, the F-88's convertible top folded into a well, covered with a flush-fitting, pivoting lid.

The fuel filler was placed just behind the top well along the fore-aft center line of the car with the deck lid opening cut around it. Space limitations of the trunk were mitigated by placing the spare tire under the trunk floor and made accessible with a drop-down, center bumper section. This concept (inspired by some European models) was adopted the following year for the Chevrolet Cameo and GMC Suburban pickups.

A common feature on GM's 1954 dream cars was a drop-down door for access to the spare stored underneath the trunk floor. The Olds F-88 was among those with this feature. Note the chrome-plated trunk hinges on either side of the fuel tank.

The F-88's body sat on a Corvette frame modified to accept the Oldsmobile V-8. This car's wheelbase remained the same as the Vette's at 102 inches. Overall length of the car stretched 167.25 inches, and its overall height with the peak of the windshield frame was a low 45 inches.

Powering the F-88 was a modified 324-ci V-8 with a single 4-barrel carburetor coupled to a Hydra-Matic transmission, perhaps the only serious drawback for the sports car. However, Olds would not offer a 4-speed transmission for quite some time. Output was boosted from 185 hp (the maximum offered for the production Eighty-Eight and Ninety-Eight series) to 250. Accounting for some of the increased performance was a compression ratio bumped up to 10:1. As a result it required premium fuel. (Indeed, a label was applied to the fuel filler cap specifying that 94- to 100-octane fuel must be used.) Writers for *Motor Life* magazine (April 1954) speculated that the top speed of the experimental car would be approximately 150 mph. No top speed or other performance figures appear to have been made public.

Designed by Jack Humbert, the interior of the F-88 was befitting a sports car. It featured bucket seats, a steering wheel covered in pigskin, and a set of competition-style instruments arranged in an upside-down "L" layout across the driver's position then turned downward to the transmission tunnel. The vertical stack of instruments fabricated from the 1953 Oldsmobile parts bin were mounted within three round housings. At the top was an odometer combined with a 150-mph speedometer and a 6,000-rpm tachometer laid out concentrically; the center one was divided into the amp (above) and temperature gauges; the bottom housing contained the fuel gauge in the top half and the oil pressure gauge occupying the lower half. The console finished in chrome and textured metallic gold hardware carried a chronometer, shifter, radio, and radio controls. A bulkhead behind the bucket seats had cutouts around the seats' backrests to provide additional room for fore and aft adjustments. A radio speaker grille was placed on the bulkhead in between the seats. Fresh air vents in the cowl, along the cowl edge of the dash, and in the kick panels as well as flip-up air scoops in the windshield header helped to provide flow-through ventilation with the top raised.

Other F-88s

Harley Earl loved sports cars, and at his direction General Motors started producing a sports car, the Corvette. However, there appears to be no record of Earl actually owning any Corvettes until after he retired, and those were designed under Bill Mitchell. The early Corvettes

Chapter Eleven *Harley Earl's Personal F-88s*

had a long way to go before they were truly sports cars, but that did not stop Earl from having a sporting type of car, the Oldsmobile F-88, which of course never went into production. The fact it was not production did not prevent Harley Earl from having a few of them.

Only three of the XP-20 F-88s were constructed according to a surviving Oldsmobile Engineering Logbook owned by a retired Olds engineer. Listed in it were the show car for the GM Motorama, one for Harley Earl, and another for Sherrod E. Skinner, GM vice president of the accessory group and the former general manager of the Olds division.

Despite the Olds logbook, which records three 1954 F-88s, there are enough configurations shown in dated photographs made by GM Photographic to prove four were actually completed. Indeed, the Shop Order books of the GM Heritage Center list four XP-20 F-88s: Shop Order (SO) numbers 1768, 1939 (the Motorama display car), 2292, and 2264. By the way, shop order numbers were assigned to such cars as a means of keeping track of expenses for the accounting department.

Strangely, SO 1768 is listed in GM's Shop Order books as a 1953, whereas all others are identified as 1954s. Perhaps it is simply a typo, or perhaps not. There is no additional documentation on SO 1768 at the GM Heritage Center. Other documents refer specifically to individual F-88s as "F-88 number 1—Motorama show car" (SO 1939), F-88 number 2 (SO 2292, built for Harley Earl), and F-88 number 3 (SO 2264, built for Sherrod Skinner). All of these were known as 1954 models. If a singular F-88 was completed during model year 1953, it would perhaps account for identifying the three 1954s as numbers 1, 2, and 3.

Harley Earl's SO 2292, Also Known as F-88 Number 2

Olds F-88, SO 2292, appeared at the 1954 Chicago Auto Show and other venues. It also served as transportation for Harley Earl and, at his direction, underwent numerous revisions over the years. It ultimately became the 1957 F-88 Mk. II. Fortunately, a significant amount of documentation on this particular F-88 has survived and is stored at the GM Heritage Center.

His car was equipped with a modified Olds V-8 displacing 348 ci and side-mounted oil coolers resembling side-mounted exhaust pipes. This car underwent many

Harley Earl's next F-88 underwent a tremendous number of styling and mechanical alterations. Originally it was painted yellow with a black interior; next it was painted black and the seat inserts were changed to yellow, resulting in a two-toned interior. By 1957, its body had been changed into the F-88 Mk. II. (Photo Courtesy GM Media Archive)

refinements during 1954 and 1955. Among the early changes were deleting the louvers on the lower quarter panels, changing the windshield and frame assembly to one without header vents, and having the seat adjustment mechanism modified for smoother operation. In late May, an order went out to have the car repainted black and to change the seat inserts to yellow. The cowl

In 1955, Harley Earl's second F-88 received styling revisions to the grille and body, as well as a repaint in silver-blue. Shown in this photo from January 1956 is a clay mockup of the revised front end along with a set of pods under the far ends of the bumper-grille surround. However, these were ultimately not installed on Earl's car. Note the mesh-type grille and driving lights; the mesh grille was eventually used. (Photo Courtesy GM Media Archive)

vents were deleted as well. Furthermore, because Harley Earl was so tall (6 feet, 4 inches), the underside of the instrument panel needed modification to provide him with additional foot room. A more serious issue became apparent as the car suffered from fuel pump vapor lock. A simple fix was suggested in a June 17, 1954, memo to Harley Earl from Bob Lauer (staff assistant to Bill Mitchell): Cut heat vents into the fiberglass panel separating the engine compartment from the front fenders.

In July, 35 additional changes were ordered for SO 2292, including a reworked honeycomb grille, new hood with a revised scoop, new fiberglass front end, new seats and seat trim, and deleted oil coolers. In addition, conventional rocker panels, new door panels, and new backup lights were installed. The Autronic Eye was relocated to inside the hood scoop, while a glove box light was installed. In August, a new transmission, an Oldsmobile Whirl-Away Hydra-Matic, was ordered installed. The car was to be made available for this upgrade on September 13 for about four weeks. About one month later, a removable fiberglass hardtop was requested. By November, Harley Earl viewed a plaster mockup of the top. He rejected it and specified one that simulated the look of a convertible top with a cloth covering be designed. It was to be lightweight and have a plexiglass backlight.

On January 3, 1955, an order for a McCulloch supercharger was sent out. Furthermore, a new set of change orders was issued about 10 days later. Among them were new front and rear wheel openings with stainless-steel mesh exposed wheelhouses, removal of "88" numerals from the fenders, new wheel discs, and a bright surface on the front of the honeycomb grille.

In a lengthy letter dated March 4, 1955, a multitude of deficiencies was ordered remedied. The letter began, "On Saturday, February 25, 1955, Mr. Earl returned the subject car to the Styling Section and pointed out that the car was unsatisfactory for driving. A meeting was held Monday morning. The purpose of the meeting was to demonstrate some of the major deficiencies and to provide a means for their immediate correction."

Among these deficiencies were the seat cushion, instrumentation lighting, gas fumes entering the car, gear selector without a distinct feel between gear selections, and rear springs that needed raising, with a possible change needed to a higher spring rate. Minor adjustments were also needed to the hood latch control, radio reception, and kick-out spring pressure in left-hand door

A feature added to Harley Earl's F-88 was a detachable hardtop styled to resemble a convertible top. Note the revised wheel openings and wheels.

lock. These changes were considered important enough to delay a development program for the Le Sabre, which Earl was apparently still driving from time to time. Additional improvements were soon reported as needed for the convertible top and heater control simplification.

By late April, the fixes had been made. Evidently, Harley Earl finally found his F-88 to be suitable to drive. In a brief memo he wrote on May 3, 1955, to his staff, he said, "The job you fellows did on the F88 was tops. The car is very comfortable and the lighting is excellent and the ride good. I would not hesitate to drive to Florida in the car now."

On September 14, Earl ordered the design and fabrication of a quarter-inch thick, one-piece tinted transparent bubble top to be completed while he was in Europe. Nine days later, work was stopped on the project for an unspecified reason. Perhaps Earl learned just how uncomfortably hot sitting under a bubbletop would be.

A memo dated September 30, 1955, ordered SO 2292 be given acceleration tests without the blower equipment, then be given the tests again prior to October 20 with a 1956 version Olds special manifold and carburetor installed. However, other testing had evidently been conducted earlier. On October 1, the car was acceleration tested at the proving grounds with the supercharger and 1954-type carburetor and manifold still in place. The 0-60–mph run required just 8.0 seconds and one-half mile took 25.6 seconds. Total weight of the car with driver, passenger, and a half-tank of fuel was 4,550 pounds. The later test without the blower and the 1956-type manifold and carb showed a 0-60–mph time of 8.95 seconds. Top speed was 118 mph. The car was then loaned to Cliff Goad, Group VP of the new GM Tech Center, which formally opened the following year.

The following November, testing was also ordered with various axle ratios: 2.78, 3.07, and 3.23:1. A memo

Earl's restyled F-88 was powered by supercharged, twin-carb Olds V-8 bolted to a Hydra-Matic. The 4,550-pound car was clocked from 0–60 mph in 8 seconds.

issued on December 23, however, stated a new 3.70:1 gear ratio "high speed cruise ratio" had replaced the 3.42:1 unit.

During November 1955, Earl's F-88 was repaired in the shop. A head gasket was blown, number-two cylinder wall was scored, and the wheels were bent according to a handwritten note dated November 26. "Too soft tires; need racing type with stiff side walls" was a comment made regarding the bent wheels. Also minor power steering trouble (unspecified) was also to be corrected. Four days later, a Chevrolet power steering pump was on its way. Noted was the need to use special fittings to install it.

Finally, by December 13, 1955, SO 2292 is referenced as SO 90020 on an order to make cowl and instrument panel revisions and to install a new windshield by February 1. It was to be ready in time to send the car to Florida for Earl's use during the GM Motorama in Miami and later at Daytona Beach. The memo also noted the clay and plaster model of the F-88 had been scrapped with Mr. Earl's approval on August 12; therefore, there was nothing available upon which to model the new hardware. This made for the possibility of making a partial cast mold from the car in order to perform the modeling if deemed necessary. At the time, Earl's F-88 was in Lansing for engine modifications. Then another change was requested for completion before the trip to Florida: replace the current grille with a new egg crate insert. The work was apparently completed on schedule since Earl did make the trip, along with his mechanic, Leonard McLay.

Earl's F-88 was repainted white just before it was used in an annual Shriners Parade in July 1956. Afterward, it was stripped of its several layers of paint and repainted white again as shown in this September 1956 photograph. (Photo Courtesy GM Media Archive)

Transformation into the F-88 Mk. II

A February 7, 1956, memo outlined an extensive makeover for SO 90020. In the end it was partially rebodied as the 1957 F-88 Mk. II; an entirely new front end (ahead of the cowl) and rear end (behind the rear bulkhead) were fabricated to replace

Earl's F-88 was converted into the F-88 Mk. II for 1957. Its original body was cut away ahead of the cowl and behind the bulkhead located behind the seats. Newly designed panels were then grafted in place. (Photo Courtesy GM Media Archive)

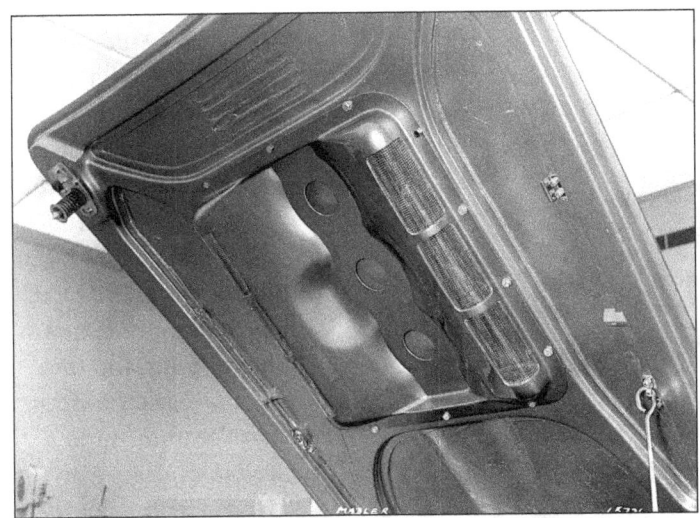

The air filters for the F-88 Mk. II carburetors were integrated into the underside of the car's low-profile hood. (Photo Courtesy GM Media Archive)

The freshly completed F-88 Mk. II was taken to Harley Earl's Florida home for his use while there during the spring of 1957. His visit to the state likely coincided with a Sports Car Club of America race or other car race event. (Photo Courtesy GM Media Archive)

the earlier components. The Mk. II was given a monotone color scheme of metallic blue. Its front end resembled the 1958 Corvette. It featured quad headlights and a blacked-out grille with OLDSMOBILE appearing in individual chrome-plated letters spread across it. At the rear were tail fins, which were low in height and stopped well short of the rear of the car.

The instrument layout remained essentially the same, but the interior color was changed to match the exterior of the car. Several publicity photos of the Mk. II variant were made in Florida at or near Harley Earl's home. One set shows Grand Prix race car driver Piero Taruffi sitting in the driver's seat. Among his wins was the 1955 Florida Grand Prix.

The latest memo available in the files of the GM Heritage Center regarding this car is dated July 10, 1957. It was in regard to the routine maintenance and minor changes performed, such as the installation of a fire extinguisher and new floor mats. The most notable action reported was in regard to the set of Traction Masters installed on the rear axle. They were soon removed when they were found to provide too little ground clearance.

Mystery F-88

Harley Earl used another F-88 (Shop Order 1768), painted bright red, for transportation, and I was able to determine this by process of elimination. This is the car listed as a 1953 model in the GM Shop Order books. It does not appear to have served as a major show car, although it did appear at various public events such as the Sports Car Club of America (SCCA) road races at Andrews Air Force Base and Atterbury Air Force Base in May 1954, according to a story published in the October 2003 issue of *Collectible Automobile*. There appear to be no documents on this particular F-88 at the GM Heritage Center. There are few photos of it as well.

The red car is definitely not one of the other three F-88s simply painted red for a time, as photographs of the car inside as well as outside the GM Design building prove. (The photo of it inside the building appears in my previous book, *Motorama: GM's Legendary Show and Concept Cars*.) That structure was being built during 1955 while, (1) Earl was driving the F-88 SO 2292, (2) the gold F-88 was still gold and still being exhibited, and (3) the car built for Sherrod Skinner was being shown on the Parade of Progress. Incidentally, the GM Design Center was formally dedicated on May 16, 1956. The noted photograph was taken during the "Dome Show," according to GM Media Archive records (no date is available), which indicates the facility was open at the time, thus giving evidence to support the conclusion the red F-88 was, indeed, one of four such cars.

F-88 Mk. III

Harley Earl received one more F-88 (XP-88, SO 90388) as a farewell gift to the retiring GM design chief. Known as the 1959 F-88 Mk. III, it was the definitive version of the series. The vermilion fiberglass-bodied car was equipped with a stainless-steel retractable top, wraparound windshield, tubular frame combined with a 1959 Olds front suspension, and various experimental components, some of which proved to be troublesome and required the car to be transported from Earl's Florida home back to General Motors in Warren, Michigan, for repairs.

In front, it had a Ferrari-inspired air scoop grille, quad headlights, and thin wraparound bumpers similar to those of a contemporary Corvette. Engine compartment heat vents were located just behind the front wheels. A

The 1959 F-88 Mk. III was posed with two of Harley Earl's other dream car creations, the 1951 GM Le Sabre and the 1959 Cadillac Cyclone. The F-88 had a Ferrari-inspired air scoop grille, quad headlights, and thin wraparound bumpers similar to those of a contemporary Corvette. Engine compartment heat vents were located just behind the front wheels. (Photo Courtesy GM Media Archive)

As was the custom when developing a new automobile, a full-scale clay mockup was made of the F-88 Mk. III. Faired-in headrests are clearly shown in this view.

The F-88 Mk. III is shown here in an advanced state of construction. Note the extensive use of tape to protect the cosmetic finish of engine components. Also note the twin fan shrouds.

A power-operated, brushed stainless-steel top retracted into the trunk compartment of the F-88 Mk. III.

push-button door release was installed rather than a conventional door handle. Headrests for the two seats were faired in and tapered across the deck. Wheels were slotted aluminum-cast units with integral brake drum with cast iron brake liners. A fuel-filler was located on each side of the rear of the car just outboard of the headrests. Overall dimensions were a length of 177.6 inches, width of 73.2 inches, height of 46.2 inches, and a wheelbase identical to that of the Corvette's at 102 inches. The stainless steel top retracted into the trunk compartment via a switch on the console. Its operation was fully automatic, but in the event of electrical failure, a five-step manual system was provided to raise the top.

Under the hood of the F-88 was a modified 1958 Oldsmobile engine with two Solex side-draft carburetors, according to the July 1959 issue of *Speed Age*, which pictured the unique car on the front cover. The July 1959 issue of *Hot Rod* also ran a story on the car, stating the two Solex carburetors "were mounted far forward on a special water-heated aluminum intake manifold." Other sources state an experimental fuel-injection system built by Rochester was installed. Both induction systems were tried; the Rochester B setup appears to have been installed a little later. Reportedly, though, the FI system was troublesome and replaced with the carburetors. A low-pressure (7 psi) Delco Brougham fuel pump mounted in the 25-gallon fuel tank delivered fuel to the high-pressure (80 psi) pump mounted on the cross member aft of the rear seat partition. The muffler and exhaust outlets were located ahead of the front wheels. A cross-flow aluminum radiator cooled by two fans allowed for a low-profile hood.

The engine was bolted to a Detroit Transmission X-10 Hydra-Matic with six forward speeds obtained via a 3-speed automatic gear set and a 2-speed rear axle. Reportedly, this transmission required constant repairs and was replaced with a conventional Hydra-Matic. If so, then clearly the transmission needed more testing before declaring it ready for use.

In back was a low-pivot point, swing axle suspension similar to that used on a contemporary Mercedes-Benz. Steering was through a variable-ratio power unit designed by Saginaw. The driveshaft passed between the front bucket seats. A chrome-plated, ribbed console was situated over the tunnel through which the driveshaft passed. The console housed the gear selector shifter, glove box, rain sensor switch (to automatically lift the top and windows if it rained), courtesy lights, seat adjuster, backlight window switch, and of course the switch for the convertible top. Between the seats mounted on the rear bulkhead was a radio speaker. On the driver's door panel was an "easy-entrance" switch. Pressing it energized the lifting motors in the backlight bow, causing the header to rise away from the windshield frame to facilitate egress, according to the operations manual for the car. Mounted above the easy-entrance switch was an electrical push-button switch to open the door. If the electrical system failed, both doors could be opened by pressing toward the rear a short lever located in a slot in the center of the door pull recess on the door kick pad, actuating the lock mechanically.

A full complement of gauges provided plenty of operational data to Mr. Earl. These included oil pressure, coolant temperature, fuel level, ammeter, air temperature, and vacuum gauges. Other features included cruise control, air-conditioning, Speed Sentinel (an alarm set to alert the driver when traveling beyond a preset speed), an eight-day Air Force clock, and compass. Interesting innovations were the two rotating discs directly ahead of the driver and positioned at the top of the instrument panel. One was for the 150-mph speedometer and the other was for the 7,000-rpm tachometer. Of course a radio was also included, but its whip-type antenna was concealed within the strut for the outside rearview mirror; only the projecting pull knob was visible when the antenna was retracted.

The F-88 Mk. III made its public debut, along with the 1959 Cadillac Cyclone, at the first Daytona 500. The cars were driven around the track prior to the start of the race.

After Harley Earl died (April 10, 1969), his F-88 Mk. III was reportedly to be displayed in an as-yet-to-be-built NASCAR museum. (Earl and NASCAR founder, Bill France, had known each other for years.) Ultimately, though, Bill Mitchell allegedly asked NASCAR officials to return the Mk. III to General Motors. Some time later it was trucked back to Warren, Michigan, and the car was ordered scrapped by Irv Rybicki or Bill Mitchell, purportedly due to its deteriorated condition.

A Latham supercharger was fitted to the Olds F-88 Mk. III engine by late October 1959.

CHAPTER 12
STYLING THE 1959s

"We need to drag their eyes down with low chrome."

– Harley Earl to his design staff

For nearly 30 years, Harley Earl had been nearly perfect in his quest to give General Motors the leadership role in styling. However, by the end of his career many of his stylists thought their boss had lost his way. The only engineer to work at GM Design under Harley Earl, Ken Pickering, said, "As powerful as Earl was during most of his career, his magic touch failed him near the end of his time as vice president. Younger designers were changing the rules and beating Earl at his own game. In the past, when his designs were setting the trend and others were starting to follow, Earl would always say, "It's time to cross 'em up." Not all of the 1958 models had been well-received by the public, and few of the stylists working on the early designs for the 1959 models thought they were going to "cross 'em up." These early designs were reworks of 1958 styling with even more heavy applications of chrome.

A Rebellion within GM Design

At first the designs for 1959 were based upon the 1958 models. But not long after the first proposals began to be rendered, GM's management made the decision to drop the 1958 A-body used exclusively for Chevrolet and Pontiac and merge them into the yet-to-be-designed 1959 B- and C-bodies. The move saved General Motors millions of dollars, but it forced a redesign of everything. Harley Earl supervised some of the early revisions and then made his annual trek to Europe to attend the auto shows. During his absence some major changes transpired.

Prior to the fall release of the 1957 models, GM stylist Chuck Jordan took a look at what Chrysler Corporation had done under Virgil Exner, who worked under Earl in the 1930s. (Exner had hired Homer LaGassey away from

A variety of two-tone paint combinations were offered for the 1959 Oldsmobile. This 98 Holiday hardtop wears Emerald Mist and Crystal Green. (Photo by Jim Jordan)

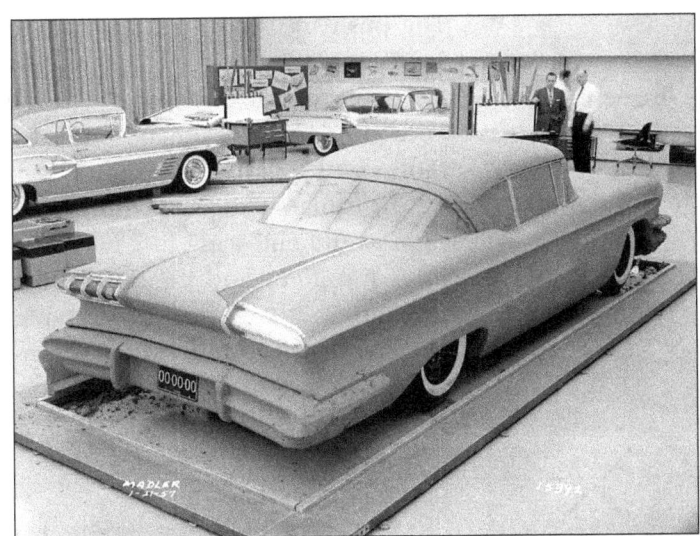

During the early phases of styling the 1959 GM cars, Harley Earl continued to favor the rounded contours used in the past. The designs were based upon the 1958 cars at this point. Seen here is the direction in which Pontiac was headed in January 1957. Note the massive, wraparound rear bumper and fin on the deck lid. Common practice was to have differing ideas sculpted into each side of a clay model, thus the varied taillights and fin on one side. (Photo Courtesy GM Media Archive)

General Motors and had him lead the design of the very 1957 models Jordan went to view.)

Regarding his fortuitous trip over to the Mound Road plant, Jordan was quoted in part one of a two-part article by Michael Lamm for the September–October 1991 issue of *Special Interest Autos*, "Chrysler had this big holding pen back behind the plant, and I used to go past there because I wanted to see next year's cars before anyone else did. Well, in the fall of 1956, through the chain link fence, I saw all these brand-new 1957 Plymouths, and wow, it was really a shock. They looked so clean and lean with that thin roof and the nice proportions of glass; just the opposite of what we were doing at General Motors at that time."

Jordan immediately told Bill Mitchell about the all-new cars from Chrysler; the cars stunned him, too. Others began the trek over to the plant to look and were just as impressed. Harley Earl favored a beefy, massive look, massive bumpers, domed hoods, arched roofs, and heavy applications of bright trim. Illustrating an example of the latter is the story from Buick's assistant chief, Stan Parker. While working on the design of the 1958 Roadmaster, he was ordered by Earl to "add 100 pounds of chrome; that's only 80 pounds. Put on some more!" Harley Earl's approach was definitely "opposite" to the "clean and lean" Chrysler products. To make the adjustments needed to the designs for the 1959 models, a crash program was instituted, resulting in a couple of months of seven-day work weeks and many hours of overtime each day.

While General Motors was searching to find a direction in styling and design, the competition was having its own problems, too. Chrysler was hit especially hard later in the 1957 model year; its new cars, while beautiful, had virtually no resistance to corrosion. Its reputation quickly suffered as a result. Mercury's Turnpike Cruiser had been a flop going against Oldsmobile and Buick, and the new 1958 Lincolns and Continentals failed to compete with Cadillac. Ford's new Edsel proved to be a sales disaster as well.

Prior to Chuck Jordan's peek at Chrysler's cars, Harley Earl was under some pressure from company president Harlow Curtice, as well as some of the divisional managers, to get away from the 1958 styling. Jordan's advance look at Chrysler's 1957 models finally led to a dramatic change in GM's styling for 1959. While Earl was away, a rebellion occurred, something previously unthinkable. Earl was an intimidating figure at General Motors. What Harley Earl wanted, Harley Earl got. Why not? Earl was helping General Motors make hundreds of millions of dollars. However, many of the stylists believed he had lost his way and new ideas were required.

Bill Mitchell, who soon took over Harley Earl's position, oversaw the alternative designs. When Earl returned from his trip, he was taken to the GM Design courtyard where he was shown a 1957 Plymouth two-door hardtop rented by GM Design engineer Ken Pickering. Earl was not impressed, and according to Pickering, Earl candidly stated, "I wouldn't piss on it!" He went on to add, "There really was a 'palace revolt' in redesigning these 1959 cars and when HJE returned for Europe, there was great uncertainty as to how he would react. Frankly, we had seen the 1957 Plymouth and sisters and were deeply worried that we were losing our design leadership. HJE could have fired on the spot most of the instigators, but instead, he accepted the new direction. Maybe he was relieved that he had been 'saved' by his design people.

"Harlow Curtice was very active while HJE was in Europe. He identified a slim, quiet designer named Ed Mueller in the Pontiac Studio and would walk into the studio, stride directly over to Mueller's desk and ask, 'What do you have for me today, Ed?' On Curtice's order, Mueller was transferred to the Buick Studio to work on the 1959s. Curtice also dictated that the 1959 Buick would be the lead car, and all other divisions would use Buick doors with specific appliqués."

Harley Earl soon realized that Harlow Curtice, along with the GM divisional managers, favored the new designs created under Mitchell's direction. Earl

The Le Sabre-based 1959 Buick is not the only distinctive model that was canceled. This Buick Special "B" exhibits the bulbous shapes of the early designs considered for 1959. (Photo Courtesy GM Media Archive)

The push for such ideas led to odd headlight treatments, three-finned arrangements (center one on the deck lid), fins on top of fins, and more. Most of the far-out proposals were ultimately rejected but some, such as the gull-wing fins for Chevrolet and Buick and the tall tail fins for the Cadillac, went into production. Other features, though, were not so far-out such as the thin roof pillars applied to all body styles and the "flying wing" roof for four-door hardtop models.

Earl, who was to reach the mandatory retirement age of 65 on November 22, 1958, let Mitchell run the show as he was soon going to do so anyway. But even after the palace revolt, GM's management evidently had not lost complete confidence in Harley Earl. His retirement contract prevented him from participating in the design of competing products, and he continued to serve as a consultant to General Motors.

eventually accepted the situation, thus General Motors moved in a new direction. However, some of the more bizarre styling proposals came *after* the revolt. Those 1957 Chrysler products must have been especially unsettling to the group at General Motors, and it explains why there was a strong push to think in terms of nothing being too weird to at least consider.

Indeed, according to part two of the two-part article for *Special Interest Autos* published in the November–December 1991 issue, Dave Holls, who was senior designer of the Pontiac Studio at the time the 1959s were in the works, said that any designer who did not develop "wilder and farther-out" ideas could lose his or her job.

While GM's lineup of flamboyant 1959 models had mixed results, its cost-cutting and higher prices gave it its second highest profit in the history of the company. Market share had dropped from a fraction over 50 percent to 48 for 1959. Competition coming from American Motors, with its smaller cars, as well as from the smaller offerings of foreign automakers, such as Volkswagen, was putting a dent in sales. Some were evidently beginning to tire of the big, finny, chromed cars offered by General Motors.

This odd lighting arrangement was considered but prudently rejected for the 1959 Pontiac. The four-point star grille was far removed from the split grille ultimately produced. However, the front bumper was close to production ready. (Photo Courtesy GM Media Archive)

Centrally placed headlights were considered for the 1959 Oldsmobile. Note the "88" numerals between the center lights. (Photo Courtesy GM Media Archive)

Chevrolet: Slim-Line, Fresh and Fine

Following the successful, new 1958 Chevrolet line of cars was another newly redesigned line of Chevys, with the exception of the Corvette, which received only minor styling changes. The economic recession, which gripped the country through most of 1958, had receded, thus leading to increased new car sales. As it had for the 1958 model year, Chevrolet again finished narrowly ahead of Ford for the 1959 model year despite the 1959 Fords being awarded the gold medal of the Comité Français de l'Élégance at the Brussels World's Fair "for exceptional proportioning and elegance of line." Ford's heavily re-skinned lineup of big cars was quite conservative in comparison to the radically changed Chevrolets. Despite ad writers claiming the new Chevys had "slim-line

The Impala became a stand-alone model this year and took the top spot in Chevy's lineup. Hardtops received a simulated air extractor on the back edge of the roof. Impalas also received a vinyl interior with an alternating patterned insert.

This set of photos reveals two very different approaches to the rear styling of the 1959 Chevrolet. The clay model (left) photographed in December 1956 has an awkward high deck that was wisely rejected. However, this design eventually morphed into the production version's "winged" deck. The photo at right taken about seven months later has a very different-looking deck. The profile was close to the final product. (Photo Courtesy GM Media Archive)

Chevrolet's styling for 1959 was nearly settled when the clay version was photographed with a fiberglass model of a proposed 1959 Buick Limited, which did not go past this phase of the design process. (Photo Courtesy GM Media Archive)

design" and were "fresh and fine," some Chevrolet loyalists were not persuaded; many of them switched to Ford this year, although not in enough numbers to help Ford out-sell Chevrolet, which out-produced its archrival by more than 42,000 units. Sales of more than 1.4 million units put Chevrolet close to pre-recession (1957) production.

The most dominant styling characteristic of the 1959 Chevys was its deeply sculpted fins. An early report in *Popular Mechanics* on the 1959 Chevrolets said of the car, "Styling is the thing with the new Chevrolet. Its low, flaring rear end is as expansive as the deck of an aircraft carrier and looks almost as wide from the driver's seat. Horizontal taillights squint, like giant cat's eyes, from under chrome eyebrows." Bob Caderet is credited with those gullwing fins. Harlow Curtice liked them so much that he passed the idea along to Ned Nickles, head of the Buick Studio. As mentioned earlier, Curtice still had a soft spot for Buick, a division he managed for a number of years before becoming GM president. Fisher Body tried to axe the idea because of the large number of spot welds required, but once the decision was made final, a stainless molding was used to cover the weld seams.

A 250-hp 283 with fuel-injection was an extremely rare sight on the big 1959 Chevrolets. Production of the type is estimated to have been in the low double-digits, perhaps around two dozen.

This view of a 1959 Impala convertible reveals the low-set headlights, low-profile hood, and dual air intakes with parking lights between the hood and grille, which were a part of the styling of the cars. Fuel injection, although still available, was rarely ordered. This restored car is equipped with the nearly $500 option; a special fender script notes its presence. Bumper guards, fender skirts, and spinner wheel covers were extra-cost items.

Writer Tom McCahill wrote in his usual metaphorical style regarding the rear end design, "My first reaction when I saw this rear flight deck, which curves downward from either side in a slow V, was 'what a spot to land a Piper Cub!' It's crazy . . . but craziness is good taste."

Hidden fuel fillers had become a styling trend. In the case of the 1959 Chevrolet, it was hidden behind the license plate mount that swung down for access. The mounting was placed between the taillights.

As for the front view of the car, *Popular Mechanics* had this to say: "At the front, two sets of paired headlights are set as low as the law allows to accentuate the road-hugging design." The headlights were lowered several inches and sat at each end of the convex grille composed of horizontal and vertical bars. The Chevrolet's low, wide hood added to the lower, wider look of the car. All but the Buick Division used the design.

Another new styling feature for the 1959 Chevrolets was the Vista-Panoramic Windshield. The compound curved windshield cut into the upper roof in a manner much like that of the 1955 Chevrolet Biscayne dream car, but not quite as far. This windshield was said to offer 53 percent greater forward visibility; its rear windshield also claimed to offer 47 percent more area. Presumably the stats were compared with the 1958 models.

The new Chevrolets, which were about 200 pounds heavier than those of 1958, rode a wheelbase 1.5 inches longer than that of the 1958. Atop a new X-frame chassis, roofs sat 3 inches lower, and bodies measured more than 2 inches wider overall. However, the X-frame proved to be a weak point. A number of GM cars with this frame split in half in side impact collisions over the ensuing years. However, General Motors was stuck with it through 1964.

Performance

Chevy's standard engine remained the familiar Blue-Flame straight-6, although buyers could still obtain any one of several optional V-8s at extra-cost, which included carryovers from the 1957 model year: the Turbo-Fire 283 2-barrel as well as the Super Turbo-Fire 283 4-barrel. Also, the 250-hp Ram-Jet fuel-injected 283 was retained, as was a companion 290-hp version dubbed Ram-Jet Special. The latter engine was largely identical to the 1957 version rated at 283 hp, but with a more accurately advertised horsepower rating.

The fuel-injection equipment introduced for 1957 soon showed it needed some "bugs" worked out of the system. It received upgrades that increased reliability on the 1958 cars; further refinements were made for 1959. Compared with the original 1957 setup, the fuel-injected engines operated on a leaner mixture, air leaks around the nozzle anchorages were sealed, each injector nozzle received filter screens, and a simpler manifold vacuum-operated valve replaced the complex arrangement involving a solenoid for cold starts and a micro-switch to bypass the solenoid for hot starts.

For its final appearance on full-sized Chevys, minor mechanical changes were incorporated that included a unique air cleaner, which was required due to the lower hood profile of the 1959 Chevy. Other modifications resulted in simplified repair procedures. Those equipped with the Rochester FI setup had the fact noted with a unique fender-mounted emblem and script.

The two versions of the fuel-injection engines had significant differences. The 250-hp Ram-Jet had cast-alloy aluminum pistons with notched heads, while the 290-horse Ram-Jet Special received pistons with slipper skirts and domed heads. Compression ratios in the respective engines were 9.5:1 and 10.5:1. The Ram-Jet had hydraulic lifters while the Ram-Jet Special used mechanical units. Valve size was 1.72 inches for the intake and 1.5 inches for the exhaust on both engines, but the tolerances differed. For the Ram-Jet engine a tolerance of +/- 0.005 inch was specified, but on the Ram-Jet special the allowed tolerance was zero. Rod and main bearings were different between the two engines.

The big news in terms of engines for 1958 Chevrolets had been the new 348-ci V-8. For 1959, the same was true. It was offered in three states of tune during its first year (and these are detailed in Chapter Seven). This series continued for 1959, along with new additions. Offered at the start of production was a single 4-barrel version of the high-compression engine rated at 300 hp (also reached at 5,600 rpm). The upgraded version of the 348 became known as the Special Turbo-Thrust, while the three-deuce 315-hp engine took on the title of Special Super Turbo-Thrust. During January 1959, a pair of even stronger 348s was added to the list. Both featured 11.25:1 compression ratios, dual valvesprings, centrifugal distributor, and scavenger exhaust headers. The 4-barrel version had an output rating of 320, while the other with its three, 2-barrel carburetors pumped out 335. Multi-carburetor engines were not legal for NASCAR competition, where Chevrolet managed a number of Grand National victories. Fuel injection had been banned from NASCAR tracks, too, at the midpoint of 1957.

Most performance buffs believed in the old adage, "There is no substitute for cubic inches." And, for 1958 the cubic inches did increase when the 348 was introduced. By 1959, the expensive fuel-injected 283 was old news. The option had developed a reputation for being unreliable, although that was not really justified. Many technicians were not familiar with how to properly tune the Rochester system, and it did need more attention than a carburetor. Fuel-injected engines were not common, so mechanics seldom needed to know how to work on one. The Ramjet option was very expensive, adding roughly $500 to the price tag, while the Super Turbo Thrust was priced at under $270. Even so, fuel injection was very exotic for the late 1950s, thus it had some appeal to a few buyers. It was discontinued on the big Chevys by the time the last of the 1959s had rolled off the assembly lines, but Corvette fans could still buy the "fuelie" through 1965.

Tom McCahill reported in the November 1958 issue of *Mechanix Illustrated* that his 280-hp 348-powered, Sport Sedan test car managed a 0-60–mph time of 13.1 seconds and 40 to 60 mph in 6.2 seconds. His 0-60 time was considerably slower than the 10.3 seconds he achieved testing a 1958 model.

Several transmission choices were available. A 3-speed manual was standard issue with any engine, while a 3-speed manual with overdrive and a Powerglide 2-speed automatic were optional for the non–FI 283s. The Super Turbo-Fire, the Ram-Jets, Turbo-Thrust, and Super Turbo-Thrust could be had with the close-ratio 4-speed and floor-mounted shifter. The latter was in great demand, but the strike by the employees of BorgWarner, the company that supplied the units to Chevrolet, made acquiring a 4-speed rather difficult, so much so that Chevy had to give preference to the Corvette when the 4-speed gearbox was ordered. Many customers who ordered the 4-speed on their full-size Chevy finally settled for a 3-speed unit to speed delivery of the car. The Turboglide automatic transmission was again offered as an option for the non–high-performance V-8s.

Chevrolet was not the only American automobile maker to offer fuel injection during the last years of the 1950s. Chrysler Corporation released it as an option for the 1958 model year, but very few of the units were ordered. Most of the cars ordered with it were retrofitted with carburetors. American Motors' Rambler also listed fuel injection as an option for 1957, but apparently none of its cars left the assembly line with the setup. After some Ford Motor Company officials heard rumors indicating Chevrolet would offer fuel injection for the 1957 model year, it elected to respond with a Paxton supercharger as an option for the 312-powered cars.

Model Lineup

The Impala was in its second year but was moved out of the Bel Air series, making it a stand-alone model. Furthermore, body style offerings expanded from just the two-door hardtop and convertible to a full array composed of a four-door sedan and a four-door hardtop,

In response to Ford's car-based Ranchero truck, which first appeared for 1957, Chevrolet released its car-based El Camino for 1959. The model, which did not sell in significant quantities, was dropped at the end of the 1960 model year. Wire type wheel covers on this example are not factory issue. (Photo Courtesy Brian Laurance)

labeled as the Sport Sedan. A top-of-the-line, four-door station wagon dubbed the Nomad was included as part of the Impala series, but "Impala" script did not appear on it; instead, Nomad was spelled out within the side molding in the same manner and location in which "Impala" was spelled out on those models.

The Sport Sedan was new for 1959, and all divisions offered this body style. Its flattened roof, with thin A- and C-pillar posts and wraparound windshields front and rear, offered excellent all-around visibility. Its rear overhang also helped shield rear seat occupants from direct sunlight, at least when the sun was well above the horizon.

Next in line was the Bel Air series composed of the two- and four-door sedans, a four-door Sport Sedan, as well as two station wagon models called Parkwood and Kingswood. The Kingswood was approximately $100 more expensive than the Parkwood.

At the bottom of the hierarchy was the Biscayne series. The Del Ray, which had previously been Chevrolet's lowest priced series, was dropped. Biscayne body styles were composed of two- and four-door sedans, a two-door utility sedan (no backseat), along with two station wagon types in two- and four-door sedan form, both labeled as the Brookwood.

Pontiac: Car of the Year

In 1958, Pontiac dominated the Daytona Speedweeks Trials, but many car buyers were not impressed enough to purchase a Pontiac that year; the styling of the cars

This Cameo Ivory and Sunset Glow 1959 Pontiac Bonneville is a largely unrestored original car. Bonnevilles were recognizable by their additional length over the lower series Pontiacs and by the set of four simulated vents on the quarters.

was a turn-off to many potential Pontiac buyers. That fact, combined with the economic downturn that year, dealt a blow to sales. The 1959s had to be better. Fortunately, they were better and well accepted.

The public loved the styling of the 1959 Pontiacs, split grille, Wide Track, and all. Automotive writer Tom McCahill praised the 1959s in the December 1958 *Mechanix Illustrated*. He wrote, "The Pontiac boys . . . eagled the hole and came up with the best looking car in the General Motors line and quite possibly the best looking 1959 car on the road." *Motor Trend* was sufficiently impressed enough to award its coveted "Car of the Year" award to Pontiac. Other prestigious publicity came as the result of a 1959 Bonneville convertible serving as the official pace car of the inaugural Daytona 500 stock car race and "Fireball" Roberts' 145-mph practice laps in a 1959 Pontiac during qualification trials for the race.

The Custom Star Chief series was composed of only three body styles: two- and four-door sedan and a four-door Vista roof hardtop like this gorgeous Canyon Copper and Cameo Ivory example seen here. (Photo Courtesy Brian Laurance)

Models

Model offerings for Pontiac totaled three: Catalina, Custom Star Chief, and Bonneville Custom. The latter was divided into two series: 27 and 28. Only the Bonneville Custom Safari station wagon was in the former, while the series 28 was composed of the four-door Vista hardtop, two-door hardtop, and the convertible.

The economy model, Catalina (series 21), was composed of seven versions: the four-door sedan, four-door Vista hardtop, two-door Sport Sedan, two-door hardtop, convertible, and six- and nine-passenger station wagons. Next up in the hierarchy, the Custom Star Chief (series 24), offered just three body styles: four-door sedan, four-door Sport Sedan, and a two-door Sport Sedan.

The Catalina, Custom Star Chief, and Safari each had a 122-inch wheelbase; the Bonneville Custom wheelbase was 2 inches longer at 124.

Powertrains

For 1959, Pontiac offered a larger displacement V-8 again. The bore remained the same as the 370s at 4.0625, but the stroke was increased from 3.5625 to 3.75 inches, resulting in a displacement of 388.9 ci, which was rounded up to 389.

The Tempest 420 389 was the base engine for all models but in differing states of tune, depending upon the model and transmission choice, and it created a somewhat convoluted set of possibilities for the buyer.

For the Catalina and Custom Star Chief, the standard engine was the 2-barrel version with 8.6:1 compression producing 245 hp at 4,200 rpm when coupled to the standard 3-speed manual transmission; when equipped with the optional Strato-Flight 4-speed Hydra-Matic, it had 10.0:1 compression and was rated at 280 hp at 4,400 rpm. A 389 4-barrel hooked to the standard 3-speed and 8.6:1 compression produced 260 hp at 4,200 rpm was an extra-cost option. This one was standard issue for the Bonneville. With the optional Hydra-Matic (10:1 compression) it was rated at 300 hp at 4,600 rpm.

The Bonneville engine was a $20 option for the lower echelon models. The 389 Tri-Power offered 315 hp at 4,600 rpm regardless of transmission choice and was an across-the-board option. A NASCAR-certified 389 was also an option; with the single 4-barrel it produced 330 hp at 4,800 rpm and with the Tri-Power setup, 345 hp at the same number of revs. Dual exhausts were standard with the NASCAR versions. A more fuel-efficient economy version, known as the Tempest 420E (E for economy), with an 8.6:1 compression ratio was also available for all series as a no-cost option and produced 215 hp at 3,600 rpm.

The SafeT-Track non-slip differential was a $42 option with gear ratios remaining almost the same as those offered for 1958.

Wide-Track Chassis

As already suggested, some of the public's attraction to these Pontiacs was due to the so-called Wide Track chassis. The wheels were moved outboard, thus producing a wider track. Front and rear track dimensions spanned 63.7 and 64 inches, respectively. A wider track provided for a better handling car, but that fact was only of secondary importance; the real purpose of Wide Track was simply for styling. Fortunately, what looked great was also functional. Chuck Jordan proposed the idea of widening the front and rear tracks to push the wheels out farther while working on a mid-size concept in an advanced studio. When the idea was adopted for Pontiac, its advertiser coined the term Wide Track for marketing purposes.

Styling

Joe Shemansky, who replaced Paul Gillan in December 1957 as the chief of the Pontiac Studio, is sometimes credited with the split grille of the 1959 Pontiac. However, dated photography of the clay mockups with the split grille show the idea existed as early as July 1957 when the studio was still run by Gillan, who is at times also credited with the design. Regardless of who actually first rendered the split grille, it was initially rejected, only to be reinstated. The split grille was dropped for 1960, but complaints about its absence brought it back again for the 1961 model year.

According to one source, the idea was actually first proposed by Gillan for the 1955 model year, but it was rejected by Harley Earl. My best guess, then, is that Gillan conceived the idea some years earlier, and Schemansky was responsible for the 1959 version of it. According to the previously mentioned story on styling the 1959 models published in *Special Interest Autos*, Bill Mitchell did not favor the design the second time around, but Pontiac's general manager, Bunkie Knudsen, liked it and Earl approved of it, too, thus it went into production. The twin-finned quarters, on the other hand, were actually first used on one of Harley Earl's original 1959 designs based on the 1958 A-body.

The stylists did their job well for the 1959 Pontiac. The top-of-the-line Bonneville brought 77,891 orders; this figure breaks down into 27,769 two-door hardtops, 38,696 four-door hardtops, and 11,426 convertibles. In all, 383,320 Pontiacs were built for the model year, which was nearly a 75 percent increase over the output for the previous year.

Another Pontiac styling direction looks more like something from Chrysler than from GM Design. Rocket body-side trim blended reasonably well with the blade-like quarter panel shapes in back but was nevertheless a bit over the top. (Photo Courtesy GM Media Archive)

Oldsmobile: The Linear Look

The "Linear Look" was the marketing lingo used to advertise the 1959 Oldsmobiles, but it just as easily could have been the "Rocket Look," something that would have been more fitting since a rocket had been Oldsmobile's theme since the release of its V-8 for 1949. Granted there were straight lines composing the styling of the new Oldsmobile, but the cars literally had a rocket profile grafted to them.

The Olds design was sculpted under Art Ross and Irv Rybicki. After developing a "much cleaner, crisper form," as expressed by Michael Lamm for an article on styling the 1959 GM cars for the June 2006 issue of *Collectible Automobile*, while Earl was away, it was reworked upon his return. A full-size clay model was completed when Earl came into the studio soon after his return from the European auto shows.

According to Lamm's article, he noticed a 10-foot-high rocket form sitting by the studio entrance. Ross had put it there some time earlier. Earl told Ross to get that rocket sitting next to the clay then said, "That's what I want you to do, Irv; create a rocket up there at the beltline." Roughly 100 variations of the theme were tried before the final one was accepted. That is how the 1959 Oldsmobile acquired its rocket-like form from the beltline and across the top of the quarter panel. A subtle tail fin capped with a bright molding emerged from the oval taillights. A tall, thick fin had at one time been considered.

That Rocket Performance

Writer Ray Brock in an article for the June 1959 issue of *Motor Trend* wrote, "When we watched Lee Petty in a 1959 Olds edge out a Lincoln-engined T-Bird for first place in the 500-mile stock car race at Daytona Beach, Florida, last February at an average speed above 135 mph . . . we decided that we had better test one of the new models." The title of the story strongly indicated their findings: "Olds . . . '59 Class Leader."

With a full tank of fuel for the best rear wheel traction, the optional 394 with Hydra-Matic, and 3.23:1 axle ratio, the Super 88 Holiday two-door hardtop test car accelerated from 0 to 60 mph in 8.4 seconds, from 30 to 60 mph in 5.2 seconds, and 50 to 80 mph (simulated passing) in 8.5 seconds. The quarter-mile elapsed time was 16.7 seconds at a terminal speed of 83 mph. Brock noted, "By virtue of size, weight, and springing, it would seem that Oldsmobile is more interested in a luxury car than performance model, still yet, it keeps the low gear in for acceleration." In regard to the front coil springs he wrote that "they are definitely intended to provide a soft ride . . . and if you plan to go road racing, you'll have to do like Lee Petty did at Daytona Beach, throw out the stock springs and stick in a pair about three times as strong." Braking was evaluated and the newly redesigned brake drums were found to be "quite satisfactory." Brake fade only occurred after repeated high-speed stops, but all stops were made in a straight line with no steering correction required.

About the only faults Brock found with the Olds was its seating and the ill-proportioned glove box. In regard to the former he stated, "Seating position is very low and to provide support beneath the thighs, the front edge of the seat cushion is raised much higher than the rear portion, resulting in a sharp angle between cushion and back. Once you are wedged into this angle between seat and back, you are there to stay. It's almost impossible to squirm around while driving to relieve the tensions of long drives. This is the price the passenger pays to permit the low body height

This striking Ebony Black 1959 Oldsmobile Super 88 convertible is one of only 4,895 built. Oldsmobile's advertisers coined the phrase "The Linear Look" to describe the styling, composed of straight lines. (Photo Courtesy Jack Milford)

Top of the line for Oldsmobile in 1959 remained the 98. The four-door Holiday hardtop like the one shown here was the most popular style in that line with 36,813 finding buyers. Note the Vista Panoramic windshield, which curves into the roof. (Photo Courtesy Scot Taylor)

of today's cars, and it isn't restricted just to the GM line." He found the interior finish to be "excellent."

Ray Brock also wrote, "Driving the '59 Olds is an easy chore. The engine is quiet, there is very little wind noise, throttle response is excellent, brakes are good, workmanship is good, and after a few days, even the awkward front seat can start to feel OK."

The Olds Lineup

Three tiers of models were offered. The economy model was the Dynamic 88; next up was the Super 88, and the top-of-the-line was still labeled Ninety-Eight.

The Dynamic 88 and Super 88 were largely identical cars sharing a 123-inch wheelbase but differing in their respective standard engines, transmissions, and level of trim, both inside and out. For the first time in several years, the low-level Olds came with a smaller displacement engine; it was a 371 2-barrel rated at 270 hp at 4,600 rpm. The Super 88 came equipped with the 394 rated at 315 hp at 4,800 rpm, as did the Ninety-Eight series. Not surprisingly, the Ninety-Eight was longer, with a 126.3-inch wheelbase and came standard with the Jet-Away Hydra-Matic, power steering, as well as some extra external trim and a lavish interior.

Body styles for the Dynamic 88 numbered six and were composed of a two-door sedan, two-door Holiday hardtop, convertible, four-door sedan, four-door Holiday hardtop, and a four-door station wagon. Those of the Super 88 were nearly the same with the two-door sedan not being available. The Ninety-Eight series also lacked the two-door sedan as well as the station wagon. The three-seat wagons offered previously were dropped this year, although they returned the following year.

Regardless of model, the new Twin Contour instrument panel with a Safety-Spectrum speedometer was included. The speedometer used a moving color bar that glowed green up to 35 mph, then glowed orange up to 65 mph, and finally red above that figure.

While Chevrolet used an X-frame and Buick a K-type with side rails, Oldsmobile used a little of both in its X-frame with side rails.

Air Suspension

Air suspension returned (dubbed New-Matic Ride in Olds factory literature) this year, but in a simplified form; only the rear suspension had the leaf springs replaced with air bags this time while the front coils were retained. One serviceman quipped that Olds had eliminated half the problems of air suspension with the new setup,

A symmetrically styled dash was a new feature of the 1959 Oldsmobiles. Note the use of two-toning in the dash as well as the upholstery. An electric clock was standard and positioned directly ahead of the passenger side of the seat on the instrument panel between the stylish "Ninety" and "Eight" script. (Photo by Jim Jordan)

Harley Earl planned for a special Buick model with styling based upon his beloved 1951 Le Sabre to be included in the lineup for 1959; the project was labeled as the XP-64. The result as seen in this photo of the mockup sitting with a 1958 Buick was not especially successful and was nixed. (Photo Courtesy GM Media Archive)

Two different rear designs can be seen in this 1959 station wagon styling clay mockup. On the left side is the design for the 1959 Buick and on the right, the 1959 Olds. (Photo Courtesy GM Media Archive)

This 1959 Buick Limited design from March 1957 featured three fins in back with the center one going through the rear windshield! Within a few months the center fin was removed, but ultimately this Limited was not produced. (Photo Courtesy GM Media Archive)

Only the tall hood and grille pattern of 1958 made it onto the virtually all-new styling of the 1959 Buick. Harley Earl had a preference for tall hoods, which implied a powerful engine underneath. (Photo Courtesy Eric Bernard)

This Glacier Green Electra four-door hardtop is equipped with the optional set of Super DeLuxe wheel covers; they were standard issue on the Electra 225. A four-spoke centerpiece on the DeLuxe wheel cover was what made them "super." Wheelbase was 3.3 inches longer on Electra and Electra 225 series than that of the Le Sabre and Invicta at 126.3 inches. (Photo Courtesy Eric Bernard)

implying that it would eliminate 100 percent of the problems if it just dropped air suspension altogether. Despite the improved dependability, very few buyers opted for it, likely due to the reputation for trouble established the previous year as well as the high price. Less than 2,000 Oldsmobiles were so equipped.

Sales Results

Sales of the 1959 Oldsmobile totaled 382,865 units, which fell a bit short of the approximately 400,000 sales predicted by Jack Wolfram, the division's general manager. Pontiac knocked it out of fourth place.

Buick: The Car!

Harley Earl planned the original Buick design for 1959 as a kind of distinctive "swan song" car. It was to be a 1951 Le Sabre–inspired Buick sedan. However, everyone except Earl knew the proportions of the original Le Sabre could not be enlarged to become such a car, but no one was going to argue with the boss. The completed clay mockup was hideous. Earl had planned to unveil it to Harlow Curtice upon his return from Europe. Bill Mitchell knew Curtice would not approve, so he wired photos of the clay model to Earl while he was still in Europe. Upon receiving the images, he realized what everyone else had known all along. The project was abandoned, but something else had to replace it.

Whatever styling was finally chosen, it needed to be right. With the 1958 model year bringing a recession, objectionable styling, and greatly decreased sales, having objectionable styling again would only further compound the difficult situation for Buick. The design was

This special interior, along with the sunroof, was included on the Buick Texan show car shown at the 1959 Chicago Auto Show. The interior in slightly modified form (and without the rifles) became an option for the 1960 station wagon. (Photo Courtesy GM Media Archive)

based upon a survey conducted by the Buick Division that asked what buyers wanted in a new model. It responded with such traits as longer, lower, and futuristic looking. Thus, customers got what they said they wanted. The cars looked nothing like the popular Buicks of the past.

The so-called Delta Wing 1959 Buicks proved to be much better engineered cars than the previous 1958s. Road test reports such as Tom McCahill's for the October 1958 issue of *Mechanix Illustrated*, were very complimentary. McCahill test-drove a car nearly identical to our subject car, an Invicta four-door hardtop. His test car, which he drove at GM's Milford Proving Grounds, was equipped with the optional air suspension.

At the end of McCahill's opening paragraph of his report, he practically summarized his evaluation of the 1959 Buick by stating, "When Better Buicks Are Built, 1959 Will Be the Year to Beat," a twist of Buick's old ad slogan of "When Better Cars Are Built, Buick Will Build Them." One of his first impressions of the new car was in regard to its improved suspension. He noted the redesigned Air Poise air suspension was much better due largely to being less complex. However, it ultimately proved to be of little benefit and quite troublesome despite the engineering

The Le Sabre was the economical Buick of the four-car series that included Invicta, Electra, and Electra 225 (all were new model names for 1959). Second most popular of all of them was the four-door hardtop version of the Le Sabre with 46,069 being sold. (Photo Courtesy Joe Chow)

XP-75/Skylark III: A Buick with Italian Flare

While the 1959 models were under development in 1957, an unusual project was underway. It was labeled XP-75 and later formally named Skylark III. Ned Nickles was appointed by Harley Earl to lead the styling effort for the XP-75. The project netted two special cars with bodies constructed by Pinin Farina in Turin, Italy, with each featuring styling based upon the production 1959 Buicks. Interestingly, they received alterations even beyond 1960, which was the final year for the basic body style to be used.

Two 1958 Skylark IIIs (originally designated as the XP-75) were designed by GM Design and constructed by Pinin Farina in Italy. The second car was built for use by Fisher Body president J. E. Goodman. (Photo Courtesy GM Media Archive)

The earliest photographs available through GM Media Archive related to the XP-75 project are dated June 10, 1957, and show mockups of the interior. Photos dated June 21 show a completed full-size clay model of the car that was referred to as the Skylark II. By mid-August a running car had been assembled, but was labeled as the Skylark III.

Pinin Farina assembled the body on top of a mock chassis. Upon completion of the body, it was sent via ship to Buick in Flint, Michigan, where it was placed upon a modified stock chassis with a 110-inch wheelbase. Overall length of the Skylark III measured 204 inches, overall width spanned 80 inches, and overall height was a low 49.6 inches. It was painted silver and featured a sculptured metal side treatment similar to what appeared on the 1960 model Buicks.

Inside were leather-covered bucket seats and a console containing the gear selector for the automatic transmission and an armrest. The dash was gullwing-shaped and had a vertically designed radio in the center (a featured that would appear on the second-generation Corvette). Ahead of the driver was an instrument cluster similar to that used for production of the 1959 model Buicks. On the passenger side was a recessed upper panel upon which appeared Skylark III script, and beneath it was a padded panel with vertical pleats. Bright moldings surrounded these areas. Other features included a special steering wheel, paddle-type inner door handles, power windows, and air-conditioning.

A second car was ordered not long after the first one, but exactly when is not known. It was built for use by Fisher Body president James Goodman. His car was painted ivory. One of these cars (probably the silver one) had a white interior, at least for a while.

Both cars may have made appearances at various auto shows, but the only documents available through the GM

The ribbed lower body molding of the Pinin Farina–built Skylark III was similar to that applied to the 1960 Electra 225. Two Skylark IIIs were built, with one of them confirmed as scrapped in 1964. This is the number-one car. (Photo Courtesy GM Media Archive)

The XP-75/Skylark III CONTINUED

Heritage Center reveal that at least one of them was shown nationwide; the first showing was in August 1958 at the GM Golden Milestone parade in Flint.

These limited documents also reveal the cars underwent various changes even as late as 1963. The ivory car, though, was scrapped on or about July 28, 1964. As for the silver Skylark III, it was placed in storage in 1964 and then transferred to the Buick Division on June 13, 1967. What became of it afterward is a mystery.

Inside the Skylark III were leather-covered bucket seats with a console containing the gear selector for the automatic transmission and an armrest. The dash was gullwing-shaped and had a vertically designed radio in the center, a featured later adapted for the second-generation Corvette. (Photo Courtesy GM Media Archive)

refinements. Thus it was dropped after the 1959 model year. According to McCahill, "The front coil springs give the car the stability it needs on turns, bends, and in braking. The rear air bags are there to sop up violent road shocks without losing the roadability properties of the whole car." He also noted the "surefootedness of the Buick" was due to the increased width of its wheel tread.

Motor Trend also published a report on the 1959 Buick in its October 1958 issue. Buick's chief engineer at the time, Oliver Kelley, told writer William Carroll, "We've spent a lot of time on things that may not show the first time you drive the car. For example, the roll center has been raised 1.4 inches in front, 3 inches at the rear wheels so that weight is now suspended, rather than pivoted as before. As a result, we have a car that handles. Another thing you'll notice is that the '59 is quieter. We found that by moving the radiator and fan forward 6 inches, and throwing away the fan shroud, we reduced air turbulence under the hood and made the engine quieter." The writer noted the "lines are good and clean. It appears fast just sitting." His road test of the 1959 test car was made against a 1958 model.

Carroll noted the much-improved handling as compared to the 1958s, which he said, "Felt icy. The wheels seemed to be off the ground so much that I was flying by the seat of my pants with little control left for steering. On the other hand, the 1959 felt more solid, as though something could be done if you wanted to change direction of the car in a hurry." The bigger engine and improved transmission pleased Carroll, too: "Lots of low-speed torque in the new engine tied to a turbine transmission provides plenty of zip to 35 miles an hour, then acceleration flattens out and a climb to the century is slower, but smooth." Fuel consumption was reported as 19.2 mpg at 30 mph, 18.5 at 40, and 15.6 at 60 mph. At the time this was considered economical.

Brakes were improved versions of the 1958 finned aluminum front drums. A new process was developed, which allowed a steel liner to be bonded to the drum, providing a better contact area.

Both the Twin-Turbine and Triple-Turbine transmissions were much improved, but the latter proved to be very costly to manufacture.

The Invicta series, the next rung up in Buick's price ladder, also offered the four-door hardtop body style. This Arctic White and Copper Glow color combo was limited to Canadian-built cars, like the one shown here.

Another new feature for Buick this year was the 401 V-8; it powered the test car and helped produce 0-60–mph times ranging from 9.4 to 9.6 seconds, along with a 122-mph top speed. A so-called economy V-8 displacing 364 ci was also offered.

Even though the five GM divisions shared bodies, they did not necessarily share frames. Buick used a K-type with side rails.

Initial sales of the 1959 Buicks appeared to foretell of a good year, but sales did not stay on that pace. Despite the many improvements, the final model year output was disappointingly low at 284,248 units sold. Even though this figure was an 18 percent increase over the prior year's results, Buick fell again, this time to seventh place. The recession had ended and sales rebounded across the board, but even more so for Buick's competition. Buick would not begin to recover until the 1961 model year. So, despite General Motors giving potential Buick buyers what they said they wanted and the ad writers exclaiming that the 1959 model was "The Car!" Traditional Buick buyers did not see much "Buick" in the new Buick.

Cadillac: Motoring Majesty

Cadillac's ad writers used phrases like "Motoring Majesty," "Cadillac . . . universal symbol of achievement," and "Shimmering Elegance" to describe the new 1959 models. Evidently many luxury car buyers agreed. A total of 140,170 Cadillacs (not counting 2,102 commercial chassis) were built, which was a figure exceeding that of 1958's production by about 20,000 units. It far outsold competitors Imperial (less than 17,300 built) and Lincoln (less than 27,000 built) whose *combined* production for 1959 was not even one-third that of Cadillac.

Like GM's cars for the other four divisions, the Cadillac was completely different in appearance as compared to GM's preceding models. An article printed in the October 28, 1958, issue of *Look* magazine noted the changes appearing on the 1959 Cadillac: "The car that originated the upswept fin now sends this style feature sweeping rearward to accentuate its low lines. The hood is wider, and the glass areas are enlarged to provide greater visibility for the passengers as well as the driver."

While the 1959 Cadillac's styling is one of the major reasons some refer to the 1950s as an "era of excess," the car was well-accepted by much of the public and as a result gave the Cadillac Division its third best sales year of the 1950s.

Model Offerings

In all, there were five series of Cadillacs subdivided into 13 offerings (not counting the Series 62 export sedan, of which only 60 were built) for this model year. At the low end of the price range was again the Series 62 available as a four-door sedan, four-door hardtop, two-door hardtop, and convertible. The next step up was the De Ville, which could be had in any of these same body styles except the convertible. More upscale was the Eldorado Seville (two-door hardtop), the Eldorado Biarritz (convertible), and the Eldorado Brougham built by the Italian firm Pinin Farina.

All models came standard with a 325-hp 390 V-8, Hydra-Matic, power steering, power brakes (with a new direct-acting booster), and automatic-release parking brake. The 390 was an enlarged version of the previous 365; its stroke was increased by 0.25-inch to 3.875 inches and its compression ratio was bumped up a quarter-point to 10.5:1. It was a continuation of the advanced overhead-valve V-8, which first appeared in 1949, then displacing 331 ci.

Styling

With the shock of Chrysler's 1957 models' spectacular styling still fresh in the minds of those at GM Design, Ed Glowacke, Cadillac Studio chief, knew whatever came off the drafting boards had to out-Chrysler Chrysler. Cadillac had to maintain its "Standard of the World" status. Glowacke, with David Holls and others, had a challenge; the challenge was made

Unlike some of GM's other cars of 1959, the Cadillac was well received by the public. The upscale Eldorado series remained comprised of the Seville, Biarritz (shown), and Brougham. The Biarritz outsold all the others with 1,320 built versus 975 of the Seville and only 99 of the Brougham.

A Fleetwood Sixty Special was again offered by Cadillac, as it had done since the model's inception in 1938. A total of 12,250 were built for the model year. Exclusive to the model was special side trim and simulated scoop. The color was labeled Wood Rose. (Photo Courtesy Cadillac & LaSalle Club)

a bit more complicated by the fact the Cadillac had to share doors with the Buick as a result of the body-sharing decision made by top management. The rear taper in the Buick door determined the Cadillac's rearward taper, a major component of its profile appearance. Without the taper, the tall tail fins would not have been practical. So, the 1959 Cadillac was built around the Buick door.

The November 1958 issue of *Motor Life* noted the freshness of the Cadillac's styling: "No second look will be necessary to identify Cadillacs for 1959 as completely new cars. They retain some basic styling resemblance, but to a much less degree than has been true for some years. The process of evolutionary change hasn't been discarded completely but it definitely has been accelerated."

Although it was similarly sized in terms of length and width as the 1958 models, the overall height for the new 1959s dropped approximately 3 to 4 inches, but the amount varied depending upon the model. The greatest change in height was that of the Eldorado Biarritz, which was 4.4 inches lower at 54.4 inches. Wheelbase for all the 1959 Cadillacs, except for the Series 75, spanned 130 inches; as for the Series 75 it measured to 149.75 inches. All body styles sat on a tubular-center X-frame, which allowed for the lower body.

Streamlined nacelles attached to the fins carried the paired taillights. Reportedly, a total of four taillights were chosen because the setup just looked more expensive than two. In front, a horizontally bisected, complex, jeweled grille also added to the "expensive" look; its design was mimicked in back in the panel running between the reverse light pods. The jet-engine nacelles on the new Boeing B-52 used by the U.S. Air Force must have inspired the parking light pods integrated into the massive front bumper of the Cadillac. Stylist Dave Holls confirmed the jet-age as providing inspiration for automotive styling. An article published in the August 1998 issue of *Collectible Automobile*, he was quoted as saying, "By the mid-1950s, jet aircraft were the thing."

Regardless of the body style and model, the glass area of the new Cadillac was huge. Excellent all-around visibility was provided because of it, as well as the barely intrusive thin pillar posts. The wraparound front windshield curved upward into the roof this time; the compound curved windshield was a feature of some of GM's dream cars exhibited at the 1955 GM Motorama.

Inside appearance had to measure up to the Cadillac standard, too. Bob Scheelk headed interior design. One of the few women working in styling, Sue Vanderbilt, was also a part of the team responsible for the look of the 1959 Cadillac's interior. The instrument panel was quite a work in itself. It was deep because the cowl was designed around the raked-back, large wraparound windshield. The section curved around on the driver's side and provided a place upon which to install switches for the windshield wipers and the power windows. Just inside this location to the right was where the pod for the optional cruise control was placed, as was the control switch for the headlights. A pod on the opposite side of the instrument panel housed the clock, below which was the ignition switch. The arrangement provided a pleasing symmetrical design. In between were a 120-mph speedometer, coolant temperature gauge, fuel gauge, and odometer/tripmeter.

Looping body-side molding and distinctive wheel covers helped to distinguish an Eldorado from other Cadillac models.

Fabric for the seats of the Sixty Special offered a challenge to design. Its metallic fibers were found to firmly grip the outer hairs of women's mink coats, a condition completely unacceptable. After some research and testing, this problem was remedied.

Options

Among the options offered were the Eldorado (or "Q") engine, Autronic-Eye automatic headlight dimmer, bucket-styled front seats, cruise control, Turbine Vane wheel covers (standard for the Eldorado series), tinted glass, and air-conditioning.

Eldorado and Eldorado Brougham

Until the 1957 model year, the Eldorado was the ultimate version of a Cadillac. It was surpassed by the limited-production Eldorado Brougham that year. For 1959 and 1960, construction of the Brougham's special body was farmed out to the Italian firm, Pinin Farina. Pinin Farina badging did not appear on the car because Cadillac designed it.

As was the case since 1956, the Eldorado came in two body styles: the convertible Biarritz and the two-door hardtop Seville. They were available in 20 colors, although 5 of those were exclusive to the Eldorado: Olympic White, Argent, Argyle Blue, Persian Sand, and Hampton Green.

Powering the Eldorado series, as well as the Pinin Farina–built Eldorado Brougham, was a 345-hp version of the 390; its additional 20 hp came from a trio of 2-barrel Rochester carburetors. Other standard equipment for the Eldorado included an improved air suspension system. While it provided a soft ride, it still proved to be troublesome and many of the cars eventually had the setup replaced with conventional coil springs. Many luxurious features were standard, such as fog lights, remote deck lid release, radio with rear speaker, power antenna, power windows, power vent windows, power door locks, and six-way power seat. Interior appointments also included lights in door panels, deep-looped pile nylon carpeting, full leather upholstery, storage pockets in the back side of the front seat, and license plate frames. On the Seville, the buyer could select combination leather and cloth over full leather at no extra charge.

Both the 1959 Eldorado Biarritz and Seville were priced at $7,401. For the money spent, the buyer actually received a car that was less distinguishable from lower series Cadillacs as compared to the 1957–1958 versions, which had their own distinctive rear end treatment. A looping stainless steel side molding, vinyl-coated fabric top (Seville), lower fender-mounted, small-block letters spelling out ELDORADO, the appropriate title of Biarritz or Seville on an oval panel mounted beneath the vent windows, and Turbine Vane wheel covers were the only visual cues providing the model's identity.

Of course the rich, powerful, and famous were among the owners of an Eldorado. GM's Fisher Body division built a special Eldorado Seville landau for Egypt's former King Farouk, at a reported cost of $100,000. The car featured cut-down fins, a continental kit, Sabre-Spoke wheels, and anodized gold accents and landau irons. Singer Fats Domino also owned a 1959 Eldorado, specifically, a Biarritz.

The Eldorado Brougham was for the very wealthy with a price tag of $13,000. It was distinctive. Body panels did not interchange with any other Cadillac and use of lead was extensive for the hand-built cars. Its styling was more like that of the early 1960s Cadillacs; the fins were shaped much like those used for 1960, and the roof design was adopted for use on the 1961–1964 models. The hood panel was front-hinged, the rear deck sloped more, and the roof was also different. Most of the outer pieces such as the grille, headlight bezels, front bumper, most of the rear bumper, and some other trim were standard 1959 Cadillac components, though. Much of the inner hardware was the same, too, such as seat structures, instrument panel, and door hinges. The windshield was *not* the wraparound type, representing an early move away from the type. Indeed, wraparound windshields, like fins, would soon pass into history. Carpeting was either Mouton or Karakul.

No longer included were the vanity items (perfume atomizer and mirror), digital clock, and silver cups, as on the earlier Broughams. Upholstery choices were reduced to 15 from 44.

Only 200 Eldorado Broughams were assembled for 1959–1960.

Pinin Farina was commissioned to build the Eldorado Brougham in 1959 and 1960. Body panels did not interchange with any other Cadillac model. This is an exquisite original 1959 version, one of only 99 built. (Photo by Joe Chow)

CONCLUSION

Harley Earl's retirement became effective on December 1, 1958. There have been a number of successors to the title of GM VP of Design (now Global Design) over the decades that have followed. However, none of them held the title anywhere nearly as long as Harley Earl's three decades.

With the "palace coup" at GM Design led by Bill Mitchell, Earl realized he was taking General Motors in the wrong direction and, therefore, largely left the man who was going to succeed him in charge of styling GM's 1959 models, as well as those for the 1960 model year, the last one for which Earl had any influence.

While many have had their time in the spotlight, Harley J. Earl enjoyed essentially two eras in it: the pre–World War II years and many years afterward. He transitioned through those years with designs that constantly caught the public's eye and forced the rest of the auto industry to follow.

Today, collectors of GM's automobiles treasure Harley Earl's works like fine art. Many have brought six- and even seven-figure bids at auctions in the recent past. Cars such as 1930s and 1940s Cadillacs, 1949 Cadillac Coupe de Ville, 1953 Corvette, and 1955–1957 Chevrolet are among the most sought by collectors. Some have been bestowed the status of "classic" by the Classic Car Club of America, or are considered "milestone cars," as determined by the Milestone Car Society.

At least a couple dozen of his dream cars have survived and are preserved at the GM Heritage Center, the Alfred P. Sloan Museum Buick Gallery, and in private collections. Some may still yet be found in garages or barns in the near future; they are a kind of Holy Grail to vintage car enthusiasts. The dream car, or concept car in modern-day parlance, is one of his legacies as they are still created by auto manufacturers for the same reasons.

Harley Earl would not be able to accomplish what he did in today's corporate world in which committees and accountants shape decisions about automobiles. Federal regulations also limit the freedoms of the stylists. Still, designers manage to produce stylish cars such as Chevrolet's Camaro and Corvette. The latter was his creation more than 60 years ago, and there is no end in sight for its production.

Styling still matters, thus Harley Earl's impact on automobile design continues to resonate. He was the right man in the right place at the right time.

The 1960 GM models received mild, but distinctive, updates. These were the last to be designed under the influence of Harley Earl. Earl's handpicked successor, Bill Mitchell, was largely responsible for the styling. Clockwise from upper left are the Chevrolet Impala, Oldsmobile 98 convertible, Buick Electra 225 six-window sedan, and Cadillac Eldorado Seville. (Photo of Buick Electra 225 by Jim Jordan)

INDEX

A
Agramonte, Jules, 27, 27
AMA, 75
Anderson, Edmund, 99, 122
Anderson, Harry W., 51
Arkus-Duntov, Zora, 59, 60, 64, 66, 74–76, 80
Arnold, Dagmar, 156
Art and Colour Section, 9–10, 17, 18, 26, 33–43, 45, 153
Auto Age, 67, 132
Autocar, 38, 47
Automotive History Review, 106
Automotive News, 93

B
Baldwin, Jimmy, 13
Barr, Harry, 74
Bartholomew, Bob, 68
Bassett, Henry, 16
Bloch, Bill, 63

C
Caderet, Bob, 68, 87, 176
Cadillac-LaSalle Series Chassis Parts List, 31
Cadillac, Standard of the World: The Complete History, 32
Canadian National Exhibition, 58, 132
Carpenter, Sue, 12
Chayne, Charles, 45, 48, 49, 52, 55, 57–59
Chevrolet, Louis, 13
Chick, John, 26
Christiansen, Tom, 59, 122
Clearing House, 23
Cole, Edward N., 62–64, 66, 74, 76, 78–80, 87, 122
Collectible Automobile, 53, 54, 99, 104, 119, 122, 169, 181, 188
Coppock, Kenneth, 37
Corvette: A Piece of the Action, 38
Corvette: America's Star-Spangled Sports Car, 63, 66
Cunningham, Briggs, 60, 61, 67, 72, 115
Curtice, Harlow, 43–45, 47–51, 69, 70, 78, 88, 96, 105–108, 110–113, 133, 141, 155, 173, 176, 184

D
Darrin, Howard, 60, 62, 122
De La Salle, Robert, 21
De Palma, Ralph, 12, 29
Dieboll, Bob, 87, 92
Donaldson, Ed, 93
Dreystadt, Nicholas, 26, 40
Du Pont, Pierre S., 13, 16
Du Pont, Lammont, 37
Durant, William, 13, 16, 20

E
Earl, Jerry, 69
Edwards, Sterling, 60
Estes, Elliot, 97, 100
Exner, Virgil, 91, 172

F
Fish, William E., 82
Fisher Body, 10, 13–15, 21, 22–26, 28, 33, 37, 39, 41, 51–53, 76, 87, 135, 153, 176, 185, 189
Fisher, Albert, 14, 36
Fisher, Charles, 14, 36
Fisher, Frederick, 13, 14, 20, 36
Fisher, Lawrence P., 13, 14, 16, 20, 26, 36
Flight of the Firebirds, 151
Ford, Edsel, 45

G
Garret, Paul, 153
General Motors Styling, 1927–1958: The Genesis of the World's Largest Design Studio, 33
Gillan, Paul, 92, 96, 122, 180
Glennie, Ruth, 156, 160, 161
Glowacke, Edward E., 49, 53, 54, 116, 119, 122, 187
GM Motorama, 11, 15, 18, 58, 59, 61–63, 65, 67–69, 73, 76, 78–80, 83, 87, 92, 95–97, 105, 112, 116, 119, 122, 124, 125, 127, 131–152, 155, 157, 164, 166, 168, 169, 188
Goad, Cliff, 167
Goodman, James, 185

H
Hershey, Frank, 115
Hertia, Hans, 87
Hill, Ron, 119
Holls, David, 9, 12, 32, 119, 174, 187, 188
Humer, Frank, 36
Hunt, O. E., 36

I
"I Dream Automobiles", 9–12, 143

J
Jenkins, Ab, 96
Johnson, Kelly, 115
Jordan, Chuck, 43, 59, 76, 129, 130, 133, 172, 173, 180
Kaptur, Vincent D., Sr., 41, 45
Kavanaugh, Gere, 156
Keating, Thomas, 78
Keller, Kaufman T., 91
Kelley, Edward, 79
Kelley, Oliver, 186
Kettering, Charles, 152, 153
Knudsen, William, 26, 30, 42, 50, 87, 96, 97, 180
Krebs, Jeanette, 156, 157
Kurtis, Frank, 45, 144

L
La Salle: Cadillac's Companion Car, 20–32
LaGassey, Homer, 43, 54, 172
Lauer, Bob, 87, 167
Lauve, Henry, 108
Lee, Don, 12, 13, 16, 17, 33, 56, 103,
Leland, Henry, 126
Lenz, Arnold, 95
Life, 58, 62, 108
Linder, Jeanette, 160, 161
Longyear, Sandra, 156, 161
Los Angeles Times, 12
Lutz, John, 36

M
Macauley, Ed, 45
MacKichan, Clare, 75, 76, 78, 83, 87, 92, 122
McDaniel, James S., 46
McLay, Leonard, 168
McLean, Robert, 63
Mechanix Illustrated, 67, 178, 179, 184
Mitchell, William L., 19, 30, 37, 38, 40, 43, 54, 69, 70, 76, 105, 149, 163–165, 167, 171, 173, 174, 180, 180, 190
Modern Motor, 128
Motor, 21
Motor Life, 62, 71, 143, 165, 188
Motor Trend, 44, 45, 48, 49, 62, 66, 103, 179, 181, 186
Motorama: GM's Legendary Show and Concept Cars, 133, 169
Mueller, Ed, 173
Muntz, Earl, 60
My Years with General Motors, 16, 17

N
National Automobile Show, 88
New York Auto Show, 47, 72, 75
Nickles, Ned, 106–108, 112, 122, 123, 138, 141, 176, 185

O
O'Leary, Howard, 36, 37
Olds, Ransom E., 43, 44, 99
Olley, Maurice, 64, 80
Opel Passenger Car Development Project, 13, 61, 62, 76, 122

P
Parade of Progress, 43, 142, 152–155, 169
Parks, Jack, 87
Petty, Lee, 103, 181
Pew, Ralph, 33
Pickering, Ken, 43, 48, 52, 53, 69, 87, 107, 108, 112, 135, 172, 173
Pohlman, Marjorie Ford, 156, 162
Pollins, Helene, 156
Product and Exhibit Studio, 43
Progress on Parade, 153
Proving Grounds, 23, 45, 56, 58, 75, 106, 167, 184

R
Ragsdale, Edward, 106, 107
Renner, Carl H., 68, 73, 121, 122
Road & Track, 71
Rose, Mauri, 65, 143
Ross, Art, 105, 122, 137, 164, 180, 181
Rother, Helene, 156
Russell, Bob, 94

S
Sauer, Peggy, 156, 158, 161
SCCA, 38, 59, 69, 75, 146, 169
Scheelk, Bob, 119, 188
Science and Mechanics, 55, 56
Scott, Bob, 94
Seaholm, Earnest, 26, 33
Sebring 12-Hour Sports Car Grand Prix of Endurance, 19, 47, 68–70, 74, 75, 146
Setting the Pace: Oldsmobile's First 100 Years, 94
Shaw, Harry, 26
Shemansky, Joe, 45, 180
Skinner, Sherrod E., 100, 166, 169
Sloan, Alfred P., Jr., 13, 16, 17, 20, 37, 43, 44, 106, 141, 149, 152, 153, 190
Snyder, George, 45, 46
Special Interest Autos, 45, 48, 173, 174, 180
Speed Age, 171
Sports Car Illustrated, 67
Stebbins, Charles (Chuck), 77, 78, 122

T
The Art of American Car Design, 37
The Buick: A Complete History, 108, 111
The New York Times, 133, 163
The Saturday Evening Post, 9, 10, 11, 12, 21, 143
The Self-Starter, 45
Thompson, Dick, 67
Tochman, Bill, 87
Turley, Joe, 52

V
Van Alstyne, Jane, 156
Vanderbilt, Suzanne, 156, 162, 163, 188

W
Walter B. Ford Design Associates, 19
Wilson, Charles E., 51, 100, 138
Wozena, Pete, 120

Additional books that may interest you...

MOTORAMA: GM's Legendary Show & Concept Cars *by David Temple* Motorama expert and experienced author David Temple has comprehensively researched the show, the cars, and the personalities to create a fascinating story with new photos of these magnificent cars. Temple goes into detail on the body, frame, engine, drivetrain, and special features of each showcase model. He has also retraced the ownership histories of some of these cars. This book features fascinating period photography of Motorama cars at the show, in development, and at different locales. No other automotive show rivaled the extravagant and elaborate Motorama for stunning productions and awe-inspiring cars. Hardbound, 8.5 x 11 inches, 192 pages, 400 color and b/w photos. *Item # CT533*

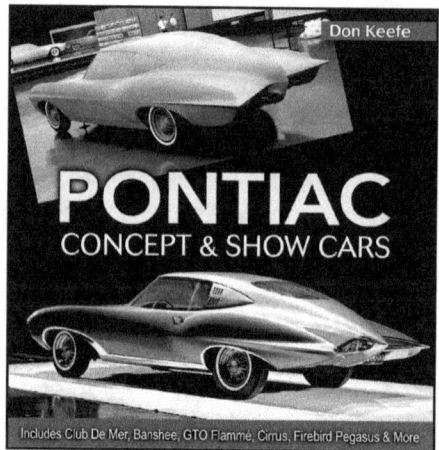

PONTIAC CONCEPTS *by Don Deefe* During the 1950s, Pontiac concept cars such as the Bonneville Specials, Strato Streak, and La Parisienne wowed the public at the Motorama show. During the 1960s and 1970s, the GTO Flamme, XP833, Firebird Pegasus, Cirrus, Banshee, and others piqued interest and kept enthusiasts coming back for more. These fascinating and innovative Pontiacs from 1939 to the 1980s and beyond are examined in exquisite detail. Pontiac fans, as well as auto history buffs, will enjoy reading and learning about these cars as well as Pontiac's Project X car program. Hardbound, 10 x 10 inches, 192 pages, almost 300 images. *Item # CT546*

DAVID KIMBLE'S CUTAWAYS *by David Kimble* This book reveals the secrets, techniques, procedures, and the dedication to craft that is required to produce these amazing illustrations. Kimble covers the step-by-step procedures while producing fresh artwork for this book featuring a McLaren Can-Am car as well as a vintage Harley-Davidson. Although the procedures covered here are unique to Kimble, and pretty much a pipe dream to mere mortals, this title provides an inside look into how he does it. Also included are the stories and tales of how it all started, traveling the world to illustrate cars, behind the scenes with manufacturers, the Corvette years, as well as a gallery of many illustrations. Never before has David Kimble shared the procedures for bringing these beautiful technical illustrations to life. Hardbound, 11 x 8.5 inches, 192 pages, 210 color images. *Item # CT535*

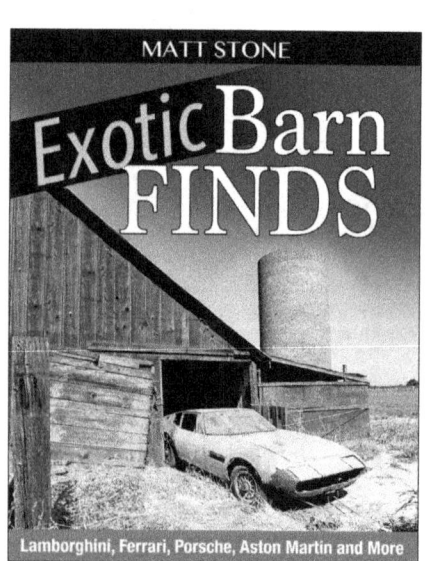

EXOTIC BARN FINDS *by Matt Stone* Veteran author and historian tells the story of more than 25 barn finds. The unique twist? Rather than the usual prewar or muscle car era product out of Detroit, these cars are all beloved imported sports cars of a bygone era. Think Ferrari, Lamborghini, Jaguar, Aston-Martin, Porsche, Maserati, Alfa Romeo, and others. There is even a Jay Leno-found 300SL Gullwing in the mix! Although there is no shortage of "barn find" tales surfacing these days, no collection covers exclusively the imported sports car icons that have become household names from an era past. All the tales are told with full detail on how they were found and why they are special. Softbound, 8.5 x 11 inches, 144 pages, 350 color photos. *Item # CT541*

Check out our website:

CarTechBooks.com

✓ Find our newest books before anyone else

✓ Get weekly tech tips from our experts

✓ Get your ride or project featured on our homepage!

Exclusive Promotions and Giveaways on Facebook Like us to WIN! Facebook.com/CarTechBooks

www.cartechbooks.com or 1-800-551-4754